Despite the immense pain and suffering it causes those who go through it, the world now accepts divorce to be just about as normal as marriage. But at The Marriage Foundation, we refuse to accept divorce as normal at all. We think of divorce as abnormal and abhorrent. We classify divorce, along with unhappy marriages, as society's number one disease; destroying millions of innocent lives.

However, we discovered that for individuals who are determined to keep their family together, by getting the education they need, and making the effort, it proves to be the best choice they ever made. We know people succeed when they have the right knowledge, and determination. And we want to help you, too.

The ideas, processes, methods, and education in this book are rooted in natural, biological and mental laws. They will help you, or anyone else, who is willing to set aside selfishness, and then be rewarded with the kind of marriage everyone wants.

Test these marriage saving principles, philosophies and doctrines yourself. Vigorously use them, and discover for yourself what marriage is meant to be.

We want you to have the greatest marriage ever.

Paul Friedman

Founder and Executive Director

The Marriage Foundation

Dedication

The effort to present these marriage saving principles and instructions are dedicated to my son, Joey Friedman, who, though certainly in a better place, left a great void in the hearts of his family, friends, and all who knew him.

Breaking The Cycle

Revised 2012

◇◇◇

We do not advocate you stay together for your children alone.
We advocate you make your marriage so wonderful, through education,
that the idea of splitting up would be unthinkable. ™

◇◇◇

Published by: The Marriage Foundation
Originally published as "Lessons For a Happy Marriage" © 2007

The Marriage Foundation -

Patent Pending

978-0-9885940-0-5

www.TheMarriageFoundation.com

Never give up

Your marriage is not over. Nor should you believe it is even close, even though it may feel that way with all you have been through, and are still going through.

From now on, to the best of your ability, you can live according to positive marital principles. As your understanding and abilities improve, so will your marriage. All your good intentions, even if your past efforts have not always been the right kind, still count as an investment into your marriage. With your everyday efforts more in synch with the right kind of thinking, your lives will improve. **Do not give up.**

Statistics have nothing to do with your own family. A truly failed, unrecoverable marriage is extremely rare, but too many couples sadly buy into the modern idea that divorce is the best way to go just because things seem "impossible". They give up too early, dooming their easily salvageable marriage. There is no impossible as long as you keep trying.

Success is inevitable when you use the right methods. The old adage "right tool for the job" has no less meaning when it comes to marriage repair. Most marriages deemed as unsalvageable only need a few intelligent adjustments.

All couples who go the distance are glad they did, because when they get over the hump they find the joy they sought from the beginning. They discover their effort is tiny, compared to the results they get, and their children are far better off! Only in very rare cases, when safety dictates, divorce is unfortunately the only way to go.

Learn how to be married

Learn how to be married and apply what you learn. Discover marriage is not an endurance contest, but the most joyful relationship imaginable, so you will be among those who know they know a good marriage is incomparable to life's other offerings. Make the most important relationship you will ever have the most glorious relationship you ever dreamed.

The science is reliable

It is your choice to do the best you can in your particular situation. However, if you are still struggling, even using this information, we want you to ask us for help. We will do all we can to help you understand, and we'll do all we can to help you apply what you learn to the betterment of your family. Reach us on the web at www.TheMarriageFoundation.org

www.TheMarriageFoundation.com

Follow the chapters like a course

The chapters are assembled and illustrated in such a way that you will not only learn the information, but will be able to explain it yourself.

If you can explain something, it means you know it well enough to live it

Contents

- Chapter One -
Introduction to Marital Education

◇◇◇

*Most failed marriages were lost to little things, which grow out of
proportion. Couples don't see it happening.*

*Even worse, they never learned those little things could have be removed,
and their marriage could have been made whole and happy.*

You don't have to suffer the same fate.

◇◇◇

Your marriage, children and family are worthy of every effort you can possibly make. We will show you how to make the right kind of effort to create marital and familial happiness.

Chapter One

Introduction to Marital Education

When you were married, you were handed keys to a glorious mansion of love and connection. Now, as you discover the principles of marriage as your education increases, your marriage will become far more than you first hoped for.

Pain will be replaced with happiness

If you pick up a pebble in your shoe, the pain will gradually build until it is unbearable. Over time, if you ignore it, a tiny little pebble will soon cause blisters and terrible sores. That pebble will cause so much pain that eventually you will be crippled, and walk with a limp. However, as soon as you remove the pebble, you feel immediate relief; and what you first thought were permanent wounds, soon start to heal. In no time, you forget all about the nasty pebble(s). Your gait becomes normal, and walking becomes a pleasure again. Of course you eventually learn, and then you become a lot more careful about where to step, as you consciously avoid pebbles.

Marriage is like that. The destabilizing pebbles are mistaken and unintended misbehaviors, which gradually cause tremendous pain and grow into ongoing terrible suffering. But as you learn to identify and recognize those crazy behaviors, you gain the power to pluck and avoid them. Once you know what to look for, you will seek the higher and safer ground of intimate connection, and the pebbles will no longer be cripplers. They will just be pebbles.

Serious problems need simple solutions

As frustrating and confusing as your particular situation may be at the moment, as frightening or overwhelming as things are and have been, or as close as you may be to contemplating or discussing breaking up your family; we know the truth, and we want you to know it too. What it takes to change your marriage into a dream relationship is much less of an ordeal than you may think. The issues and problems you think and feel to be cripplers and killers, are most likely only pebbles.

Your marriage is worth investing whatever it takes on your part to make it what it can be, and you will be relieved when you gradually realize how much simple common sense comes into play. You will get what you want, when you know what to do.

It is not too late

It is anything but too late. You can still reclaim the connection and intimacy you always craved, no matter how awful things seem to be at the moment. For one thing, your current focus is probably on all the pain and problems, so without intending to minimize what you are feeling, more than likely things are not half as bad as you may think. It is normal to be fearful, but because too many marriages fail, you may imagine yours can fail too. But it is probably not true. Your marriage, if you take the right action, will probably succeed in ways you never dreamed of. And we intend to show you the way.

Success comes to those who apply the right effort to the real problems

Learning the "whys" for wrong behavior will give you the insight to change

Do not trust the scary predictions and so called signs of trouble you read in magazines, or hear about on TV or from your friends. They cannot judge your experiences or your marriage, much less predict the outcomes. They cannot see the big picture of your marriage, with all the unique intricacies or the foundational love, and your sincere commitment to your soul-mate. Only you know how important it is to save your family. You know what you are willing to do.

You are willing to move heaven and earth, but you will not have to. You will only have to learn, and then change your own behaviors to do what works.

Marriage is an amazingly resilient relationship

Rarely considered during times of trouble, when there is so much overwhelming confusion, is that marriage is an amazingly resilient relationship. There is literally no other relationship in this world that has as much potential for resurrection, no matter how much damage has been done. You will soon discover, step by step, what we have discovered; that just about everything about marriage and family is a set up for success.

Marriage is not a set-up for suffering and failure. It is a set-up for fulfillment

Yes, your fears are perfectly understandable, and it is not really your fault that you would be uncertain. Everything on the outside of your marriage, from divorce trends to gross misunderstandings of marriage relationships, pushes couples into feelings of discouragement and hopelessness. Couples are surrounded by doom and gloom stories, so they do not realize how simple it is to bring back and actually rejuvenate a troubled marriage. And to make matters worse, people in trouble are mislead into thinking divorce is a "positive" option. If not for the blitz of misinformation, the vast majority of hurting families would never contemplate divorce for a minute, but would put all their attention on solutions, as they should.

Some who seek information about marriage solutions do not think their marriage is on the brink or anywhere near it. In that case, what you find here will be just as useful since core marriage information is universally applicable whether you have the jitters, just want some improvements, or think your marriage is on its last leg.

Good solutions exist

The hope and help you need will literally be found within your marriage, so all you have to do is learn what to look for. It is love, commitment and the marital structure itself that make marriage so uniquely resilient and exciting. Your marital connection and intimacy are treasures you cannot find anywhere else. And the conditions for success can be created by you, when you know how. You do not need to be a genius or anything special. You just need to learn what is spelled out in these pages.

Four steps to success

The four intertwined steps to acquire the knowledge which lead to achieving your dream relationship once and for all time are simple, practical and understandable

1) Determine to have the best marriage on Earth-enthusiastically do what you need to do, to improve your marriage

Do not give up or settle. Determination to succeed is the number one qualifier for success. You cannot succeed without determination, and you cannot fail if you have it.

Never give up. The failure rate of marriages would dramatically decline if success stories were as wide spread as stories of failures, but we have to live with what is out there.

Discouragement, which easily comes from identifying your own situation with so many stories of failure, causes people to give up; and giving up causes certain failure. Giving up is the final step for troubled marriages because there is no more effort to look for solutions or make any more real effort, even when solutions are right in front of you. Couples give up far too easily. How can you possibly succeed if you do not try? Do not consider giving up.

2) Learn the science of what makes marriages work- learn what creates predictable results, and focus on them

How can you succeed if you do not know how? What will you work towards if you do not know what you should expect from marriage? The divorce rate in an educated society would be more like 2%, not 50%, if we paid more attention to meaningful education.

The success of your marriage is dependent on your own knowledgeable and sensible efforts which make the difference, not statistics. You will soon know enough to make failure a non-consideration.

Nobody can know how much happiness is possible when they are off track and fighting for survival. But you will learn and see the highest goals of marriage are both practical and attainable. You will learn what makes a marriage, *your* marriage, work, and work well. There is no need to settle for a 'less than' marriage. We want you to have it all.

3) Understanding the pitfalls and obstacles- You can avoid trouble when you know what it looks like

Without understanding the nature of pitfalls and obstacles or why you keep banging your heads against the same walls, sometimes fooled by different wallpaper, you are too often like mice in a maze. But you will learn all about the pebbles and pitfalls, and what to do to avoid them. It will soon be more like stepping over curbs than tripping over every single crack and bump.

4) Proactively enhance your relationship- The vision of an ideal marriage needs to be perfectly clear to you, as well as the steps you need to take.

We all want connection and intimacy; that is why we got married. Though obviously not the only reason, they are certainly the big prizes. These grand prizes are exclusive to marriage and should be sought without fear or shyness; they are part of marriage.

You will learn how intimacy and connection are effectively worked for, and then experienced. Because these two prizes are usually obscured by imitators such as lust driven sex, we discuss the differences between sex and intimacy, as well as the beneficial utilizations of sex, so you can go beyond the shallow ideas currently making the rounds. You will also be able to articulate what you already feel to be true.

Divorce in a marriage educated society would be well below 5%

We all want connection and intimacy; that is why we got married

You don't have to be perfect to have a perfect marriage, but you have to know what to avoid and what to try

Misery enjoys company

In our societies, the reasons for divorce have multiplied, while the pathways to blissful marriages have become obscured, or pushed aside. Our friends and families have all been primed to expect us to have a failed marriage; and as much as they would like to help us when we get into trouble, they do not have the tools to provide us hope or help even if it were their most sincere intent. Very few know how to have the marriage of their dreams; so many of our friends are secretly delighted when we run into trouble, too. A few are jealous of others having marital success, but most would just rather not be the only ones suffering in their marriages.

It is not their fault they are not supportive of you having an incredible marriage. So do not share your fears or woes, or you will invite negative 'support'.

In order to have the best results in your family, we found it is very important for you to keep your marriage, and all that happens within, a closely guarded secret. We advocate and explain the benefits of a private life of joy within your marital home, and discuss how to keep it so. If you want to help a friend with information from The Marriage Foundation, we suggest you let them know anonymously, so you don't have to share what your own family's problems were.

The Foundation's role

None of us as individuals have the luxury of the time it takes to research and prove principles and philosophies we need in order to create our marriages from the bottom up, so people rely on those who take it upon themselves to help others. This reasoning is why The Marriage Foundation and others like us are invited into the lives of those in need. We gather what you need to strengthen your marriage, and then pass it on in as many ways as we can.

As human beings, we are still evolving and learning. As we mature and learn, not all of the best information is always readily available, nor can everyone attest to what is the best of the best in marriage coaching and counseling, but we try to be the cutting edge.

The Marriage Foundation strives to be an exemplary source of practical marital information, which has been thoroughly tested and accredited. We are intent on tracking results and making revisions as discovered and needed. We want your family to succeed.

It is our mission. We want the current anomaly of marital misery to end, so we are doing all we can to validate what we offer. Our revisions will continue as couples report their results to us. Our work is dynamic.

Divorce and marital unhappiness is far too common

People desperately need a way out of the polarized positions they find themselves in when they hit some of the snags, or major impediments in their relationships. The trouble is, and it is obvious with a 50% divorce rate, couples are not being shown how to save their marriages, but rather are too often funneled into a system designed to expedite separation and divorce. In our society, far more energy goes into expediting divorce than into preventing it.

The personal and societal problems of divorce directly impact you, your family and your society.

The trinity of tragedy that comes from divorce

1) What happens within our society impacts all of us

The social and monetary cost of divorce is staggering. The raw statistics tell us how bad things are. The scholastic dropout rates are much higher than for kids from intact families, as are the suicide attempt rates (70% come from broken families), the prison population (90% come from broken families) and poverty (over 50% of divorced families experience poverty after divorce).

Then there are the drug and alcohol abuses, pornography, shoplifting, prostitution, depression and a myriad of other issues, all of which dramatically increase due to broken families, and does so within every socioeconomic demographic.

The costs to our society weaken our communities and our nation. Our country has gone from being a nation of families to a nation of individuals because of divorce. We have lost our grounding. The psychological impacts on our children cannot be given a financial cost, but we can see the increase in greed and other abnormal attitudes which can easily be traced to children growing up without the security of a protective family.

It certainly does not take a psychologist to tie the insecurities of being raised without the united protection of a mother and father to the inevitable need to over-protect oneself.

2) What happens to the children of divorce

If we could truly feel the internal and often repressed pain of each child who watches their mother and father turn on each other, at worst, or when they abandon each other, also at worst, we would be incapacitated with sadness. One friend who does many divorce mediations describes it as a child going to a hostile planet with two bodyguards who turn on each other. The Marriage Foundation came into existence for the primary purpose of protecting children by protecting marriages.

3) What happens to a divorced couple is far more tragic than publicized

Individuals get married with certain expectations of themselves, and each other. They also have expectations of the benefits they will derive from marriage. The number one expectation, which acts as a foundation for so many others, is that they will remain together until the end of life.

The decision to marry the person you married was the most important one you have ever made to date, more important even than having children. It was not made lightly. So ending a marriage means failing at the most important endeavor, the one that holds more promise than any other effort of life. The impacts create a sense that

1) If you can fail at marriage, you can expect failure in anything else you attempt

2) Life is completely unreliable, as you will always wait for the other shoe to drop

Few would subject their children to divorce if they knew how terribly they are impacted

The decision to marry the person you married was the most important one you have ever made to date, more important even than having children

No need to delve further into other impacts. We bring these up because the seriousness of marriage and devastation of divorce have, for the most part, been swept under the carpet. But we do not want you to ignore these eye opening realities. Preferable, is for you to determine you will not give up, and you will make every effort to have a blissful marriage.

Determination to succeed is the number one qualifier for success. You cannot succeed without determination, and you cannot fail if you have it. Never give up.

Divorce is far from painless

Despite noble rhetoric and good intentions, divorce courts, because of materialism based laws, emphasize material issues such as individual incomes and property division. Couples are forced to divide houses, assets and pay legal expenses. Commitments for child care are also fought over, due to its monetary value in the court's eyes, at the expense of facilitating effective co-parenting from the children's point of needs.

By design, there is little true humanity to be found in a court of law. Well intentioned, but overburdened people put programs in place which were adapted by concerned legislators, but the courts are simply too overtaxed and under personalized to help many children. No family court person can argue this unfortunate reality.

Too many social workers, who just do not have the time to help any family get to a good place, reluctantly end up acting as facilitators of the divorce rather than protectors of families. Some very good people with good intentions become cynical slaves of the court system instead of doing what they dreamed of, which was helping families.

The way laws and rules divvy up money, primarily based on percentages of child custody, inevitably leads to competition and slander, rather than cooperation. Add to the mix psychological experts proving themselves to courts so that they have future assignments, by creating fancy well crafted reports, often despite common sense solutions which should have included marital education and suggestions for reconciliation.

Then parents use lawyers to probe one another to find parenting and psychological weaknesses, instead of validating each other's value. It is obscene how many couples divorce when experts see and know there is hope. But it is not their jobs to create hope, and we do not blame them.

Two wonderful people, who originally found each other and committed their lives to one another, find they are now in a horrible battle, pushed on by fear and anxiety, fighting for their individual lives instead of their lives together or for their children. So, they hire the best lawyers they can afford, to attack with all their might, the one who they loved with all their heart. The whole thing defines irony.

The love couples sought is not gone! But the love and mutual regard is so overshadowed with the crazy break-up reality of insecurity and struggle, that their minds are overwhelmed and barely functioning. Nobody knows which way is up, while mutual compassion and selflessness, so vital to a family, is almost nonexistent.

Many individuals who are going through a divorce resort to psychotropic drugs, which helps them (barely), stay afloat, while others turn to alcohol or drugs. Still others binge

Despite noble rhetoric and good intentions ... children are fought over based on their monetary value

on meaningless relationships or empty sexual encounters. But there is no relief, even in the best of divorces, for many years. The sense of failure, the inevitable blame, and the choosing of sides among friends, all change lives forever, not for better.

If couples learned the truth, that if they put a tenth of the energy into their marriage, which is forced out of them by the divorce process, they would have a very successful marriage.

Divorce is (almost) completely preventable!

Folks rarely actually really want to end their marriage. The threat of divorce is usually a cry for help. Many even naively think a lawyer or mediator they consult with will compassionately guide them to a path that will help them save their marriage.

But why would a family law lawyer ever tell you to not give up on your marriage? It would actually be unethical and is certainly not how they earn their living. Why would a family law lawyer inform you that no child from a broken home does as well as their counterparts from intact families? It is not his or her business to help you stay together. They assume, by your contacting them that you have already made up your mind after exhausting every possible avenue to repair your marriage, and save your children.

You will soon discover that divorce is almost always preventable

Truly good people who could no longer take the pressure of a malfunctioning marriage, and erroneously believe divorce is the only way out, find zero encouragement to look for alternatives to divorce from the family law world. They find themselves caught in a funnel towards failure.

Statistics which should be well known

Did you know it is a rarity for both husband and wife to give up at the same time? Divorce is usually pushed upon one parent by the other. The knowledge that divorce is usually foisted by only one presents an opportunity to save a marriage, even at that stage. People generally do not understand it is not the role of a divorce lawyer to be anything but a hired advocate, but we know very well that most marriages can be saved at that point.

You can turn your marriage in the direction you always wanted with knowledge and resolve

Very few find the way to break the vacuum pull and momentum towards completing their divorce. But you should know the truth. Your marriage does not have to end. You can completely turn it in the direction you always wanted, with the person, your spouse, you are with now.

We do not hesitate to grab couples off the edge of the divorce cliff

The genesis of The Marriage Foundation was discovering ways to save those who were committed to divorce, but were still willing to give it one last shot. The knowledge we gave to those who were interested in continuing with their marriage was effective in most cases, and will be in yours. Our information is usually not what you will find in most book shelves, but what really sets it apart is how obvious our discoveries are, and how effective our solutions are, whether your marriage is just a wee bit scary, or collapsing in a heap of lies and disgust. We seek your family's success. We want your children to be safe.

There is no final divorce until the judge calls it so

In many states, there is a set time for cooling off, often six months. When an individual goes to a family law lawyer, they are told the period of time in their state before a divorce can be final. In some, there is no waiting period. Few lawyers actually tell their client the real purpose for the time is to give the couple a chance to reconcile. Some lawyers make it sound as if it just a formality.

In a few cases, the family law lawyer will also tell their client that many legislators have created safeguards so couples can discuss issues without undermining their case, but not many do so. Family law is different than all other legal cases. Typically, clients in a lawsuit should not discuss a case with the person they are suing, but it is different in family law. Reconciliation, whenever it comes about, is (almost) always the best path to take.

No matter how long the separation of the parents lasts, it is always a good idea to try to find common ground, so the children will not have opposing parents. It is very important for parents to do all they can to get along and act as if they are still connected, even try to learn how to be married again, so their family can be reunited. It is not unusual for us to see couples emerge from the worst possible squabbles and find the family they want is the one they are walking away from. But it cannot happen with just determination. There have to be real educated changes made, too.

Education

The truth is without fundamental marital education all the determination and all the counseling in the world will only help so much. Individuals need enough information about marriage so they can face most marital problems with knowledge and confidence.

The knowledge you need in order to have a sound marriage is a lot more than a few tips about what to do in this or that situation. All of us need to understand marriage from the bottom up. We need to know why things work the way they do, so we can improvise according to what is needed when it is needed.

There is hope! A properly functioning marriage brings so much joy it sometimes seems unreal. No matter how bad things are today, your marriage is still a marriage; so by making positive changes and then allowing the changes to become normal behavior, your marriage will become exceptional, better than you ever dreamed! Don't imagine you are with the wrong one, or somehow next time will be better despite your failings.

Second marriages fail more than first ones

People do not generally realize second marriages (and third) have a much higher rate of failure. It should be obvious, but we, our society, like to pretend a tough time or two means our marriage is a mismatch or…whatever.

What it really means is we need to learn how to be married. We need to learn to forgive ourselves and our spouse, and then do what it takes to make our marriage wonderful, instead of staying on the old tracks that lead to pain and suffering. You have free will. Once you know what you have been doing that causes pain, you can change your ways to do that which causes happiness.

Save your children

Ninety-nine percent of us never hear the statistical truth about what happens to children during and after divorce. We believe most individuals would never consider divorce an option, no matter how much they would suffer by staying married, if they knew the whole truth. Yet, somehow the statistics remain hidden.

Those of us who read the statistics about what happens shed many tears, even though we are familiar with them. Just hearing them again reopens the ache. Most of us would never stand by while an animal is treated cruelly. We even cringe when a litter of dogs or cats is removed from its mother, yet we close our eyes to the trauma imposed on children of divorce. Parents need to know.

We, the foundation, would be negligent if we did not share the most compelling reason for staying together is to protect your children. We know many of you are also products of broken homes. Do you want your children to suffer as you did, losing out on all the benefits of an intact family, as you did? Children adapt, but they still suffer so much. How could it be otherwise? They come to a hostile planet, and their two bodyguards become enemies. They need security to grow up and face this world.

We do not advocate you stay together for your children alone. We advocate you make your marriage so wonderful, through education, that the idea of splitting up would be impossible. Break the cycle!

Understanding marriage as a "thing" allows a scientific view of it

Practical, practical, practical

We all know there are no such things as magical solutions. There are no fairies and magic wands. We need comprehensive understanding of marriage as a whole. We need something that indisputably works in real life.

Thankfully marriage is not as complicated as it first seems. What is missing for everyone who goes the separation route is the knowledge that marriage has more to offer than any other venue of life. When couples know what they are striving for, then their efforts to get there will seem like trading pebbles for pearls.

Marital education

If you look at marriage objectively, it is as obvious as frosting on cake that trying to be married without education is like a sixteen year old trying to drive a car in big city traffic without ever going to driving school; good luck with that!

Why not use science to make your marriage your greatest happiness

When we began the foundation, we looked at the current places you can go for marital education. We are fine, if not delighted, with any training that works; but statistics tell us many courses are not working as well as they should. Statistics reveal those who take religion based courses, for instance, have no better chance than the general population.

Naturally, there are tremendous concepts within many programs, but we feel what you learn about marriage has to be universally foundational and applicable, and always work when applied, *every* time. It cannot be something that only works if you are a Christian, Jew or Mormon, American or Spanish. What works has to be scientific, no matter what religious or secular basis inspired it. Information has to work because it works with human and spiritual natures, regardless of individual culture or beliefs. So with great appreciation for their often underappreciated work, we garnered some of their ideas as part of our many sources, and assimilated what we found to be universally applicable.

They, as well as we, know you shouldn't have to belong to a particular denomination or even believe in God to have a successful marriage. Marriage works when it works because a system you use works with who you are as human beings. Any system has to take everything into account. It has to work regardless of culture, creed, income, intelligence or anything else. Like gravity, it has to work because it conforms to natural laws. So, although we are unaffiliated, we are supportive of any idea that will help a family remain together and prosper.

"I literally thought my marriage was done. Now it is not even a thought in my mind"

Our system is universal

We define a "happy marriage", as a design of positive interactions and ultimate gratifications based on selflessness. We also outline what marriage has to offer in ways we have not found anywhere else, and we pass on how to achieve those ideals. We unabashedly define what makes marriage unique and spectacular.

Prepare yourself for this education

Before you get started, it is a good idea to compare what you want in marriage to what you have now. Make this experience personal, so you are involved and invested.

Do you want peace; but have tension and arguments. How about trust, caring, support, intimacy, and love? Instead, is every petty problem eclipsing what you want?

Some explanations of certain concepts or methods that work well are expanded in this revision, as more explanation is needed than we originally thought, but for the most part what we share is as logic driven as could be, and built upon what we already knew and shared in earlier iterations.

Of course, this is not a claim that what we share will absolutely work for everyone in every single case, but the logic is sound, and we would never ask you to do something counter to what you believe will work. Your results are what we live for, and we are not afraid to revise and refine our information as often as we need, to make sure we save as many families as we can.

Thousands have been helped, millions more will follow

We have unearthed almost every nuance of all the important principles anyone has to learn.

Here is a typical example of feedback

Hi Paul,

I want to thank you for sending me your book. I am about half way through and it has immediately impacted my life. I explained to my wife, Lori, our meeting and the book and she has just about completed it. . . .I am not a very religious person but I do believe in divine intervention. I am beginning to believe our chance meeting just wasn't that, chance. . . .

I can't begin to tell you how much I appreciate what you had shared with me/us. Our marriage is now on the right track of recovery. When I met you on Friday, I literally thought my marriage was done. Now it is not even a thought in my mind.

Again, thank you and if I run into you at Starbucks I owe you a coffee . . . it's the least I can do.

Brad

The book has been revised and includes much more than what Brad was given.

For those of you in a troubled marriage, this knowledge will show you how to end your suffering. You will be encouraged all along the way and learn how to move beyond the hurt, which is sometimes the hardest part. You will learn how to behave in ways that create joy and security. Those of you in newer marriages, but who are already feeling some tension, will discover marriage is wonderful, when you understand it.

Very few marriages that end in divorce are lost because of insurmountable issues, such as complete mental instability, which leads to physical danger and/or other radical problems. Commonly perceived big issues like infidelity, mistrust, loss of respect, financial problems, and emotional suffering are actually symptoms of one or more of the three killers, discussed at length, thrust upon people who have no idea what they are doing to themselves and to each other. The so-called big issues are forgivable and forgettable when understood in proper context. Couples learn how to forgive and move on, for very good reasons.

When you make your marriage into something truly wonderful, everyone wins. Isn't that how it is supposed to be, where everyone wins? Many of you good people are hanging in there for the sake of your children, but now is the time to get the joy back into your marriage so your kids will not be the only reason to be married. Your children will benefit when you are happily married. What a difference! Also, please do not entertain the notion that your best hope is a marriage that you can 'live with'. You deserve to have a marriage you will not want to live without.

We meet people all the time who believed they already lost a marriage they did not want to lose. Some already moved out, lived in separate rooms for months or years and/or had begun the legal process of divorce. We were their last shot. Do not give up! Ninety-nine percent of the time, both partners make the effort after a bit, but mutual agreement is not a prerequisite for happiness. You can lead the way. Yes, of course you will have to make changes, but only changes that make sense to you. The proof will be in the pudding, and you will see it. Once you understand the underlying principles, correct behavior is obvious, which it should be.

You deserve to have a marriage you will not want to live without

Learn these lessons as conceptually as you can. Don't get hung up on every word or detail. There are different ways of hearing things, and this book contains more information than any normal person needs. Our goal is to get you going in the right direction as efficiently as possible. You will not hear it all even if you read it all; neither will you need to. You will hear what you are ready to hear, and it will likely be enough.

Everything is presented in a definite order, so it is better to not skip around until you have finished the book at least once. There is a natural compounding of knowledge that will come from reading this book in the order written. Especially, do not read the chapter on intimacy until you have assimilated the foundational principles built one upon the other in the previous chapters. Sex without intimacy is shallow and crude; not close to the connection you can have when you deepen your friendship. But general misunderstandings abound, so we want to ease you into the real deal so it makes sense enough to utilize.

Now smile; you are embarking on a new and wonderful beginning.

Is divorce ever an option?

There are those who are not willing to change, or they have a deep belief in something to the exclusion of anything else. Those folks take a bit longer to try new approaches because some concepts need to be thought about, and experimented with, first. They should not lose heart, but try harder to change according to useful ideas.

Unfortunately, however, there are some extremely rare relationships in which, sadly, one or both partners have fallen so far that they are abusive by any standard. Threatening conditions cannot be taken lightly. Each of us has to take personal responsibility for our children's safety, and our own.

We also worked with couples, not many, who admitted to living with some violence or minor drug (including alcohol) abuse, because we want to help all; but not all were successful. Some children must be kept from their own parents, so you have to get professional help if your situation is dangerous, please. Don't get scared by shadows, but be honest if things are explosive or dangerous.

Most of us get the happiness we strive for

Don't allow the despair of your current situation to destroy your expectations for happiness. When you do what is needed, your efforts will help you achieve your good goals. A plant that is mistreated will usually come back when you know, finally, how to treat it. Your marriage is a lot more resilient than a plant. Do not give up!

Your religion is not your marriage but your marriage may be your religion

We do not promote God in these lessons but we encourage those who have a connection to pray, pray and pray some more. Praying cannot possibly hurt a thing, and focuses the mind on the bigger picture.

. God bless your family! We want you to have it all, and you can.-P.F.

Don't allow the despair of your current situation to destroy your expectations for happiness

- Chapter Two -
The Three Marriage Killers

❖❖❖

Everything you do in life is challenged by specific destructive forces.
But success is assured to individuals who are able to identify the behaviors
and attitudes which are avoidable, and then replace them with constructive
and protective behaviors. The same is true for marriage.

Your knowledge will serve your needs.

❖❖❖

Marriage killers are like con artists, unseen for what they are. But when you learn to see through their disguises they are wolves without teeth. You will soon know them and destroy them. Then you will be able to focus your efforts on marriage builders.

Chapter Two

The Three Marriage Killers

If this was a marriage manual for newlyweds, we wouldn't start with three killers, nor address them as such; because when they first crop up, they aren't killers. They are just ugly behaviors. When people are educated, and behave the way they should, the killers never show up.

But couples in troubled marriages have to focus on stopping their detrimental, or killer, behaviors, which show up in the forms of thoughts, words and actions. That has to be your absolutely highest priority.

Once you determine to stop the things which sabotage your marriage and things cool down, then you can explore the beneficial marriage enhancing ideals of positive attitudes, loving communication and selfless behavior; but killing the killers is the first order of business.

Newlyweds easily avoid the killers

Marital education for newlyweds begins with defining the greatest visions of marriage, which creates a 'destination' to move their marriage towards.

They also need descriptions of what it is like to live in an ideal relationship so they are inspired to do what it takes to build security and happiness in a natural way.

Then, we illustrate how to build upon selfless love and positive expectations, showing many ways to enhance the strived for goals.

Learning about killers is valuable if your marriage lacks harmony

Starting a marriage fresh, without all the debris that comes from not getting along, is completely different than fixing a marriage that ran off the rails.

This specific approach is tailored to your situation. If you prioritize your efforts with ending the destructive behaviors first, your progress will be accelerated.

Little problems only grow because they aren't recognized for what they are

We cannot stress enough the importance of keeping intentions and behaviors focused on relationship building and making your married life about happiness. Exposing and bypassing the temptations to misbehave is important, of course, but the emphasis will be on fueling happiness producing connection.

The killers are present now, but they will not be here for long. Yes, you need to see them for what they are, and yes, you need to abolish them. But this is not about getting rid of the killers and going on with your lives. There is too much to be had from going further, and we want you to see that.

Couples in troubled marriages have to focus on stopping their detrimental, or killer, behaviors, which show up in the forms of thoughts, words and actions

Sometimes the bottom line seems pretty far up

The minor mistakes, the pebbles, became killers for you because, like termites hiding within the wall, they grew and multiplied until your marital home was threatened. You didn't see it coming.

And, it's unfortunate some new marriages are in trouble right from the start and need education designed for troubled marriages. But for the most part, learning about marriage killers is for those who need it after trying everything else and failing, regardless of how long they are married.

Still, the base line is starting in a place where the killers aren't running your lives.

Education for troubled marriages needs a special focus

Putting an end to all your misbehaviors takes a bit of time, but not months or years

For those who are not getting what they want from their relationships, who are wondering where all the promised connection is, this will help you. Dealing honestly and determinedly with the killers will be a great investment into your marital future, but we see it as just getting this stuff out of the way.

Couples who get married without any kind of practical and extensive marital knowledge, like you did, are almost sure to have troubles and get discouraged. The same thing would have happened to you if you started driving without any driver education.

Although we forget how tricky and scary it was to get on the highway the first time, you managed to pass your tests and now drive like you were born with the ability. Well, you just jumped right into marriage, without realizing marriage is much more complex than driving!

Eventually, everyone can learn to drive successfully. Everyone can also learn how to be married successfully; education just makes sense. But driving isn't all about avoiding danger or going through mental checklists in your head, and neither is proper married life. You can only get so far in your relationship before a lack of knowledge was going to cause some real problems. That does not mean your marriage is over. All it means is you have to stop doing the wrong things you do, the things which work against achieving what you want.

You will have success by moving in the right direction, with determination

Putting an end to all the misbehaviors takes a bit of time, but we don't want this to take years, or even months. So you need to put in a lot of upfront effort. At the same time you have to get started on getting the joys your marriage has to offer.

Your marriage is alive, and it will heal. If you follow our guidance it will heal faster than you can imagine. But there is no getting around the fact you have to deal with the reality of a marriage filled with hurt, anger, frustration and weariness. You can't just skip the steps you have to take to end the scourge of the killers.

The pebbles have to be removed and you will heal, but you also have to stop picking them up. Your efforts gain traction, and you will see your marriage will for sure bring you joy. But you need to be reminded often. It will be fine as long as you keep trying.

The killers have to be subdued

The first thing to do is stop the killers, the incompatible and destructive actions; they are no joke. Marriage killers are not some random "outsiders" who slipped in to kill your marriage. They are there because you, yourself, brought them into your marriage, and you keep them there.

Misguided speech and behaviors need to be squelched and replaced. They hurt you and your spouse, keeping you in a state of pain. The killers have a life of their own now, and they rule your marriage.

There is nothing more precious than the connection you sought, and still seek

You will discover why good behavior was evasive and how you can bring it back into your lives like you never had it before. By the power bad habits have they have literally taken you over, making you do things you would never condone if you were in your right mind.

And they are not just killers of your marriage. They destroy you as individuals. They reduce you as people, and slowly eat away at all you once were, and all you can become.

They are relentless killers which need to be identified and stopped.

The killers are sneaky

A big problem is you cannot see them for what they are. You actually see your reactions and inner resentments as normal, as you blame the circumstances for outrageous reactive behaviors. So the killers have to be clearly pointed out, and identified, exposed and scrutinized.

You have to be able to see them as they happen

They have to be thoroughly understood, so that in the future you are able to admonish yourself for including them. Until you understand the killers are your enemies, you cannot defeat them. However, once you see what you are doing to yourself and your spouse, you can take the necessary steps to rein them in, by intelligently catching them.

You have powers over habit

Because they have become habits, you can apply the necessary wisdom of introspection and discrimination to scientifically change everything you need to change.

Habits are reversible! So, as your destructive thoughts, words and behaviors can come under your control, as you simultaneously begin the process of building your marriage in a way that brings you true happiness.

Maybe it seems a bit vague at this point, but the reality is your marriage is a lot more than just salvageable. Your marriage will become what all marriages are supposed to be.

But you need to get it on track as fast as you can. There are just three killers, and the main one is as good as dead as soon as you make up your mind. You can do this!

Marriage killers are in your marriage because you brought them in, and keep them there

Habits are reversible!

The destructive power of inconsiderate communication has to be replaced with marriage-building words and actions

Over-familiarity is the first killer

Thank heaven that the first killer, which is giving you the most trouble, is also the easiest to recognize and conquer. Once pointed out, it is remedied with progressively greater and more targeted effort. We will show you exactly what it looks like, and how it slips into your marriage. We will also show you exactly how to get it out; then how to keep it out.

When you immediately put your focused attention on the first killer, over-familiarity, which is most fundamental to all your problems, you will advance the furthest in the shortest amount of time.

By tackling this killer first, your subsequent efforts will fall right into place. When you replace over-familiar speech and behaviors with supportive respect, everything you think, say or do will lead to harmony, love and connection. As your efforts to dislodge over-familiarity become a deep habit, the pace of improvement is steady, and encouraging.

The second killer, Poor Communication, is well known, but hardly understood

We distinguish marital communication from all other forms of communication.

In a marriage, the destructive power of inconsiderate communication has to be replaced with marriage building words and actions. Because communication is at the heart of marriage, everything you learn will tie together as one form of communication or another.

But using rules of communication that works in every other part of life will betray you; it will not work. Your spouse is not a co-worker or friend in the normal sense. Communication in marriage is very special, and your techniques have to be appropriate.

We call the third killer Marital Materialism

You didn't get married to form a corporation where each of you works for, and protects themselves. You want and need love, connection and intimacy.

In marriages that have suffered for a long period, we have seen how too many couples reduce their marriage down to a business deal. When this mentality rules, the efforts to rekindle love turns into a "who goes first" standoff.

Expectations in a happy marriage are expectations that one has of themselves, to please and honor their spouse. Expectations in a materialistic marriage are the same selfish expectations found in everyday life. That isn't what you want.

This particular killer is not so easy to kill because of how social environment pushes us into selfish thinking. Thank goodness it is the rarest of the three.

Kill the killers first, and then move on to the good stuff

You do not want to get stuck killing the killers for the rest of your life; just enough to get them out of your lives. You will see, no matter how long it takes to gain self-control; once you have, you will have stopped driving your marriage towards disaster.

Once you will learn to control yourself, you can put your efforts into creating the happiest marriage on Earth. Then, you will realize the connection and intimacy you dreamed of is right where you hoped it would be, in the sacred relationship of your marriage.

You can leave the pain and suffering behind forever!

There is a shortcut to killing the killers. It is to recognize the rules which we share are not "thou shall not" orders from above, so to speak; but are great guardrails, which keep you from making the same mistakes over and over again, when you remember them.

The idea of following rules is not fun for everyone, but they define safe limits

When a marriage is off track, the quickest and most certain way is to follow some of those universally applicable rules until you see for yourself, how they keep you safe.

If you absolutely hate rules, make these rules an exception to your rule of hating rules. The benefits you receive from following them will make you glad you did.

Do what you should, not what you want

Doing what you should do, instead of what you want to do, will create more happiness than frustration. In other words, avoiding established bad habits, despite the nagging impulses, will make all the difference in the world.

When you learned to drive, which is admittedly less complicated than creating a successful marriage, the first things you learned were the rules of the road, mostly learning the don'ts. The don'ts relate to things which get you into trouble, even if done innocently.

Don't drive on the wrong side of the road, don't drink and drive, don't accelerate in unsafe conditions, and don't get mad at other drivers etc.

There are different kinds of rules

Some rules are blatantly obvious. Staying in your prescribed lane and not texting while you drive, do not need explanations. The benefits of other rules make sense after a brief explanation, like the rule about applying ice to a bruised body part.

Then there are more complex don'ts, which need to be explained in more detail, like the rule about not eating mucus causing food when you have a cold.

Other rules just need to be accepted, like not sharing a secret about an acquaintance, even if you are dying to tell someone, because the wisdom of those who have studied the results benefits us.

Marital rules are very reasonable in context

For your marriage, we try to explain everything very well, so you have no doubt about the wisdom of any of those rules we share with you. We want you to know what you are doing and why, well enough to explain it back to us if we asked. That way we hope, you will want to adhere to what we suggest.

Doing what you should do, instead of what you want to do, will create more happiness than frustration

When you are able to consciously define the don'ts which keep you from perilously impacting your marriage (they really should teach this stuff in school), you will be much safer.

As you become familiar with the marriage killers, you will soon notice the most destructive behaviors in your marriage fall under the over-familiar category. You will see how you unknowingly ignored the early warning signs and reactions, as your marriage slowly transformed into a war zone, or maybe a cold-war zone.

No blame

Blaming either you or your spouse for messing up your marriage is wrong. The fact is even though you may have done some counterproductive things, it is not entirely your fault.

Feelings of guilt delay the process of learning

Who learned in school, or somewhere else, what they should do to have a good marriage? Marriage, considering how many of us have one, is the most misunderstood relationship there is. Nobody, but nobody, should feel guilt for what went wrong.

The don'ts are very useful

The rules you establish for your behavior will protect you from the killers by acting as internal guardrails. Paying attention to the don'ts, just as you did when you learned anything technical, will make a big difference.

Like with everything else, the don'ts for marriage eventually become second nature. Marriage is what you do 24-7, so having so much opportunity to practice your positive efforts will soon make them second nature.

Not everyone does everything wrong, of course. Nobody, and no marriage, ever needs a complete revamping to have the happiness you seek. It is actually the eclipse effect that causes everyone so much trouble.

The eclipse effect

The don'ts you ignore create so much trouble because they overwhelm all the good you have in your marriage. They eclipse your loving and positive behaviors, all of which might now seem absent to your spouse because of the buildup of misbehaviors and pain.

Marriage doesn't have a tally sheet where you can balance your good and bad behaviors. There is no scorecard. Bad actions immediately block your views and memories of all the good things in life, no matter how vast; just as your hand can completely block the entire sun from your view.

It distorts reality

Even though both of you are really good people, and your good traits far outweigh your bad habits like a thousand to one, because of the eclipse effect it is hard to feel the underlying and desired joy you deserve. No matter how much love there is, it seems so distant when there are behaviors and communications which eclipse the love you feel.

The same thing happens when a minor part on your car goes out and the whole car shakes like a jalopy. A flat tire, one tiny but important part of your car, can make driving completely impossible. Or think about how the absence of one button makes a shirt un-wearable.

The good news is just as fixing one small part will have you back in the shirt or driving a great car again, and moving your hand away from your eyes will open you up to the world. So removing small bad habits, which undermine your marital happiness, allows the innate joy of marriage to fill your lives.

Understanding the common origins of the killers

All three killers come from the same troublesome roots, which produce all sorts of various bad habits. In order to change the habits, you have to be aware of instincts and drives.

We won't spend an inordinate amount of time going over the manifestations of the killers, which can be endless, but we apply laser like focus on explaining the root causes of misery producing thoughts, and behaviors.

Removing bad habits allows the innate joy of marriage to fill your lives

You need to know where the trouble begins

You need to learn how to identify and eradicate them at the source. Just about everyone finds these explanations fascinating and enlightening. Everything will change for you as you learn so much about yourself and your spouse.

You will learn how to halt insensitive and unthinking things you do to hurt your marriage. There are deep hidden controls you have over your life, so you can permanently become the best spouse who ever lived.

Most people, in most unhappy relationships, try to control the things they can't, and don't try to control the things they can. It's about education.

Marriage is everlasting

The world currently (it is a temporary trend) advertises marriage as disposable, but don't fall for such illogical nonsense.

No normal person wants to give up the biggest commitment and dream of their life

No normal person could ever reasonably want to give up on the biggest commitment and dream of their life. Individuals are just afraid of getting caught off guard, so they think or talk about separation, special compromises or divorce. Forget that nonsense!

Show your spouse you mean business about wanting your marriage to endure, by being a great spouse, perhaps the greatest spouse who ever lived.

Then, why shouldn't you shoot for the highest heights? You definitely should have a great marriage, and if you refuse to give up, and apply your will to changing you, you will almost assuredly get what you want.

Make good things your habits of choice

Compassion and understanding will replace condemnation and criticism when you act on your love instead of your fears. And that makes complete sense.

But nobody told you to keep up your good efforts after your wedding. The deeply sincere words of your vows (recall how you felt when you uttered them) were beautiful, but were not practical with the limited and worldly education you had around communication.

Now you need to shift your attitude to align with the reality of what is actually required to make your marriage work. Push the rest of the world, with all its gimmicks, out of your marriage, so your relationship is not violated by fears or negative fantasies.

The basics are there

When you got married, nobody taught you to share, or communicate with your spouse in ways that kept the budding relationship moving towards intimacy and connection. It was nobody's fault. It is just that most people do not actually know how to be married.

Nobody could explain what they did not themselves know, how happiness and the yearning to be together that was felt so strongly during courting could continue, or how you could make it expand beyond anything imaginable.

You did not hold your tongue when you were upset, nor did you learn to express your love and loyalty with patience. You had no guidance, so you made one mistake after another.

It isn't too late

It is not too late to start fresh. Your good educated efforts will change your future. Marriage is not something you studied. You didn't know you should make it a priority to be skillful. Despite its importance to you, and the seriousness of marriage being a lifetime commitment, you jumped in unprepared.

Nevertheless, your unspoken expectation, and theirs, was that you would have the closest ally possible for the rest of your days. You still can have the gifts of marriage, but not without expending the energy you should have expended before.

Had you at least expressed and talked about your needs for connection, with all its ramifications, things would have definitely been better today. Had you put your ideas out on the table together, before you became engaged, you would have established an understanding of intentions, and would have known what was expected of yourselves.

But nobody suggested it, and it never occurred to you that there might be a system to marriage, so you plunged into what you expected to be an ocean of bliss, without knowing about the hidden dangers, or the hidden blessings.

Nobody taught you to share or communicate with your spouse in ways that kept your relationship moving towards intimacy and connection.

- Chapter Three -
Over-familiarity

◇◇

*The term over-familiarity seems unclear until you are shown
how it is the perfect way to describe how you and your spouse
behave towards each other, and how it has been the foundation
for all your marital woes.*

◇◇

You and your spouse dance together without realizing there has been three of you; you, them and your over-familiar thoughts, words and misbehaviors. When you finally see it, you will realize how inappropriate you have been, and you will want over-familiar out of your lives forever.

Chapter Three

Over-familiarity

What is unbelievable is how you got so comfortable with your spouse that you forget to treat them with the most basic respect and kindness you would treat anyone else.

It only happens because nobody warns us about the disease called over-familiarity, which loosely translated means you think just because you are close to each other you somehow have the right to ignore the most basic reasonable respectful boundaries of another individual.

You take each other for granted, all because you think you know each other well enough to ignore basic rules of getting along and even ignore your love for them, which is supposed to be your number one guiding principle. There is nothing alright about that, nothing at all.

It is not intentional, of course. Nobody in their right mind actually wants to hurt the person they want to receive love from. But you must admit it is pretty ironic.

Over-familiarity will destroy every relationship all by itself, long before the numerous issues that arise from it; it is extremely toxic! It is the most common killer, where excuses for being mean, even when the situation demands being kind, abound.

Disrespect is an ever growing cancer that progressively erodes every hurting marriage

Being over-familiar does not necessarily mean you insult each other or throw things. Sometimes, in fact, the outer appearances can be very subtle or discreet.

Not every couple demean themselves with shouting matches or nasty texts. It shows in many ways, both overt and passive aggressive. The various ways it manifests is always in layers, too, where you can see how mean you were only after you remedied an obvious offense.

No one knows better than you the ways you mistreat your spouse. Nobody feels the pain of your behavior more than your spouse, either.

There is no doubt you are on the receiving end as much as the giving end, too. The problems stemming from over-familiarity are endless. Fortunately, in spite of its pervasiveness and destructiveness, over-familiarity is the killer most easily fixed.

Yes, it can be fixed

At first, it almost doesn't seem possible that such an embedded killer can be permanently removed and everything can be back on track, but it is true.

When you learn how and why the terrible habit of disrespectfulness is able to establish itself in the first place, you can start to nip it in the bud whenever it tries to sneak in. But

Over-familiarity is the most common killer where excuses for being mean abound

In spite of its pervasiveness and destructiveness, over-familiarity is the most easily fixed

first, you need to understand all the ins and outs, beginning with individual rights.

Learning where your spouse's boundaries are is your obligation of love and respect

Your spouse, like everyone else in the world, has every right to their personal space. Nobody has the right to go into another's space to judge or criticize them etc. Nor does anyone have the right to define the space of another.

There are generally accepted personal space norms, which most people agree everyone has a right to, and then there is space based on an individual's choices. Either way, when it comes to interactions with others, we are obligated to respect the boundaries of every single person according to their personal particular desires.

Society has volumes of written and unwritten laws about personal space, which describe when it is ok to intrude or not. So much is covered by laws and social norms, like when and how parents or teachers discipline children, or what is acceptable when a person is arrested.

Because of over-familiarity, every couple in trouble has ignored primary considerations within their marriage, and they all have paid the price. So naturally the first, if not the most important rule, is to behave respectfully and lovingly toward your spouse. This is a rule you must never break in even the slightest way. The number one rule for happiness and harmony is

Treat your spouse respectfully
regardless of any reason that may make you want to forget this rule

Remember, what worked before you said "I do" still works now

When you first met, you treated each other with kind and cautious respect, which is normal when getting to know someone. You didn't want to blow it.

Then, as you began to see the potential for a deeper relationship which would lead to marriage, both of you began to ratchet up your attractiveness. Both of you made progressively greater effort to show each other your best sides. This was good!

You were patient, kind, and attentive. You were sweet, funny, considerate, noble, and appreciative; right? You were oh-so-polite, always smiling, constantly complimenting each other, and you easily laughed at each other's jokes, even when they were not all that funny. You dressed to impress, washed behind your ears, and bent over backward to do special little things for each other. You bought flowers for each other, made cookies, maybe called or texted each other all the time.

You treated your squeeze correctly! You were on a mission. You now need to get back to being on a mission!

You may laugh now, when you recall some of the things you did to ensure you were the kind of person your crush would be impressed with, things only you will ever know. No matter who you are, you tried to be romantic and sexy, and no matter who you are, your efforts were appreciated.

Treat your spouse respectfully, regardless of any reason that may make you want to forget this rule

These gestures were not so crazy. You wanted your crush to appreciate your efforts, and love you enough, based on your sincere intentions, to choose you as the one.

Couples do not keep up the effort because they do not know about the benefits which come after the wedding. If they did, they would keep redoubling their efforts every day.

You were trying to win their love and respect. Perfect! Start doing it again!

Never worry about going over the top for fear of appearing phony. Trying to impress your pre-spouse was not phony then, and will not be phony now!

Your desire to impress was never supposed to be extraordinary and different behavior, designed and used only to ensnare them, and get them to marry you. You showed your good side, and you need to always show your good side.

They know about your other sides only too well

Your other sides are the sides you need to work on, not force others to accept. Keep your bad sides to yourself.

If something, some flaw you are working on slips out, that is different. We all have slips and have to live with the slips of others. It is the expectation that they only love you if they accept what is in your toilet that gets you into trouble. But it is neither fair nor reasonable to expect your spouse to live with childish behavior as proof they love you. You can and should control yourself, always to the best of your ability.

Expressive loving behavior was and remains practical. It always has its place because it creates closeness and connection, which makes your partner feel safe and appreciated. Bring it back.

In the beginning, you expressed the real you, instead of what you knew were unattractive habits you thought might be a turn-off. What is wrong with that?! Your habits are not you, anyway. It's the ones you know about that we are talking about, not the ones they know about.

Behave respectfully again

It is normal for you to have been considerate; otherwise you did a bait and switch. Now, it is only fair for you to create new special habits that make your spouse feel even safer with you, and more loved and appreciated.

Intentional thoughtful consideration is an essential mode of behavior for your marriage, which will automatically steer you away from the risk of over-familiarity.

This is why newlyweds, who keep it going from engagement without stopping, never have to worry about the killers. While pushing forward in the right direction, it means you are not going in the wrong direction, because you cannot go in two directions at the same time. You just cannot go in two opposite directions at the same time, so you have to be sure you stay consistent.

Trying to impress your pre-spouse was not phony then and will not be phony now!

Intentional, thoughtful consideration automatically steers you away from over-familiarity

Authenticity

Some say they want to be real. They genuinely think it's not real to control their ideas, speech and automatic reactions to their spouse's speech and behavior.

But don't forget, you are endowed with free will, and you have the ability to change your thoughts and especially your attitudes any time you wish. Of course you can be automatically irritated, if it is an automatic reaction. Or you can use your will to shift your attitude to compassionate and patient.

It is up to you whether you will be an automaton or not. You are not phony just because you change your thinking. You are just using your free will effectively and positively.

You are endowed with free will, so you have the ability to change your thoughts and attitudes any time you wish

You control yourself all the time. You behave well for any person who is important to you, like your boss or a customer, and you now need to include your spouse in the category of those for whom you control yourself.

Be desirable

You also act your best anytime acceptance is important to you. You should strive to be accepted by your spouse.

Your spouse's acceptance of you was not and is not a grace you should think of as a given. You are not automatically entitled to their acceptance, even though you need to give unconditional acceptance to them. Can you see how crazy it is to think otherwise? If everyone acted the way they felt, there would be constant conflict…hmmm.

You used to be nice

Do you recall when you courted your pre-spouse and they were in a bad mood or had a bad day? You did all you could to ease their suffering, right? That is correct marital behavior, not just correct behavior for courting!

Impatience and annoyance are always inappropriate. Of course, you sometimes feel annoyed or impatient, but have you mistakenly learned to believe your expressions of these traits do not need to be monitored and restrained? Do you just let it rip, anywhere anytime?

It is a ridiculous idea that being a jerk because you are unhappy is being real. and that you should be able to be "real" with your spouse and that it is a form of intimacy.

No, no, no! That is not intimacy! It is a form of selfish childishness. Intimacy is what you want, for sure, and you shall have it, but it is very different from immature expressions.

When you were first together, you did not expect your squeeze to come around or snap out of it if they were upset. You were authentically concerned for them, not thinking how they might be bumming you out. You probably didn't even think of them as bumming you out because you put their needs ahead of yourself. Giving unconditional acceptance is selfless; the correct way to be towards your spouse.

At some disastrous moment, it all began to fall apart

After some time you became over-familiar with your spouse, and you stopped behaving at basic levels of consideration. Without realizing it, you slowly became all about 'you' in your relationship, while your spouse became all about them. That is when you got off the path that leads to happiness.

Can you actually recall the last time you thought about what would really make your spouse happy? When you dated and courted, you spent a lot of time thinking about what would make them happy!

You take your spouse for granted now, and resentment has become the normal response to his or her needs. You internally and externally complain about how you do not get your needs met, but never consider if your spouse, the one who you promised the sun and moon to, is getting their needs met.

You are not keeping your word

You might say you broke your word to them. What are your excuses? Everyone has a boatload of excuses, but they do not count. You did not make your promises of love and support conditional on how they behave towards you, or anything else. You cannot legitimately blame them for your bad behavior. It does not justify it.

You didn't make your promises of love and support conditional on how they behave towards you

Maybe you currently see your spouse's needs as an imposition on you. We seem to be good at deciding what is fair, and we are usually willing to listen to other points of view about what is fair; but fairness is not part of the marital equation Fairness won't work. "Unconditional" is the proper word and guiding principle. Your efforts have to be unconditional, just like you say your love is.

Understand human nature

Theoretically, most people definitely wish to serve their spouses, and many think they are doing so even though their spouse would not agree.

Fairness is not part of the marital equation

Most people actually do want to serve their spouse, but I have never met anyone who wanted to be abused by being thought of as less-than. Many women occasionally enjoy the fantasy of being a courtesan, but no woman wants to actually be treated like a whore. Most men take a lot of pride in doing "honey-dos" for their wives, but no man wishes to be the house slave.

Instead of treating each other like royalty forever, as you promised, you fell into habits of behavior you would never dare use on anyone else.

What happened to the flowers?

What happened to the smiles and sexy looks?

What happened to compliments, sweet phone messages, careful grooming, supportive chats, little gifts, funny stories, gentle smooches, loving looks, special dinners, and unasked for shoulder rubs? They have gone out the window.

You didn't just stop the good, you replaced it with awful

You replaced beneficial and appropriate behavior with ugly sarcastic comments, cold grumpy looks, critical thoughts, commands, pointed insults, stupid complaints, and nagging, and/or unfair expectations.

C'mon! When you enter someone's space with rudeness, anger, criticism, expectations, or other destructiveness, you are offensive and being rude. You will not build a loving marriage with those; no way!.

You need to get back to doing what you know worked in the past and then more. They married you for reasons you do not give them anymore. You still want to be cherished, maybe more than ever. Do you really expect your spouse to cherish you when you are mean and indifferent? Will they love you because you exposed their weaknesses?

Use your intimate knowledge to benefit your spouse

Even a sweet dog will eventually bite you when you mistreat it every day. Do you think you now know your husband or wife well enough to treat each other without consideration? Does that make any sense at all? Do you believe you have reached a point when it becomes okay to be a jerk? Is that what friendship is supposed to evolve into? No way! You are supposed to use your intimate knowledge to give more than they expect.

You literally traded the bliss, which comes from consistent loving behavior, for the perverse right to speak your mind, and act out your most lowbrow behaviors.

Being relaxed enough to be your self does not mean you can be a toad

Relaxing in the presence of your spouse is a good thing; but relaxing your efforts to be considerate, especially at their expense, is a bad thing. Think how happy you feel when your spouse is genuinely concerned and considerate. That is how you need to be towards them.

Naturally, nobody exhibits all the negative characteristics expressed here, but it only takes one example, even if it is not listed, to fit the bill of over-familiar destructive mistreatment.

You have the power

Go back to sweet behaviors, even if your spouse does not. It is still in your best interests to win your spouse's affection and appreciation—regardless of how you are treated.

You proved you can do it (when you courted) and so wondering if your efforts will work or not is a waste of time. You already know being nice all the time, and not being mean ever, will definitely work, so that is what you need to do.

If they changed, as many say their spouses have, and you are not happy with them and therefore withhold your good behaviors; it only means they can change again, when you change your behaviors.

Relaxing in the presence of your spouse is a good thing; but relaxing your efforts to be considerate is a bad thing

They are not robots. They will respond to your positive efforts.

After you got married

We have heard so many variations of "it's different after you're married". And yes, it is supposed to be different; different better!

The better you know your best friend and lover, the more you are supposed to use your intimate knowledge to be nicer in ways no one else in the world can match, because no one knows the little secrets about your spouse like you.

Instead, you unthinkingly behave in a way that says that because you are married, you may abuse each other; as if that is what you and your spouse signed up for.

You did not did not sign up for any abuse

Your spouse did not sign up for abuse

Isn't this so unbelievably simple? Don't follow the ways of the cruel world in your marriage. Over-familiarity does not work in marriage any more than driving the wrong way on a highway works for driving.

Replace your over-familiar behavior with loving and supportive behavior, and make extra supportive behavior a habit. Don't you want to be treated the way you were treated when you were courting? Would you consider marrying the person who treats you the way you are currently treated? Well, neither would your spouse.

The best way to take advantage of the security of your marriage contract is by opening your heart and expressing love without inhibition. Express loyalty and appreciation like you ought to. Don't be concerned, or worry if your spouse does not get this. Just do what you know is the best way to treat them.

You do not need to set ground rules, or make a deal to do this, because you already did that when you said "I do".

Predicate your behavior on what you know is right, rather than how your spouse behaves

You are ultimately responsible for only your own behavior. This point is critical to the success of your marriage. If you wait for your spouse to measure up before you take the next step, you will fail.

You be first

Behaving well towards a person who does not treat you as well as you would have them treat you is a sign of maturity.

We know the reasons for resentment, and we know the reasons to override those resentments. We also know how to control the mind and will show you. You, too, will soon learn how to deal with the internal objections that pop up in your mind. For now

Don't follow the ways of the cruel world in your marriage. Over-familiarity does not work in marriage any more than driving the wrong way on a highway works for driving

You do not need to set ground rules or make a deal, because you already did that when you said "I do"

though, just think about how being kind will create harmony, while being otherwise will add to your woes; its common sense.

No time limits or conditions should interfere with your efforts to behave well. You are hurting each other, and have become so used to it that you do not see how mean and ugly you have become.

You don't hear yourself when you speak to your spouse. Your meanness, in whatever form it comes, was extremely painful in the beginning; before you became numb. Perhaps it is still painful, but you hardly notice through the anger and hurt.

Your marriage is not a sitcom

The world is cruel. Make your marriage a safe haven from the world.

It's your right to notice your spouse's flaws or behavioral faux pas

Life is not a TV sitcom where it is funny or entertaining to be vicious or sarcastic. It is not comical to judge or ridicule another's weakness or unfortunate predicament or to goof on them. Nor is it your right to notice your spouse's flaws or behavioral faux pas. It is time to stop this atrocious behavior right now!

We hear so many exceptions. They are not valid. Not one. There is never a justifiable reason to be mean or inconsiderate; excuses are, in fact, a form of lying. You have no right, no matter what the circumstances, to criticize your partner. Not only is criticism simply an expression of your own shortcomings, but it never, never, never achieves your desired result, immediate or long term.

Really, what is "wrong"?

If you see your spouse doing something 'wrong', which is anything you happen to not like (be honest), quickly stop your own mind from judging. Instead, think about changing your perspective; or you can dwell upon one of the many positive traits they have.

Then, make note of your own offensive behaviors, without comparing it to your spouse, so you can be humble.

Marriage is not a contest. If your spouse has difficulty living up to standards you have set for him or her, the real problem is that you are being judgmental. Do you see the reasoning? Judgment is based on subjective evaluations seen through your eyes, and unless your spouse is evil, they are doing the best they can. Try to see their actions through their eyes. You will be surprised as you learn things you had not considered before.

It makes no difference if it is difficult, if it is the right thing to do

What is suggested here is certainly not meant as an easy thing to do. If it were, the book could end right now. There is a lot to learn about how the mind works and why this simple advice is not as easy as 1, 2, 3. In fact, telling someone to "just stop, just do this, just do that…" is like telling someone all they need to do is climb Mt. Everest. "Hey, what's the problem? I told you how to fix your marriage!"

No, we do not think it is easy, nor will reaching the goals of marriage necessarily be immediate (maybe it can be). We do know, however, that it is more than doable when you have more information. We also know the effort can be made right now. Then, you will see the hard parts, as you run into them, are far from impossible, but not until you make the effort.

The results come based on your efforts, not time

Maybe, you can reverse the trends quicker than you think. These lessons contain all you will need to be successful, so take it step by step. Each step brings you closer to your needs. You already took the first step, and made some effort by buying these lessons.

Now start watching your behaviors towards your spouse. Start being kind now. Stop being critical now. Stop saying things that are offensive and disrespectful. Shout compliments, and be gracious instead of shouting criticisms and complaints.

You know how to behave well

Being gracious means being sincere and saying something your spouse will like hearing. If you stop being mean, and start being kind, everything will immediately improve. You have the power! Do not fool yourself!

One couple I worked with told me they treated each other just fine, that over-familiarity wasn't their problem. They were numb. After some discussion, they began to see just how much they abused each other, in subtle and quiet ways.

Subtle attacks and hurts cause not so subtle pain and resentment

Because this particular couple remained polite (they worked in politics so they were really good surface communicators), they thought they were nice to each other, but they were actually very cold towards each other. That's not why you married your best friend; is it; just to be nice?

Anyone can get nice at the local coffee shop! "Insincerity is like a beautiful dead lady." Being polite just to be polite is only slightly better than remaining quiet. However, it is better to start with politeness, if that is all you can muster, rather than wait until you feel like being polite. Ending the abuses is half the battle.

Replace the awful with love

Refocus on your love, and build it again in your heart; and for now, as you adjust to the idea that you can have a great marriage, mostly focus on improving your actions. Positive actions will ease current tensions, which will make more future positive actions easier.

It can be a struggle at first for some, but others will just jump right in without worrying if they look foolish; they know what they want. Either way, if you faithfully move towards your destination of a happy marriage, even with occasional slips or detours, you will absolutely reach it.

Results come based on your efforts, not time

If you faithfully move towards your destination of a happy marriage, you will absolutely reach it

Either way, slowly, or quickly with abandon, tend to this precious plant of your relationship without applying anymore "lovicides" of inconsiderate behaviors. Force your mind, to the best of your abilities, to return to thoughts which add love to your relationship. Show your spouse you love and appreciate them.

Don't think they already know you love them. What difference does that make anyway? People respond to real time expressions of love.

Get past any excuses to not reveal your love. You will learn how to express your love in more and more penetrating ways if you are serious about it, and refuse to be less than great; no matter how long it takes or how hard it may be.

Keep your marital friendship your dearest friendship

Gossip is a primitive, if not barbaric, learned behavior

Not long ago (well at this rewrite it is long ago), I went for coffee with a couple of my friends (women), one married and the other divorced. Grace asked Lilly about her fairly recent marriage, and Lilly started to tell us the good . . . and then the bad. I told Lilly she was breaking a cardinal rule.

One must never say anything that can be even remotely construed as negative about their spouse.

Are you possibly guilty of talking about your spouse, too? Have you ever said things which might shed a bad light on them?

The world is a foolish advisor

The world says it is ok to criticize, in certain situations, but it is not. Your spouse is your choice for a lifetime companion, so speaking ill of them makes you look bad as well. Allowing negative ideas about your spouse to pass your lips is counterproductive. In some cases, it may reach the level of treacherousness.

Lilly innocently countered that she was just being truthful, and of course I complimented her for her intention, but I also reminded her that her intention to be loyal must supersede all other intentions. I suggested if her husband heard what she said he would probably be hurt, and she agreed.

I also let her know that giving hurtful facts about someone is not actually being truthful. The mind of the listener will always fixate on the negative, and then have an unbalanced and thus distorted or 'untruthful' understanding of the person who is being discussed. The listener will not have a truthful insight, just a focused and therefore exaggerated view of a mistake or flaw.

Think how challenging it is to remain positive about someone you might have heard gossip about, even though all of your previous experiences with that person were positive. When we listen to someone going on about someone's flaws, we are all ears. Some say it is human nature, but in reality it is a primitive if not barbaric learned behavior, a destructive habit that needs to change.

Here is a rule

The rule is to never allude to any possible flaw your spouse may have.

Both listening to, and sharing gossip are horrible and we all know that. Can you see how gossiping about your own spouse is traitorous; just because you are mad over some trifle of the moment? Is this cool? It is so accepted as normal these days!

Other people defensively say they only put down their spouse to a close confidant; they say they need to unload to someone or they might explode. We say, explode then, if that is the choice!

Be loyal

Why would you give ammunition to someone about your own spouse, your best friend, your soul-mate, your precious love?

Why would you want to reinforce negative feelings that may cross your mind? It is all too common to take the person we are closest to for granted. It literally defines irony! Yet, some actually feel privileged to be the one who can inform others of their spouse's otherwise hidden flaws. That's not nice!

On the other hand, it is almost as dangerous to tell all about your spouse's good, but private qualities. Too many women discover their best friends are not above approaching husbands other than their own, tempted by a blabber-mouthed wife.

It is important to transform bad habits of spreading gossip, to the opposite habit of praising your spouse. Can you change that now, if you are one who breaks this rule? Being utterly respectful of your spouse at all times, whether or not you are in each other's presence, is just common sense.

Don't try to "fix" your spouse

Let your spouse, and others work on their own flaws; you work on yours.

The reason the mind prefers to notice the flaws of others, especially your spouse's, is because it is easier to see the cause of your suffering comes from something outside of your own attitudes and behavior. That way your mind won't feel pressure to change its bad, but comfortable habits. But it is living a lie!

You are the one causing your troubles, and you have tremendous power to change your life; but not if you are busy working the flaws of your spouse.

In this case your mind is an enemy

Your mind says why not blame all your problems on someone else? Your spouse makes a very convenient scapegoat; that is the trap, or pitfall. Blaming others takes all your attention away from your own flaws; flaws you can actually do something about.

Too many women discover their best friends are not above approaching husbands other than their own, tempted by a blabber-mouthed wife

You have tremendous power to change your life; but not if you are busy working the flaws of your spouse

It is especially easy to blame your spouse because you can see all their flaws; much more easily than your own.

Remember, other people's erroneous thinking is their problem, and nothing you say or do will get them to change. Any effort you make toward changing them is not only wasted on them, it is effort not made toward changing your own nuisance habits, which then compounds your problems.

In addition, pointing out your loved one's flaws is the opposite of loving behavior.

Pop Quiz

1. Can you control your spouse's mind?

Answer: *NO, you cannot; No way*

2. Can your spouse control or change your mind?

Answer: *NOPE, not unless you allow it; which means, no*

3. Do you try to control and change your spouse?

Answer: *Of course you do!*

Yes, you do! You can protest if you want, but nearly everyone tries to control his or her spouse. It is how we are programmed; to get our way.

Trying to control your spouse in small or big ways is both offensive and useless

Trying to control your spouse in small or big ways is both offensive and useless

Be utterly respectful of your spouse's boundaries at all times, whether or not you are in each other's presence.

Control

Self-Control and the Other Kind

Everyone who is uninformed, which includes just about everyone, tries to change his or her spouse, no matter how many times they failed in the past.

Trying to correct or change your spouse is a losing proposition for both of you. This rule, by the way, is like the rule about braking when your car is in a skid; you will crash if you try, even though it seems to be the right thing to do at the time.

Try to change your spouse and you will crash; absolutely! Even though the mind comes up with many rationalizations and exceptions, we must stick to our commitment to mind our own business and to change only ourselves. This is an absolute law of human "physics"!

Your mind telling you "if only they would change" is wrong

The subconscious habit to blame and change outer circumstances, such as your spouse's behavior or thinking, leads to nothing but frustration for everyone.

Life is much sweeter when we refuse to try to change each other, no matter what; even when asked. In fact, when we remember to appreciate, rather than criticize, each other everyone is happier. Change the flaws you see in yourself. Everyone will be happier. Avoid giving advice, even when begged for it. There are much better ways to be helpful; like complimenting efforts, or being supportive of their strengths and accomplishments.

Even logic tells you not to try to change your spouse's mind

All logic dictates the futility of trying to change another person. We never allow another person to change us, yet do we actually think others will be grateful for our advice? Our minds play tricks on us! Ignorance pushes us into this ridiculous behavior; it is so common! We don't realize they can't "hear" our advice, so we repeat ourselves as if they are stupid, and then wonder what is wrong with them. Why don't they change? For the same reasons we can't hear advice given to us!

They won't change for you

We hate it when someone blames us, even when we accidentally did something wrong. Yet we think nothing of blaming someone else for whatever unfortunate event might befall us; it's crazy! What is especially self-defeating is when we blame the person we are supposed to love with all our hearts. Moreover, it is always petty and unanticipated things that bother us. Put things in perspective! Do you see the irony?

The one person you vow to love, cherish, respect, and hold dear is the one who gets your unrestricted crap. It is insane!

Replace your over-familiarity with unconditional respect

Over-familiarity, which allows any boundary to be crossed, has to be replaced with unconditional respect.

Honor your spouse. Your happy marriage will bounce back faster than you can imagine. Your marriage relationship is organic and full of life, so it will heal very quickly when you stop the bad behaviors—when you remove the pebbles.

Apologize to your spouse even if he or she cannot hear you; this will encourage contrition on your part and speed up the transition. Ask for forgiveness. Promise you will try never to be mean again. Don't allow your mind to think your spouse is rude, so you can act immaturely too.

Finding excuses for your wrong behaviors is one of the greatest obstacles to success; it is insidious

Most people will immediately see flawed behavior in their spouse, without acknowledging that critical thoughts must never be entertained in their own mind. You should not allow

All logic dictates the futility of trying to change another person

Marriage is organic and full of life, so it will heal very quickly when you stop the bad behaviors

critical thoughts to sprout into disrespectful behavior. Kick them out! Control the words and behavior. Control your mind. It is your mind, and you can control it.

Whatever works for you is usable

When you first met, you were respectful because you feared rejection. That's a fine reason! Whatever you need to motivate your good behavior is fine. That particular fear can be healthy.

Of course, it's better to behave well because you wish to please your spouse, but take the fear motivator rather than the mean treatment.

When I was a budding entrepreneur, I called my older and wiser friend who sold his chain of restaurants for $93 million dollars; a tidy sum in those days. I said, "Don, I can't even sleep at night I'm so worried." He said, "Good, fear of failure will help you succeed."

Nobody wants fear in their mind, but he knew how to turn it to his advantage. Use what you have to make yourself a better person; that is the point.

Don't be too smart!

Try hard to stop yourself from thinking or saying things like, "I knew you would do that," or "you never listen to me," or "I saw that coming".

Allow only kind and beneficial thoughts about your spouse to be expressed in your behavior and words. Assuming the positive instead of the negative is very important.

**When was the last time you dwelled on good thoughts about your spouse?
Think of some right now.**

Really; Right now!

**When was the last time you couldn't stop thinking about
how good a person your spouse is?**

Do it now!

**Make it a habit to be your spouse's most ardent supporter;
that is what loyalty means.**

If you do your part, you will have a great marriage; even if your spouse does not do his or her part, such is the power of right behavior.

Allow only kind and beneficial thoughts about your spouse to be expressed in your behavior and words

Today is your starting point

Have you, perhaps, lost your objectivity? Obviously you have; which is why your marriage is in trouble.

You are not alone! When you courted each other, you saw their good qualities and barely noticed the little flaws. Now you have to stop any thoughts, other than positive thoughts, about your spouse.

Replace any bad feelings and thoughts that sneak in with sweet thoughts. You can relive those exciting courting days by controlling your mind, words and behavior.

You cannot run away from your own behaviors

Some people actually believe, "if only I had a better partner everything would be fine". So, even while they are married, they look around for the so-called perfect partner, and by looking at the surface of others—looks, charming demeanors, and other outer traits—they gradually become more negative toward their spouse.

They do not realize that in the beginning people show only the good, just as your spouse and you did. Who in this world is perfect??

The surface of a person does not tell the whole story. When people switch partners, they only switch mirrors, and the same bad traits will show up again until you get rid of your own bad traits. Stop comparing your spouse with others. Instead, get on with making the tiny effort of controlling your own behavior instead; we say tiny in comparison with the guaranteed gargantuan suffering that comes from ignoring this reality.

When you recognize how much poison you have been spewing into your relationship, and make the effort to stop, you will have won half the battle. Damaging thoughts, feelings, and speech are erosive toxins eating away your relationship as surely as acid eats away the most durable steel.

There is one area of selfishness that works

A 'self-interested' way to look at your life is to recognize your thoughts as your closest environment; even closer than the nose on your face, or people around you. You live in the mental environment you create.

When your thoughts and feelings are miserable, you live in a self-created miserable environment. When you make your thoughts and feelings positive and uplifting, or compassionate and charitable, you live in a healthy mental environment. It's completely up to you.

As this concept sinks in, your relationship already improves, because the relationship will heal when it is not subjected to that which undermines it—the pebbles of inadvertent misbehavior.

Replace any bad feelings and thoughts that sneak in with sweet thoughts

When your thoughts and feelings are miserable, you live in a self-created miserable environment

You have the power

You didn't mean to become mean, so don't take on guilt. You don't have to follow this practical advice; it is your call. You can imagine someone else created your suffering if you want to. You have free will and will do what you want; but has it ever worked when you tried to change your spouse?

If they chose to go along with your demands when you were insistent, did it really help for long, or did you just keep noticing new flaws to make yourself miserable?

You can control a great deal in your life, and you can learn about whom you really are, by learning to control your own mind. If you make the effort to control what you are able to control—your mind—you will be happy.

Stop banging your head against the wall. Stop trying to control or change your spouse.

Stop expecting from your spouse…anything!

Stop manipulating them!

Stop asking for this or that!

One of the greatest expressions of over-familiarity is to go into someone else's space with judgment and criticism. Instead, always compliment your spouse.

Always compliment your spouse. No matter what your mind is thinking, all you have to do is shift your thinking and deliver a sweet compliment. You won't lose a thing, but you will gain much. Always compliment your spouse.

Fill in the blanks of this quiz

1. I will never _____ my spouse again.

2. I will always look for opportunities to _____ my spouse.

Answers: 1. *criticize*; 2. *compliment*

The recurring theme is for you to look at your own stuff, which is all you need to be concerned with in order to find happiness and meaning in your marriage and life. Graciously allow your spouse the space to grow and develop when and if they choose.

Savvy people never try to force growth or change upon others (except their kids) because it doesn't work. They work on themselves and never consider another person's flaws. They realize it is only their own flaws which bring pain. They diplomatically and lovingly support the positive efforts of those who wish to change, but do not presume to act as teachers of those who do not ask for their help.

The more you work on yourself, the more you will overlook the flaws of others. If you work on your bad habits, you will see the bad habits of your spouse even more clearly; but they will remind you of yours, and you will have more compassion. It is a win-win.

> *You can control a great deal in your life, and can learn about who you really are, by learning to control your own mind*

Here are some real life instances of over-familiar behavior

The following is not an attempt to cover all expressions of over-familiarity, just a way to get you to recognize some of your own undesirable expressions. See which habits you have fallen into.

Some of these behaviors are part of your own collection. Consider if they are respectful and loving, or if they should be removed from your repertoire.

Men

• Belching or worse (you know what I mean) in front of your wife

• Leaving toilet seats up (you do not need to know why it is such a big deal)

• Discourteous speech, such as swearing or yelling

• Trying to "fix" your wife's problems, when she is usually only sharing

• Expressing anger; verbally or otherwise

• Expressing impatience

• Looking at other women

• Flirting and/or responding to flirtatiousness

• Expecting sex, as if sex is owed, like some commodity

• Not defending your wife in any circumstance

• Not understanding her point of view, or trying

• Having mean or degrading thoughts about your wife

• Trying to control the family finances

• Trying to control your wife's behavior

• Making fun of your wife, even "jokingly"

• Criticizing your wife

• Assuming you know what she is thinking

There are many more ways, but we hope you can think of ways in which you have stopped treating your wife with the same level of respect you want for yourself.

When you pay attention, you will notice when you are unkind

Women are "guilty" in other ways

On the other hand, if you are a wife, you will be reading this, maybe thinking, "Uh huh, that's what he does!" If you are having thoughts about his flaws, you are doing more than acknowledging a situation; you are being critical, and thus expressing a form of disrespect.

Do not mistake flawed behaviors as a personal attack. In most cases, the habits are not intentionally aimed at you. If you assume they are intentional or loaded, you will make yourself a victim. Being a victim is a personal choice.

Women

Do not mistake flawed behaviors as a personal attack, which in most cases are not intentionally aimed at you

• Having unkind thoughts and feelings about your husband

• Talking unfavorably about your husband to your friends (so commonly accepted, and so horrible)

• Not considering family budgets

• Complaining to or about your husband

• Unkind speech such as nagging

• Ordering him instead of polite requesting

• Not dressing up or making yourself beautiful for your husband

• Criticizing your husband openly or in private

• Reading your husband's mind

• Finishing his thoughts and sentences

• Not demonstrating love and loyalty through intimacy (well covered in the last lesson)

• Manipulatively withholding affection

• Blaming your husband for misunderstandings

• Taking sides with children, or others, publicly

You are currently expressing disrespectfulness in many ways, all from over-familiarity. We hope you see your boundary crossing behavior will never contribute to a harmonious and loving relationship. You need to move your relationship in the right direction to get the intimacy and connection you want.

**There is no magic to getting the relationship you desire,
but if you do what is right, it will seem magical**

If you and your husband treated one another in an unloving manner when you were courting, there is no chance you would have chosen to marry each other; the same point to men. If you are thinking, "Yes, she does all that and more", you are critical. You need to think something along the lines of, "My lovely wife may have a few flaws, but I refuse to notice them; they are so small compared to all the wonderful traits I see and admire. I love her so much."

The main point is you both stopped treating each other with the connection building love and respect you expressed during courting. Because of the negative shift in your attitudes and behavior you are cheating yourselves out of what you rightfully expected from marriage.

Neither of you are happy with how you are treated and both of you blame the other for "starting it". Therefore, now is a good time to make a conscious effort to recognize your personal misbehavior and take responsibility for being kind from now on, regardless of how you are being treated.

This is not an opening to share this with your spouse and suggest or request. You may talk about the book you are reading, but you must not suggest your spouse read it. Self help means *your* self!

*No matter how
you are treated,
be kind, courteous, and
well-behaved*

No matter how you are treated, be kind, courteous, and well-behaved

Stop kidding yourself by imagining your life will be better if your spouse changed. Behave better because it is how you are supposed to behave. Be kind because you know it's the right thing to do.

Some of you will get this principle right away and others will have a 'no way 'attitude. All we can say is if you think you have to wait to see if your spouse is agreeable, you are never going to have a happy marriage. Not now, not with someone else, not never.

If you imagine it is different in your case, because of whatever, we guarantee you, you are making a big mistake.

*Now is a good time to
make a conscious effort to
take responsibility for
being kind*

Worth the effort because nothing else works

Deciding to accept personal responsibility for your behavior, without excuses, is a hard task. It is going to be a chore to catch yourself and change your habits. If you add to the burden by needing proof of your spouse's willingness, it will be impossible.

You may think we are being a bit strong, but this is like gravity; there are no exceptions. Last time (for now) we say it; behave like you are supposed to behave, as if you were in the company of the greatest person on Earth.

You cannot get away with blaming your spouse for your behavior

It is not your spouse's shortcomings that are the problem with your marriage. Your spouse may be the catalyst for revealing your own flaws to you. But your behavior is ultimately a reflection of how you wish to live.

Treat your spouse better than anyone else in the world, even if it appears unfair at the moment.

How you behave defines you

A favorite story emphasizes this point. This story is true. I heard it myself, from a concentration camp survivor.

Behold your spouse as your greatest friend and lover

While in a concentration camp, a prisoner was saying a prayer of thanksgiving. The one overhearing the well-known prayer was startled by his friend's prayers of sincere and humble gratitude, and asked, "How can you be grateful? Have you lost your mind? You have lost everything else! You are skin and bones, your family is dead, all is gone and you are dying! What can you possibly be thankful for?"

The inmate softly answered, "I am grateful that God didn't make me like those who put us in here."

We can explain why this is powerful

The man in this story did not allow his outer circumstances to control his self-view or behavior. His noble attitude removed him from the victim designation, despite every outward circumstance, so he felt no compulsion to retaliate.

In his mind, he was a free man who felt joy, because he did not let anyone or anything interfere with his self determined attitude. He reframed the perspective of his situation to feel his inner peace, rather than his outer temporary environment.

Powerful, yes, but you can do the same! It's not as hard as it first seems. It is a matter of training the mind to behold your spouse as your greatest friend and lover, one who can do no wrong.

Only you can make you into a victim

Ultimately, you are a victim only if you choose to be one by seeing yourself compromised, or by reacting without thinking.

Most people fall into the trap of falsely defining themselves by how they think or feel, or by imagining themselves as kind, generous, loving, passionate etc. Others define themselves as they optimistically imagine others see them.

Few people realize they are defined by how they behave, especially when in a difficult situation.

Be kind, courteous, and well behaved, so you are living your ideals. But don't waste your effort trying to change your spouse. It is better to change, through mind control, how you perceive your spouse. That doesn't mean you will be a doormat.

When you control your mind, you are never a doormat of someone else, or a victim of your past bad habits.

Your circumstances will change as you do

Circumstances will change with the right effort, but changing yourself is the most useful effort of all. The effort you make will guarantee you will be a happier person, no matter what the situation. It is the effort itself that pays off.

We rarely see a spouse not come around when the other one makes ongoing sincere effort with the intention of never giving up.

Remember, you chose your spouse to be your lover, best friend, co-parent, business partner, and more for the rest of your life. You weren't crazy or ill-informed.

Your troubles of the past cannot stop your changes from brightening your future

You are in trouble primarily because you didn't know how to behave in a relationship. Now you are learning these things, so everything will work out. Treat your spouse with the love and respect you would for the most important person on earth. If you take these lessons to heart, and practice what you learn, it may soon be time to celebrate a new beginning.

Years ago, the Thames River in England was pronounced dead. It was so polluted it looked like there were no more fish in it. The government passed strong laws, and made cleaning the river a national cause. Everybody got on board because the pollution impacted their lives in ugly ways.

Within a short time, to the amazement of all the skeptics, the river came back and is now clean and sweet. No one had to sanitize the waters or filter it. They just stopped polluting.

As an individual you have far more power over your relationship than you think. Just by doing your part, to the best of your ability, you will change everything.

The difference between marriage-building and marriage-destroying behavior is obvious

By doing your part to the best of your ability, you will change everything

Lose your expectations for how your spouse speaks with you or behaves. Focus on changing the one person you can actually change; yourself.

Be vigilant about learning to behave with your spouse

The next section, on communication, will reveal some wonderful ideas which will not only show you how much you have to gain from your efforts, but will also show you how superior your marriage is, compared to all other venues of life.

- Chapter Four -
Communication

◇◇

*Defining communication in general terms is useless for couples
who live in the unique environment of marriage. Individuals have to
be able to distinguish their marriage from other venues, and
emphasize the opportunities none but they can enjoy.*

*Instead of being harmed by the powerful tool of communication
you need to learn how to use it for love and connection.*

◇◇

*It is only common sense that you would communicate
with your spouse in a way that lets them know that you see
them as the most important person in your life*

Chapter Four

Communication

Communication is essentially any system, simple or complex, used for exchanging thoughts, feelings and desires.

While everyone knows that every married couple (in trouble) finds communication to be problematic, if not the basis of their misfortunes, marital communication is unique, and superior to all other forms of communication. Once individuals learn how to use communication to their marital advantage, it becomes wonderful.

Your marital relationship is not only unique among relationships, but is the best relationship you will ever have. Marriage is superior to any other relationship, even compared with close relationships such as sibling, parental, mentor; or any other.

Marriage is special

The most exciting feature of your marriage relationship, differentiating it from all others, is its very design, which encourages secure expressions of unconditional love.

True, the security of marriage appears to have lessened lately in our society, but only because we have lost sight of the innate and fundamental working principles core to marriage. Otherwise its integrity remains, and it is only a trendy illusion caused by "popular opinion," which you can and should discount and cast aside.

Only *your* marriage matters

Your marriage is the only one that counts. Popular opinion has no meaning to your marriage, so forget those other ones. When you recall the potential of your marriage at any time, especially just before you interact with your partner, it will make a tremendous difference in your attitude and thus how well you will connect with each other.

Your marriage relationship is inseparable from your communications

In a way, all the help for married people needs to center on communication because it is logically impossible to separate marriage communication from the relationship itself.

The relationship you have with your spouse is the greatest you will ever have. By definition, marital communication, the form of communication exclusive to your marital relationship, is superior in its potential, to every other form of communication.

So, learn to make communication with your spouse the highest and best communication possible. Your sincere effort all by itself, even without specific training, will bring both of you greater happiness. But, of course, get the training!

Marital communication is unique and superior to all other forms of communication

Your sincere effort, all by itself, will bring both of you greater happiness

You have to step out of your comfort zone

Deep and fulfilling relationships of any type do not just happen. It takes study and effort. And, of course, your desire to shift your relationship depends primarily on your individual effort, along with a growing working knowledge.

Your marital relationship will be an ever expanding source of joy, but it needs a lot of TLC to accomplish the goals of deep connection and intimacy. Striving for that connection is definitely worth the effort.

Don't be afraid to learn some things you might not have thought of before, and then incorporate them in your life. Maybe you will find some ideas are refined versions of ideas you already had, but didn't try. Others will be revelations. All will help you change your marriage.

There is always more to learn

Some folks think they already know how to nurture relationships because of their past relationship experiences. They think it is a waste of time to investigate different ideas. But everyone forgets they are often unrealistic about what they actually know about people, and can usually go much further with a little more information and experienced encouragement.

Your communication experiences are limited and not 100% relevant

The truth is, most friendships are hardly what they appear to be, so you can't trust your experiments in other relationships.

Of course, the optimist in all of us tries to see the best in what we have, thinking we have super close friends. But most friendships are not as deep as we think, or as tight as we imagine. Almost everyone has had the experience of being disappointed by a friend they believed in. But it's easier to make excuses or gloss over events that led to a falling out, than to admit to our errors.

Now is a good time to learn

Be open to learning that which may have never occurred to you.

Ironically, too many people think they already know a lot about relationships, even while they are in trouble with their marriage. That's the kind of thinking that leads to blaming their partner, instead of finding their own flaws and working on their own stuff. Be careful not to fall into those categories.

Then, beyond the above cautionary warning, in other relationships your friends have not been tested in trials that expose all possible weaknesses the way marriage does. In fact, hardly any, if any, relationship would come close to standing up to the kinds of tests encountered by two people who join their lives together in marriage.

Your marital relationship will be an ever expanding source of joy, but it needs a lot of TLC to accomplish the goals of deep connection and intimacy

And, on the good side, no relationship provides the depth and satisfaction marriage can. So, avoid comparing methods in your marriage friendship to any friendship where your friend doesn't wake up with you every morning.

Be open to applying different kinds of ideas to your efforts. Of course all new ideas seem foreign at first, but old ideas which do not work just don't work, no matter how used to them you are.

Not even parental love is as special

Parental love and protection is superior to most relationships, of course. Most parents will support their child to the end, right or wrong.

But they do that because of instinct driven love and protection for their child. That kind of love, as incredible as it often is, is at its core a compulsion, which is based on instinctive commands to protect their offspring.

It is a great gift, of course, but it is not the same kind of gift as the love which comes from your spouse, which is rooted in free will.

Marital love is based on choosing each other, which is very different. Nothing about any other relationship, in fact, comes close to marriage because of the voluntary nature inherent in the relationship.

Your marriage is a perfect structure which was created to promote the highest possible relationship. But marriage will not work, regardless how wonderful the potential for all kinds of special bonuses, when it is taken for granted; as you are now finding out.

Your marriage is a perfect structure which was created to promote the highest possible relationship

Communication is how we exchange our thoughts, feelings and intentions

Before you got married, had you known the vast differences between marital communication and lesser forms of communication, you would be living the dream relationship you sought; definitely.

You would have avoided hurtful and distance causing comments. You never would have intentionally expressed anything that might have hurt your spouse's feelings, even if they slipped, and said or did something that hurt you.

You would have stepped over all the pitfalls, and avoided any temptation to hurtfully speak your mind.

You would have learned to control your mind, mouth and reactions, instead of just saying whatever came up. You would have understood that forcing yourself to be good is a far better option than expecting your partner to be resilient.

There are simple common sense laws for healthy communication

You unknowingly took the most cherished relationship in your life for granted, especially with your communication and (temporarily) missed the normal abundant opportunities to build an expanding and deepening connection.

Rather than making the most of the psychological, emotional and physical closeness, which is an inherent part of your marriage; you unknowingly misused and even abused your spouse and the relationship that marriage offers.

By misunderstanding marriage (and how could you understand marriage in a world where we concentrate on teaching every science in our schools besides relationship science), you both spoke "openly" and unsympathetically, if not callously, in an over-familiar way, to your most treasured relation.

At the same time, you rarely sincerely praised or adored one another, even when the opportunity to communicate love and support was screaming at you. And so, instead of satisfying and inspiring each other, you became proficient in making each other miserable. You blamed each other instead of correcting your own offensive ways.

The pain is often excruciating

The pain you feel from being unappreciated is terrible, yet ironically, if not hypocritically, you probably do not think twice about condemning, criticizing or complaining to your spouse. You make every excuse for lashing out (it is never deserved, or excusable, as some try to defensively rationalize). And when you do not have a good excuse for your outbursts, silent treatments, pouts or whatever; you seriously expect your spouse to instantly forgive you, get over it and move on.

Yet you may hold grudges for days or weeks, when they are the one who may have hurt your feelings.

Change your approach and change your marriage

You can't change your spouse, even if they are really rude, too; you have to accept that. But you have the power to change and master your own reactive behaviors, and stop making your spouse so unhappy.

Then, when you shift, and attempt to make them happy, what will probably happen, when they are not feeling so maligned and abused, they will probably learn how to treat their spouse, you, better; copying your enhanced attitudes and behaviors, or creating their own.

Look at your behavior fairly

Currently you are not an example of what a person should do to have an amazing marriage! But you can change that.

An objective look at your behavior and communication is called dispassionate evaluation. When you want to improve something, anything, it is essential to look at it dispassionately; without guilt, blame embarrassment or whatever.

You need to be dispassionate, so you know how to change things. You have to be honest about how you treat your spouse.

You have the power to change and master your reactive behaviors and make your spouse happy

Make positive permanent changes

You, just you, can change everything about your marriage for the better.

You can patiently and steadily eliminate all your toxic talk. Toxic talk is like having rats in your living room. Toxic behavior has no place in your life at all.

Children are taught potty talk is a no-no, and adults have to learn toxic (blame, condemnation, criticism, complaining etc.) communication is also a no-no. Uplift your communication to a positive, user-friendly tool of love, and noble intentional praise and encouragement for your spouse. That effort alone will significantly improve your marriage.

It is unreasonable for you to continue spewing toxin, no matter what your circumstances may be

Stop entertaining expectations of your spouse, or putting conditions on them. Work on correcting yourself. Concentrate exclusively on improving your own communication.

You will soon start to see even your tiny little right efforts, as you learn and improve them, will yield enormous benefits. Then the coming greater efforts, made with continual practice, will bring your marriage to where it should be.

You can do this! If you read this and think "oh that is a nice idea but they don't understand", you are the one who does not understand.

We have seen people go from complete war, couples living under different roofs, threatening e-mails, violence, multi-affairs…you name it, we have seen it, and they still manage to achieve a happy marriage.

We know you have to break down your own resistance to change, but absorbing the principles of marriage and working with them will work for you, too.

First you have to make changes, and then results will surely come

Intentional positive marital communication effort comes before deep connection, harmony and intimacy, not from it.

Never predicted to become selfish, superficial or insincere, true marital communication was expected to deepen your connection, because it is primarily between the innermost part of you and your spouse.

But you cannot just take for granted that it is all just fine, without any of the bruises healing. When you have been tearing your relationship down instead of building it up, it takes time, sometimes more and sometimes less, to change yourself and get beyond the hurt.

Adults have to learn that toxic communication is a no-no

Even tiny little right efforts, as you learn and improve them, will yield enormous benefits

First you have to make changes, and then results will surely come

Marriages recover better than anything

It is almost always true your marriage will recover and become incredible no matter how bad it seems now, but you have to keep in mind that human physics is still all about cause and effect. Once you jump off a cliff, the ground comes up very quickly and there will be damage. The time to recover can never be completely accurately predicted.

Failures are rare, and mostly due to prematurely giving up

Never give up. Your good efforts will absolutely impact the future in a positive way. Even though there are no guaranteed one hundred percenters in life, we see extraordinary turn-arounds.

Your positive efforts will always produce positive results, in one form or another

So always do what is the right thing to do. Your positive efforts will always produce positive results, in one form or another. But you have to make some clear and decisive changes before you see the results you want.

Let's repeat that marital communication is the grandest

When you first got married, all the advice seems to be about what not to say or do, so your marriage would not get creamed.

Nobody talks to newlyweds about how to get the benefits from marriage, or, what they are, because most don't know. Friends, aunts and uncles never skip the warnings or sharing of the compromises they discovered.

But nobody speaks about the wonderful vision of a great marriage or the bonuses you can get when you know what you are doing. Advice is always about avoiding inevitable negatives.

So you get on the road to paradise and never know what to look for or how to keep your bearings.

Get positive about your marriage

When you buy a car, they tell you how fast it will go in six seconds, or how steep a hill it will climb in the snow, all the good stuff.

They don't tell you about the normal problems you will have, like inevitable flat tires, because they are selling you and want you to focus on the good things. Besides, everyone already knows about flats, future repairs and maintenance; so why dwell on the inevitable problems. They want you to enjoy your car.

But when you get married, nobody says anything about good things like connection and intimacy. They don't share how you will experience these inevitable benefits, when you do things right.

Friends with advice only tell you about the reduced free time, tough times and whatever else they coped with. Of course, we need to learn about the required maintenance and repairs, but we really should be testing the bennies, too.

Nothing is better than a smart marriage

A good marriage has no comparison when it comes to the joy you will experience, so we have to stop doing the dumb things, which prevent you from doing the smart things thst bring the visions of happiness into reality.

You will begin to understand how, and why, marital communication is so delightfully unique. We will use this fundamental reality as the foundation, upon which to build your understanding of what quality marital communication looks like and how you can develop yours. Bottom line; marital communication is different from all other forms of communication, and you really have to experience it in order for it to be appreciated.

All relationships are types of communication

One way to think about marriage, or any other relationship for that matter, is that they are all about communication.

There are a number of wonderful metaphors typically used to describe marital interactions. But the fact is that no metaphor can begin to describe all the treasures that come from a properly functioning marriage. So, we straightforwardly suggest you always shoot for the highest and best you can do. Base your efforts on getting the most from your marriage, by being the most for your spouse.

Our intentions are to help you get what you want. So we explain positive communication in concepts, and illustrated with specific behaviors. But you need to have better underlying attitudes and commitments. You have to learn the principles.

For instance, when you recognize it is your perception of what is going on that is causing you to be critical of your spouse, you will understand you need to change your perceptions, rather than change your spouse.

You have to do what works, or what you do will not get you what you want

The principle is this; **changing an outer annoyance is not the way to find happiness.** It never works, never worked and will never work; so why keep trying. You have to change those attitudes of yours, which cause your behaviors, if you want to get real change.

Sincere intentions are very important

There is no substitute for sincere positive intentions. Your intentions are everything. There is an old saying "the road to hell is paved with good intentions" that is blatantly false advertising. If your intentions are good, no matter what obstacles you encounter, you will eventually discover the right way to serve your spouse with love and support. But, of course, you have to be sincere.

Most of the useful work you will do to serve your marriage will be made toward changing how you see things. Then always try to add more sugar to your marriage, even when you reactively think you need to complain or analyze.

Marriage, or any other relationship for that matter, is all about communication

You have to do what works, or what you do will not get you what you want

You will absolutely discover that sincere effort, which you make for the right reasons, will save you from incredible suffering. But efforts made for the wrong reasons, will always be counterproductive.

It is always better to say and do what you know to be user friendly, and thus right, than to speak your mind. So sometimes that means shifting your mind, and that is what you must do.

The two following parts will describe the concepts of venues and marriage in a way that will allow you to always keep your bearings, so you will know what to do no matter what.

Part One-Venues

Venues make all the difference

The importance of distinguishing your marriage (venue) from other venues

How and what you wish to convey has got to properly fit in the particular venue, or circumstances, you are in, so your communications can be relevant, and effective.

Knowing the stage you are on and the audience you are addressing influences what you say and how you say it. It is unfortunate people do not, as a matter of course, consider the idea of systematically differentiating the various venues of life and their nuances.

Both obvious and subtle differences in various life and social situations, when meticulously studied and understood, will always give a person a better handle on their daily operations, making them much more effective while reducing a lot of stressful missteps.

Being conscious of venues makes you more successful in life; period. In fact, being consciously aware of them as you discover their importance, you cannot help but start paying attention to them and improving all your communications.

If they taught this one little thing in schools, our world will change!

The combination of stage, and audience, is called a "venue"

Those are the components that define a venue. The stage, or setting, refers to your position in relation to the other person, or people. The audience is the one or more people who you are directing your communication towards. This is universally applicable, whether you are speaking to your cat or the president of your country.

Every great communicator has an in depth knowledge of their stage and audience. Experts are comfortable in their venue simply because they studied, and understand it.

Because of their awareness they will rarely be caught off guard, so what they say will be purposeful, not just a defensive or giddy reaction. There is no magic in how knowledgeable folks handle communication, only intelligent awareness.

It is always better to say and do what you know to be user-friendly, than to speak your mind

Define your own venues, just for practice

Become familiar with your day to day venues. Then, work according to their demands within them and see how it makes life much easier. What you do and how you communicate within any venue is always about making the best use of an opportunity, no matter with whom. So the more you know about a venue the better.

With even a tiny general knowledge of the nature of venues, you can be scientific about specifically recharging your marriage (venue), as it is the one most demanding your attention. Beginning with solid, easy to learn communication skills, you can slowly master communication within your marriage.

Set your intentions

Imagine worthy goals for your communication, like connection and mutual support. Then, think about what will best serve your vision. Also, think about things you might say out of habit, which you do not want to say because it will undermine your efforts. This self-observation and planning is the beginning of creating a real plan to improve your life.

Consider this; in every different venue there are various definite limitations, as well as particular possibilities. It's the potentials and limits that distinguishes one venue from another.

Why bump up against walls that definitely exist? When you think about where the limits are, you will not have to.

Think realistically

Do you want to get the most out of a conversation? Why badger a phone center person into doing something they have no power to do, even if you convince them you are right? By ascertaining what is actually possible, you can focus your attention on what is, and is not, achievable in the particular venue. It will save you a lot of aggravation.

Make your communications scientific, based on what you know about cause and effect, even if you have to reach your conclusions by trial and error. Pay attention to results from your communications. That way you can start to take responsibility for the reactions you get.

Just don't fool yourself any longer! Don't blame someone for missing the point when there is no way they could ever get your point!

Don't expect a judge to be honest just because they are a judge, when you know they are fiends with your opponent's lawyer! Just be real!

Beginning with solid, easy to learn communication skills, you can slowly master communication within your marriage

Pay attention to results from your communications. That way you can start to take responsibility for the reactions you get.

Be real about gender generalizations

Everyone wants to know the "secret" of communicating with the other gender, but there is no reliable generalization. Each individual is different, notwithstanding the true or false generalizations, and you need to learn about your audience through logic, observation and/or trial and error.

The particular need and purpose of each relationship is what makes each venue unique. When observed casually, anyone can see at least some nuances; but when studied as in using other people's observations, we find there is sometimes more to discover than first thought. You will soon be way ahead of many dangers, now that you are learning what to look for.

We will discuss the marriage venue at great length, showing you some insights which are usually hidden or obscured, to give you a boost in the right direction. But first, we will discuss the basic concept of identifying and distinguishing various venues. That way you can see how to figure out which behaviors and communications are best for each.

Practicing consciously shifting, instead of unconsciously reacting, is a great help to instill the need to shift for your spouse.

Understanding venues

You already know the differences between physical venues, such as a bank, versus a department store, or a baseball diamond, versus a football field. You know them automatically and confidently.

But most people never think a lot about the various social, or life venues they participate in, like a party versus a business lunch. They go to each with almost zero communication preparation.

Because you are comfortable with your day-to-day interactions (maybe over-familiar), you trust (without thought) your actions, speech and attitudes will automatically adjust as needed. So, without realizing it, you leave a lot to chance.

Not thinking through your opportunities or possible social traps in a particular venue puts you at risk, and reduces your ability to realize your potential benefits. Most people leave a lot on the table.

Not knowing how to speak with a doctor, for instance, means you will only have a partial understanding of your own sick body, if you need help. Not considering your marriage as a special venue with special needs has certainly hurt you even more.

Let's make it more real

If you are in a venue of a social function, and meet a person who may someday be a potential employer, you would want to behave in a way that would get them to consider you a good hire. It would be out of synch if you got intoxicated, and told raunchy stories. It isn't more complicated than that!

Everyone wants to know the "secret" of communicating with the other gender, but there are no reliable generalizations

Nobody has to tell you that if you misbehaved, your efforts betray the results you want from that meeting, that venue.

Your behavior and communication have to be aligned with the particular dynamics of the venue you are in or you will possibly (probably) lose out. And even though the behavior would be tacky in that venue, identically crude behavior would be perfectly acceptable in another, like if you were partying at a girls night out or guys only fishing trip. The stage and audience, you see, has everything to do with how you communicate.

You can't just do your thing and hope for success

Most people miss the point of adjusting for the parameters of a venue, and much less for their own marriage.

They say things without any common sense applied. You know, it goes back to this idea of not considering anyone but themselves (we should have been taught the uselessness of selfishness in grade school).

Some folks think when they interview a lawyer they may hire, the lawyer will appreciate a good lawyer joke, not considering they may get a laugh but probably will also get a bigger bill. Lawyers do not think of themselves as pariahs, and most lawyers actually are, like everyone else, trying to be good people. How rude to put them all down!

Or, how stupid is it to ask a traffic cop if he met his quota today after he writes out your ticket for speeding? Police officers are putting their life on the line every moment of their work day!

Stop, and think about what gets you the best results

Being mindful about these things is normally automatic to most people. Most do not behave this way towards others...until they get married. Then, they abandon the most basic respectful thoughts and behaviors because they expect their spouse to put up with their bad, along with, good traits.

There are countless venues in life, each of which require various and different styles of communicating, based on your needs, the relationship, your desires and purposes and your audience. You need to not only see what you can get, but also what you can give.

Some venues are spelled out

In some venues, such as in scientific communities, the legal world of judges and lawyers, the military or governmental diplomatic departments, appropriate styles and behaviors are concisely spelled out.

In all of those, the style of talk, the vernacular and jargon, what is appropriate and inappropriate etc. are studied in classrooms and apprenticeships. "Robert's rules of order" is a great example of delineating correct behaviors in detail, and demonstrates how much detail certain venues require...but what about our poor marriage venue?! There, we need to use our best discretion to be our spouse's best friend.

Your behavior and communication have to be aligned with the particular dynamics of the venue you are in or you will possibly (probably) lose out

There are countless venues in life, each of which require various and different styles of communicating

In any venue where important decisions are made as a matter of routine, there have to be standardized rules. It is just common sense to create norms for venues in which people come from different walks of life, different cultures etc. They need a common language with agreed upon boundaries.

But following prescribed formal rules is not the norm for most of us. They are not studied. In most day to day venues, there are only some unwritten laws of communication, which we haphazardly learn, and then follow to the extent we need to fit in, and then only when we want to.

Usually, in fact, we tend to learn the rules of a venue over time, the hard way. That is what we did when we got married. We had no rules for our new venue, and so we winged it, behaved without any awareness of the results of our lack of self-discipline.

We know that when you see how much you benefit from adjusting your behavior to enhance your marriage, you will put in every bit of effort it takes to make it happen

The downside of free will

We have this little thing called "free will" that can make us pretty ornery if someone dares tell us what to do, especially when we do not want to.

Still, there are those times we follow the rules and behave ourselves without giving it too much of a thought. We know, but usually only instinctively, in many situations, the consequences of going along with our whims will be worse than exercising a little self-control.

You do not think it through necessarily, but you respond to an inner guidance system, usually based on painful memories. But, for sure, you have overridden your desires and inclinations in the past, in order to get the most out of an opportunity.

Would you agree with that? In the past, have you exercised your free will to do what you did not want to do, just because you knew it would create a better outcome?

We know you have! So, because you have trained yourself to be respectful, or whatever it took, when you wanted to, we all know you can also train yourself for your marriage to improve, just as easily, if you wish!

You have the power! We know from our experience that when you see how much you will benefit from adjusting your behavior to enhance your marriage, you will put in every bit of effort it takes to make it happen.

Your free will has to be self-managed

You cannot just do your own thing in life. Try yelling at a cop who pulls you over as if he were your kid brother who switched channels on you, or how about expressing your true angry feelings about the failures of the legal system to a judge hearing your case. You will pay a price for your indiscretions in all of those situations.

You have to choose your topics and styles based on whom, what and when; or else. The price for indiscretions is especially costly in marriage.

Shifting your communication style for different venues

During the day, you automatically shift your communication style many times in order to fit the particular setting youare in. Almost a hundred percent of the time, you shift without thinking about it.

Without thinking about it, you speak with your kids differently from their teachers and then differently to the school principle, differently to the clerk at the drugstore, differently to the traffic cop, who you don't yell at as if they are your kid brother, and differently to a minister, priest or rabbi. You even shift when you talk to yourself, or your pets.

Most never actually think about how many times they shift communication style and why, because it is so automatic and habitual; but if you did, you would have more control over your life. If you give it enough thought, you might recognize the subconscious reason you shift your communication style is to get along better, to get your needs met most efficiently and effectively.

In most cases, how you communicate has to do with what you want and who you are with.

Different venues of life call for definably different communication styles, based on needs, cultural expectations etc.

No doubt, you can list the needs for a particular style in pretty much every venue you can think of, and you will be right. You can probably come up with ways to improve your style in various venues you think are important to you, so you can get more of what you want.

Learn all about those you connect with

I am really friendly to my local baristas. They do a fine job, and so I acknowledge them, because they are good people, who just like me, look forward to positive interactions. I want them to feel good about themselves. And, I am the first to admit, I like them to remember how I like my coffee! In the marts of the world, we have to adjust our thinking, and our communication to get our needs met.

Is this your experience, too? Absolutely, it may be essentially selfish, and in the world you need to be self-protective, but you can care about all you may encounter, too.

But in marriage, your adjustments need to be selfless, no matter what the situation or whatever the predicament, if you want all that marriage has to offer.

In most cases, how you communicate has to do with what you want and who you are with

In marriage, your adjustments need to be selfless, no matter what the situation you are in

Including information about a particular individual's personality within a venue helps you better tailor your communication style. That is why it is good to observe and listen to get the most out of your interactions. In a work venue, for instance, knowing whether your boss is a tyrant or a humanitarian will help you select a more appropriate style of communication.

You also have to know as much as you can about your co-workers, all for various reasons. No matter where you are, you will always benefit from listening and observing, then thinking about how you can improve your communication.

Your knowledge about your spouse will help you serve them. If they are troubled and lashing out on you, you can try to understand their troubles rather than the trouble it causes you. That is what we mean by selflessness.

The person you know best, far better than you know yourself, is your spouse! Appropriately, it is your job to observe them, so you can be there for them just as you intended when you agreed to marry them.

Even if some relationships look somewhat similar at first glance, no other venues resemble marriage

Different venues means different communication for different situations

Most people are under the false impression that communication is communication, is communication; no big deal; but marriage is tremendously different from peer relationships, friendships, work place relationships and every other connection or relationship you can think of.

Even if some relationships look somewhat similar at first glance, there are no other venues that resemble marriage. All the rules of good communication in the rest of the world are based on getting along through give and take.

But in marriage, where selflessness is like water to a plant, it is all about give and give, without selfish expectations.

We advise those who are struggling in their marriage to become more conscious of venues, so you can learn to see what great things are possible in your marriage, which can absolutely never be possible anywhere else. This allows your focus, once you stop the meanness, to be on striving for the benefits of intimate connection.

Why allow foolish behavior to rule your lives? Why work so hard on stopping yourself from being a jerk, when you can put all your effort into being amazing so that you harvest amazing.

But first, learn to catch the jerky habits, of course. Then, explore your marriage for its potential. See for yourself what is possible!

PART TWO

The Marriage Venue

Make a vow. From this moment forward, you will treat your husband, or your wife, only in ways you think will uplift and honor them. Every thought, utterance and action, no matter how they treat you, from now on, will be your intentional gift to them.

Is that not what marriage is supposed to be? Are you not responsible to do your part, regardless of how well your spouse does their part?
Don't offer words without intentional feelings of love behind them, which only fill air time, or any hurtful words, which only create sorrow. Put forth only connection-building communications, from now on.

Remember, even when your spouse's actions trigger you, it is still to your greatest benefit to behave according to what satisfies their needs, and not yours.

When you are misunderstood, restrain your words and feelings of disappointment. You are learning how to communicate better, so it takes time to gain proficiency and time for the results to come. Never give up. The results will surely come.

Marriage is better, by far, than every other venue in life

Perhaps the most striking difference between marriage and other venues is that all the other venues you encounter are defined by the situation you and the other(s) are in, and not by you, or who is in it with you.

A police officer is compelled to act as a police officer while doing their job. You will never know them as a person. That venue is defined by his job and your infraction.

But in your marriage venue, regardless of a fleeting mood, or changing circumstances, it is your spouse, and you, that define the venue. Whether you are in line at a movie, greeting the Dali Lama, or snuggling on the couch; it is still the two of you, alone together, who define your venue.

Communicating in a special way with your spouse, with more love and respect than you would ever extend to anyone else, even the Dali lama, confirms their importance to you, and yours to them. The circumstances or location should never reduce your intentions to serve your spouse, as that needs to be your highest priority, regardless of anything else. You may want to read that again.

Protect them from your bad habits

Your old gnarly habits will certainly try to betray your best intentions.

Even when stopping yourself from undermining your marriage with 'ready to launch' depreciating speech is excruciatingly difficult, protecting your spouse from your bad habits, or harmful moods, is always worth the effort.

We are not suggesting you will always be successful in the beginning; it takes some time to

Make a vow that from this moment forward you will treat your husband, or your wife, only in ways you think will uplift and honor them

Never give up. The results will surely come

take control over the mind. But although switching completely away from being sensitive and reactive to being sweet and considerate, especially when you are super annoyed, will be super difficult, it is not an excuse to not do the best you can.

With sincere and constant effort, your habits will gradually change, and with each effort it will be progressively less difficult.

It is never the outer circumstances that make you feel how you feel anyway, but it is how you feel that makes the outer circumstances what they are.

Marriage is the two of you, regardless of circumstances

It cannot be over stated how marriage is not like a business partnership venue, social relationship venue, or any other venue in which worldly rules of engagement adjust according to where you are, when it is happening, or what you want.

Marriage is all about pleasing who you are with; your spouse. Your soul mate is everything to you, because your marriage transcends material, psychological or emotional gains or loss.

Measures of success and failure in every other venue are essentially material

Marriage, on the other hand, your connection with each other, is different because it is spiritual at its core.

The rules for your marriage venue are as radically different from all other venues as strolling a sandy beach on a sunny day is from trudging through a mountain pass in a blinding snow storm. The measure of a successful communication in marriage is security, connection and joy. Other venues are defined by much lesser measures of success.

Always remind yourself to see your spouse as your soul mate, a much higher designation than any other person has in relation to you, and your spouse's importance to you will continue to escalate beyond measure. You will be much happier when you shift your mindset to appreciativeness that your relationship is something so special.

Marriage is the unity of souls, bound by your intentional infusions of active love, which, of course, takes specific effort. Therefore, proper marital communication is uniquely superior, and is intended to bring the two of you closer together through the invisible connector of conscious love.

Love and connection are, after all, the virtuous goals sought by all individuals; individuals, couples, and spiritual seekers, alike. But it is not attainable in any other venue the way it is in marriage. In marriage, it is protected, by design, and the potential for growth is unlimited.

Missing the point of marriage is the cause of marital suffering

The greatest number of pitfalls people encounter in the course of their marriage, all of which block the experience of love, do not arise from outer circumstances (like finances or outer temptations), even though it seems that way to those who do not look past the material surface.

With sincere and constant effort, your habits will gradually change, and with each effort it will be progressively less difficult

Troubles arise *solely* (100%) from abusing your closeness; over-familiarity

Closeness, which can be a two-edged sword, is also one of, if not among the greatest blessings of the marriage venue. Only in marriage do people agree to be together forever. No other commonly known voluntary relationship is forever.

But instead of using closeness to express love, in ever new imaginative ways to increase connection, as would make the most sense, individuals abuse their spouse with their unique insider's perspective. Then, to make matters even worse, they excuse their crazy defensive intentions with petty selfish (selfishness is the hidden toxin in every destructive act) reasoning.

You still need to impress your spouse with consideration

Thinking you can tell your spouse they are bugging you because they interrupted you, for instance, is a great example of putting your needs ahead of theirs.

Any justification for not being 100% loving, 100% of the time, will only take you further away from the life you want.

Although, according to worldly thinking, it is merely stating your truth, or something else about yourself, when you complain; in marriage what works is putting your spouse's needs ahead of your own, especially when it seems patently unfair to look past their mistakes.

When it is a challenge for you to be nice, all it means is you are about to go beyond your present limitations. By pushing yourself beyond your habitual limits, you invariably become a better spouse.

Fairness in marriage? Not like you think!

The ideas of fairness in the world only have to do with what works from each individual's point of view. It is always subjective. Subjective means every single person has a different opinion of what is fair.

In marriage, what fairness means is that you always do what works for your spouse, no matter how unfair it may be for you. It is very simple that way. This kind of maturity is called selflessness, and is the best way to live.

It seems like it would work if both said they would be that way to each other, but that would only create expectations and demands. So you have to keep it your mission, without expectations. Don't worry, though. You will later see how you do better than "fair". When you feel tweaked in any way, and you think you are being treated unfairly, or a situation feels unfair, instead of reacting, it is best to

Stop; stop everything, so you can unhurriedly

Evaluate the possible outcomes, and then decide how to

Act in a way you believe will be beneficial to your spouse (some people take this concept

Troubles arise solely (100%) from abusing your closeness; over-familiarity

By pushing yourself beyond your habitual limits, you invariably become a better spouse

to extremes, imagining they must become doormats, until they learn the nuances of this new way of thinking).

Use your natural marital closeness to your advantage

Your closeness is ultra dangerous when it is used to exploit your partner's faults, because it is like misusing a surgical knife.

You have to recognize that the power you have can be used to hurt, or help. Those who misuse their power, as you (and all of us do) have done, cause a lot of trouble.

The more you learn about your partner, due to their always being in your range of observations, the better you are equipped to not only avoid triggering their weaknesses, but, more importantly, you are able to support, admire and praise them.

You have free will

It is completely up to you to decide how you treat your spouse. It is not up to them as some say "well, if they treated me better…" No matter how your spouse treats you, your behaviors have to be based on how you wish to behave, not based on how they treat you.

Predicate your behaviors on what is right behavior, not reactive behavior. Those who act with their spouse according to how their spouse acts with them, claiming they deserved it, or some other excuse, only spiral down their marriages; just as you might expect.

Your spouse is the most important person in your world, and life

Your spouse is the most important person in your life, and is never an adversary, any more than you could be your own adversary.

When you include them in your heart, they can help you live and enjoy the safest most satisfying existence imaginable. In other venues, a person is almost always on some side other than yours, and when they are on your side, it is almost always because of self-interest. Your spouse is always on your side; by definition!

Don't compete with your spouse

Your spouse is not only on the same side as you, but they are the same side as you. Never entertain the idea of, or engage in, any competition with your soul mate. It is crazy to make them a competitor, even in jest.

As you may know, competition is a polarizing game in a world of competing needs, which must not exist (and in reality, cannot exist) between you as a married couple. As long as you honor your spouse with respect and consideration, which they are due by virtue of your marital promises, you will find expressing love, respect and gratitude, in contrast to competing, comes naturally. In fact, competition between married partners is an abnormality, which causes only trouble.

It is completely up to you to decide how you treat your spouse. It is not up to them as some say "well, if they treated me better…"

Even in jest

Even "cute" competitions can potentially spiral things downward, so it is better to avoid competition regardless of any temptation. If a competitive moment slips in, despite your intentions, at least make sure your spouse "wins".

When you play a board game or tennis or some other competitive match, be sure you are always supportive of your spouse's efforts, be the first to praise good moves, and be quick to congratulate their accomplishments. Winning in those is ok but win with grace. If your spouse is sensitive to losing even in games, it is better to avoid playing.

If others put your spouse down for a bad move or sloppy effort, it is your job to overshadow any comment with praises. Some may think it is loyal to overtly defend their spouse, and in some cases when they are attacked, it is correct to get firmly on their side. But in most situations, just praises will do the trick.

You cannot go too far in being there for your spouse

Those who say this philosophy, of not being competitive, may be going too far, are not being realistic. They are merely so used to the abnormal behaviors of the world that they have not thought out the dangers of competing within marriage, or have considered the benefits derived from always being progressively more loyal and supportive.

Just as you cannot go left and right at the same time, neither can you be competitive and supportive of your spouse, at the same time.

During any moment of competition, you are choosing your side over theirs. It may not reflect your overall attitude, of course, but we think no moment should be wasted in thoughts and ideas which do not bring you together. All your words should be useful towards your goals of closeness, rather than harmful or neutral (wasted).

Your spouse knows you inside and out

Your spouse is your soul-mate. There is not one person, not your best friend, mother, father, teacher, 3rd cousin on your father's side, or anyone else who knows your flaws as well or in as many ways, as your spouse knows yours. Isn't it so obviously true?

They see you all the time, in every conceivable situation, going through every conceivable test of life. They are aware of your flaws and mistakes, weaknesses and strengths, with an objective un-obscured vantage point. They see it all. Of course they see you through their particular filters of their experiences, so some of what they see may be their own flaws. But the point is you cannot hide your stuff from them very well, if at all.

The reverse is also true. You know your spouse better than anyone else, by far.

Your husband or wife is, if you even pay only half attention, pretty much an open book. Of course, if you have been too selfish to notice them, because you have been too wrapped up in them not satisfying your needs and whims, you probably do not know as much about them as you should.

If a competitive moment slips in, despite your intentions, at least make sure your spouse "wins"

Your spouse is your soul-mate. There is not one person, not your best friend, mother, father, teacher, 3rd cousin on your father's side, or anyone else who knows your flaws as well or in as many ways, as your spouse knows yours

But even if you are the self-absorbed type, it is still likely you know more about them than you do anyone else.

The jewels and flaws, but you concentrated on the flaws

Of course, just as they see your flaws, and you see theirs, so both of you also have the unique opportunity to see the hidden jewels in each other, which nobody else sees.

That is where you need to put your attention, of course. Until you do, there is no chance for happiness. Yet, and this is so valuable, if you choose to focus on their positive traits and ignore the things they have still to work on, your lives will improve beyond measure.

How simple this formula is, yet, because of habits it is so difficult for some. The question you have to ask yourself is whether you throw yourself into pits of misery just because the effort it takes to overcome past bad habits seems difficult.

Because of popular but ridiculous beliefs, many, perhaps you too, are still living with the fantasy that they (your spouse) can, or should, change according to your design.

Even though it may be a good idea for them, on some level, what actually works is for you is to work on your own flaws, as you are willing, and for them to work on theirs.

You are way too close to each other in your marriage to include judgment and criticism as part of your lives. Besides, all they really want, really, is to be allowed to be themselves without constant reminders of their failings, same as you do.

Give what you promised

They want you to praise them and be proud of them. Just as being constantly criticized is a tremendous burden for you, it is for them, too. One of you has to stop the criticisms first.

You have to stop seeing them as their flaws. The flaws they carry are not who they are. They are a really good person, but like the rest of us, and you, they have some flaws and always will. You also have to stop reacting to every little comment as if it were a pointed attack. Even if an attack comes, it does not mean you have to stand up to it or die. You can ignore it.

The mistakes your spouse makes can be ignored, or compounded into an argument by your reactions. You have more power to avoid problems, and create more good will than you might think.

On the other hand, you also can see things about your spouse which nobody in the world has any idea exists, but is so darn cute or noble you are blown away by them.

Sometimes individuals are so burned out they can no longer see great qualities, but that's rare. Most of us only have to recall how we were impressed back when we met our spouse to break our own ice. Those are the qualities we need to focus on, and then compliment them about. Those are the treasures we enjoy, which none other can enjoy. Those are the qualities it makes sense to restrict ourselves to commenting on.

All your spouse really wants is to be allowed to be themselves without constant reminders of their failings, same as you do

Maybe it is not so easy, because of past and current bad habits, but that does not matter. When you are climbing out of a pit, you grab on to the strong ropes, no matter how much it hurts your hands, because it is how to save yourself.

Don't imagine your mind is set, and cannot be changed. It is your mind, and you can control it. In fact, it is your mind, so it is your obligation to control it.

Your spouse is not an ordinary person

Your spouse is incredibly special for you. Even when difficulties abound, nobody in the world will ever be there for you like your spouse will. Nobody will ever care for your success as much as your spouse does.

What other venue can come close to these claims? Nobody is more supportive of you having a great relationship with your children as your spouse is, and nobody can give you the love and connection you desire, or need, like your spouse would like to.

But you have to do your part, and give them room to be themselves, even when you do not understand where they are coming from, even when they falter in doing their part. You can do this.

All it really takes is a resolute commitment that you will not taper back on your efforts, even as things get better in your relationship (they will).

You would not believe the follow ups from years ago, where folks say they forgot what we shared. Keep yourself informed. Continuously ramp up your respectful love and support so your marriage gets, exponentially, better with time, till the end of time.

Your spouse will come around, they always do

Ok, maybe your spouse is not acting like the most supportive spouse in the world at the moment, but they will improve when the pressure subsides. It is far more natural to protect a spouse than to put them down. It just needs to be practiced, so you can feel the differences.

Your spouse is special. Who else in the world would even think to give you love without seeking something in return? Now turn that around! Who, but you, can give such a potent gift? The opportunity to intentionally give your spouse selfless love and support, which they cannot get anywhere else, is too great a marriage enhancing opportunity to pass up.

If you learn to give love without expectation, a lifetime effort for some of us, you will be happy. There is, actually, no other way to achieve permanent happiness. Neither is there a better venue than marriage to practice this lofty, and practical, exercise.

Great spiritual individuals treat everyone the same way you should treat your spouse. Those special souls, who give selflessly, in this cruel world, are defined by their courage. It is far from safe to give unconditional love in a world filled with man-eaters. But we mortals can imitate their nobility, with our spouse, in the safety of our protected marriages.

Your spouse is incredibly special for you. Even when difficulties abound, nobody in the world will ever be there for you like your spouse

If you learn to give love without expectation, a lifetime effort for some of us, you will be happy

This is an opportunity which should be advertised as a primary reason to get married, because of its universally understandable benefits. There is no higher or more practical purpose in life than learning to give unconditional love. The safety zone of your marriage is the safest of all arenas in which to practice unconditional love. The results are marvelous.

Your spouse is always and categorically part of your side, even when they do not know it yet, or think otherwise. They are not just on your side. In other venues of life, you give and take, you compromise and deal, always looking for the inevitable other shoe to drop or see what little edge you can get as you strategize for the best deal for your side. In marriage, the more you give for the sake of pleasing your spouse, the happier you will be. Your spouse is your side.

When your attitude is right, you will get joy and happiness from giving your all to your spouse, just like when you dated! It is confusing the goals of marriage with goals within other venues that confuses people. The only time you can lose in marriage is when you are thinking of how you can be taking care of and protecting yourself instead of your spouse, the exact opposite of other venues.

Don't worry about your own needs! This worldly hype about making sure you take care of yourself is utterly destructive in marriage. It is one of the biggest lies and destructive elements of society.

Take care of your spouse. The rest will fall into place.

People forgot why they got married, and they forget their marriage will work as long as they remember to once again cherish their soul-mate above all else

You can communicate with your spouse in a way you cannot communicate with anyone else.

Base your relationship on selfless intentions. How else can two people survive, much less grow, in such a close relationship? When you act selfishly, it is only a matter of time before you burn each other out with demands and grievances.

On the other hand, even if just one of you strives to act selflessly, as is the case for many marriages, it will completely shift your marriage. You can choose to be soul mates, or choose to be cell mates, all defined by your intentions and actions.

The deepest experiences can be shared in your marriage venue

Sex, when you are not married to the person you have sex with, is shallow and usually draining, even if you pretend it is more than a temporary release.

Without marriage, sex can still be an attempt to be close to another, but the feelings are fleeting at best. Unmarried physical engagement is mostly based on covering up insecurity. But when you are married, sex is a vehicle used to express deep love and intimacy.

Friendship is more reliable, too, when you are married to your friend. Outside of marriage, confidentiality, between even the closest friends, is usually eventually betrayed, as is loyalty and close cooperation; not necessarily on purpose.

People forgot why they got married, and they forget their marriage will work as long as they remember to once again cherish their soul-mate above all else

Even noble soldiers, who bravely fight for each other's lives, eventually depart from their deployment and slowly forget to think about each other. But the bonds of marriage daily grow stronger till the end, making each interim moment potentially fulfilling.

You were just never shown these important differences for marriage, or how to gain them! The marriage venue is where you can find them.

You need to remain mindful and responsible

Common problems come up when individuals forget to shift their perspective away from worldliness when they are with their spouse, or they might shift into an incompatible communication style, based on over familiarity, or they shift back to defensiveness, when their interactions do not go as initially planned or expected.

They might say, well I tried and it didn't work, so it is every man for himself. Not shifting your mind to marital, user-friendly mode, sets you up for marital difficulties.

Of course selflessness works!

You have to be consistent and committed, but it cannot help but work if you stick to it.

As soon as you treat your spouse as anything other than the most important person in the world, you are off on a tangent that will take you down one rat hole or another.

It makes no difference when you shift away from marriage partner mode, it will hurt you every time you do. It also does not matter when you wake up, and shift back to being your spouse's ardent support, it will quickly improve things.

Keep alert to your mental state and keep it in line with happiness. You can do this! It just takes you making up your mind and being always mindful of your marriage venue.

Don't be deceived by surface traits

Some foolish people think their spouse is not as funny, clever or maybe as sexy as some random acquaintance.

Because they are so focused of the subjective comparisons, they destroy any chance for a thriving marriage by looking at a little trait rather than the whole relationship. Once you said "I do", the surface personality traits are supposed to be as nothing, compared to the heart connection and your marriage.

Forget about your spouse's traits, other than to admire them. When you are deeply connected, you can be in love with what you see as their wonderful traits while not bothered by their little or big flaws. True connection transcends the surface. Leave the traits of your spouse to your spouse. They will change the ones they are ready to change at their discretion.

In your marriage venue, the traits are not important. Nobody is perfect, anyway.

The bonds of marriage daily grow stronger till the end, making each interim moment potentially fulfilling

True connection transcends the surface

Your attitude is all important in discussing differences

Individuals want to share their frustrations with their spouse, and of course they should be able to. As long as you are not critical, demeaning or blaming your spouse; you can usually express your feelings, regardless of how much they may differ from theirs.

If your spouse is sensitive about something, considerately try to pre-announce that what you are going to say is only your opinion, and that you will respect theirs. Remember it is always best to be considerate with your spouse, as over-familiarity has done so much damage.

Keep it a discussion, and stop everything, immediately, if your conversation begins to become an argument. However, if your frustration is with something about your spouse, it would be best to look at your own pettiness for at least a week before you say something. If after a week you still think it is them causing your frustration, you will need to look at your pettiness for a month longer. If after the second month you still think they need to change, you should consult with a good coach, or write to the foundation. Don't worry, we will set you straight!

Be considerate

Naturally, it is never wise to persist with repetitive overly passionate expressions, because it means you are too attached to your opinion. But repetitive complaining falls under another topic anyway; nagging.

In a small space, like your marriage venue, sounds have a lot more impact, so your complaints do not need to be repeated, unless you just want to be annoying.

Your spouse will not hate you just because you have different views. It is expressing your views with finality that causes trouble.

Presentation needs to thought about

If you make it seem like you feel your opinion is the only one that counts, it means all other opinions are discounted.

Also, it is rarely a good idea to take a hard stand on anything. At worst, if you are on the verge of losing it, you can always say you will think about what you are discussing. Then change the subject, or go do something else.

When naturally polarizing topics, like religion or politics for instance, come up and you find yourselves on opposite sides, unless one of your actual actions can, or will, impact your marriage, it is better to let it go. If one of you is so passionate that it cannot be set aside, it might be a good idea to get some professional help to help you create harmony.

Communicating is a form of giving

Treating your spouse to loving communications rather than selfish expressions caused by personal frustration will not minimize your own needs in any way. It is just common sense to place the needs of your spouse ahead of your own.

Repetitive complaining falls under the category of nagging

Treating your spouse, and their opinions, with respect and consideration is the kind of expressions they need, and serving their needs, if you want a spectacular relationship, must be your highest mission.

Uninformed people make too much of small points, which are so irrelevant they are forgotten in days, or even minutes. Every point that may be argued is insignificant compared to the peace and love you are better off striving towards. There is a saying we find quite applicable in married life

"do not sweat the small stuff; and it is all small stuff."

Put your spouse first

In your marriage venue, always communicate in selfless, serviceful ways, putting your spouse ahead of your own needs, even though you want to react (reactions can be immediate, or may hide in the mind for a long time).

When you stick to the rule of controlling your speech, your current usual reactions, which you do not even think about, will soon seem petty to you.

The reactive part of you is actually an unfortunate habit, which gets you into trouble time after time. Over time, your new habits will become your best. When you want to react, even if it is so powerful you cannot contain it, you still need to

1) STOP   2) EVALUATE and finally   3) ACT WISELY

Selflessness is the cornerstone of a healthy marriage venue

Selfishness stems from fear.

Admittedly, in the world there is plenty to fear, but not in your marriage. But it is natural to not shift for your mate because it was never pointed out. So, even though you have nothing to fear in your marriage, your reactions do not think "oh, I do not have to be reactive or fearful, this is my soul-mate".

Be selfless in your marriage, as you wanted to be from the beginning. You need to own the idea that protecting your spouse is more necessary than protecting your own skin, and show it in your words and deeds.

As you develop the selfless mindset you need to serve your spouse, without any expectation of getting anything in return, you will get the most from your marriage.

The greater your mastery of selflessness in your marriage, the better you will do. As you start to see how you habitually put your own needs ahead of your spouse (useful in the world but deadly in marriage), but then remember to override the selfish tendencies, the happier your marriage will be.

In your marriage venue, always communicate in selfless, serviceful ways, putting your spouse ahead of your own needs

Selfishness stems from fear

Don't fool yourself out of happiness

Some individuals are insulted by the above, and take these comments as personal accusations. But it is not an accusation at all, nor is there blame attached to asking you to recognizing the likely culprit in your marriage.

We ask individuals, and occasionally couples, to recognize that our civilization is primitive in the areas of relationships, so you need take your ideas beyond the norms of society in order to have a great marriage.

It is as hard a reality as you will ever find, that selfishness is destructive to a marriage. And though it is not easy to see ourselves, it is almost certain that if there are problems, they stem from this universal culprit. In virtually every case, when one decides to steadily and tenaciously make himself selfless, it means the likelihood for success is close to 100%.

Of course, you can well imagine that nobody wants to hear they have been doing something wrong, or they have destructive tendencies.

You can't change your spouse

Most individuals want to hear that their spouse is a jerk, and if we show them how to do such and such, they can transform them. But that is never the case; ever!

Selfishness is always aggressive behavior in your marriage, and your selfishness is the only one you can transform. So you have to gain mastery over yourself.

There is really no other way, nor should there be. What makes all the self-effort worthwhile is the amazing reality of a marriage in which you do it right. Don't worry about how long it takes, or how far you have to go. Just start, you will see how little effort you have to make to get results you never dreamed of.

Selfishness-Bad   Selflessness-Good

Modern selfishness, which is the underlying motivator in nearly every action in the world, is completely out of place in your marriage venue. With all the self-serving justifications, even though watching out for number one has become all too normal in our society, selfishness in any form is a cancer to any marriage.

Selfishness degrades both your marriage and you as an individual. When self-protection rules, when allowed in your mind and marriage, it repulses your spouse.

Remember, the whole idea of a happy marriage includes attracting your spouse, which you do with selflessness. You may fear you will lose something by giving your partner your all. Well, your marriage is better than that! Ignore those false internal paranoid messages. They are carryovers from your worldly experiences.

Civilization has primitive ideas in the areas of relationships, so you need to take your ideas beyond the norms of society in order to have a great marriage

Loving your partner is safe

Learning to love your spouse unconditionally is inherently safe and reasonable, we all know that, each by our own experience.

But we are prisoners of habits and fear brought over from worldly experiences. Putting aside fear, and doing what it takes to express unconditional love may be hard to swallow. This is the hard part for many. That's why we stress the innate differences between marriage and all other venues, so you can make the shift, regardless of what your mind is telling you.

Follow this logic about your special relationship, and convince yourself, in theory at the very least, even though it is not commonly accepted (which is why the divorce rate is so high).

Then go for it, without holding back. Push yourself until it proves itself valid in your life. Nobody will then be able to convince you that this information is anything but 100% accurate, and a lifesaver.

But you have to do the work! The harder you work at this in the beginning, the faster the results will come.

Learning to love your spouse unconditionally is inherently safe and reasonable

Your marriage is a safe place to experiment with this

Marriage is your safety zone in life. Its where you are safe, even if it does not feel like a safety zone at the moment, because of all the misunderstandings. But it remains the exact venue for giving and receiving unconditional love.

Just because you have not used your marriage as it was intended, does not mean it will not work now that you know what you have to do. The effort to improve how you behave with your spouse is a lifetime effort, but the true early benefits come pretty fast. After some time, it becomes a joy to be selfless, rather than a difficult challenge as it seems at first.

Don't settle for less than a real marriage

Without trying to love unconditionally, a marriage is not a marriage at all. If you refuse to learn to love unconditionally to the best of your ability, of course, you can have a marriage in name only. But, please, do not be frightened, thinking you have to reach some perfection to have a real marriage. Probably very few reach perfection for some years. Real results come from intention, and the best effort you can make, not an effort that is scored or rated.

Real results come from intention and the best effort you can make, not an effort that is scored

It is wrong to intentionally test your spouse's love and dedication

The idea of speaking, or should we say blurting out, whatever is on your mind, when and how you want without thinking of how it will be received or impact others, may be normal in certain quarters of our society. But it is a gross misunderstanding of what constitutes intimacy.

Inconsiderate speech is immature in every, and any, venue, but it is absolutely brutal to those who trust you to love them.

Some think when someone accepts random un-thought-through communication without complaint, it is a sign they are loved for 'who they are', but this is simply not so. When you intentionally test your spouse's love by ignoring their basic and unique needs for respectful treatment, you risk offending them, and cannot gain one thing from the offense.

The common vernacular is that you have to respect the other's boundaries, and it of course makes sense, no matter how you word it.

Anyway, once you got married all testing was supposed to stop. Your approach to your spouse was supposed to shift, completely and forever, to supporting and satisfying your spouse. You know them very well, and you need to not only accept them for who they are, but praise them for who they are.

Your communications needs to be based on your intentions to sincerely love and please your spouse

The irony

It is ironic that people put so much energy into having their expectations met with demands and complaints, but so little energy into proving their love and loyalty to their spouse, by interacting with basic respect and consideration.

How is it possible for you to show appreciation and love if your attitude demonstrates it is all about you having your expectations met? You need to shift your attitude to be someone who is there for your husband or wife, even if they are not there for you very much right now.

Looking good and sounding good

You dress to impress, and wear pleasant scents because you want to become more approachable, and your communications also need to be based on your intentions to sincerely love and please your spouse.

If you forget to consider how what you say impacts your spouse, it is a subtle sign to them of your indifference towards their needs, even though it may not be your intention.

Unfortunately, if you are like most couples, your current communication is rarely intended to please your spouse, but is almost always used for selfish reasons.

Practicing thoughtfulness is something most do not consider, but should. The marriage venue is special, yes, but you have to fill it with love.

Experiment with everything that may be positive

Make your mind up that you will develop your marital communication skills.

That is the best positive way to improve your lives, where your communication style matches your increasing love and caring. When you arm yourself with determination to establish love and support as the foundational principle of your communications, and you never, ever excuse anything hurtful that may accidentally pass your lips, you will construct the bridges of love you always wanted. Is this not simple?

A look at the possibilities

Marriage is the most important venue in your life because your husband or wife is the most important person in your life. And not coincidentally, marriage also has the most possibilities for all kinds of happiness; contentment, self-acceptance, sensual pleasure, intimacy, joyfulness etc. No other venue offers as broad a spectrum or as much security and contentment.

Those who know the joys of marriage through their ongoing efforts, never hesitate to demonstrate their feelings of love and appreciation to their husband or wife. They would rather suffer terrible humiliation rather than intentionally hurt their spouse's feelings.

Those couples enjoy every interaction, no matter how mundane or seemingly trivial. They go out of their way to make each other feel special, and appreciated. The opportunities are endless, and so are the rewards.

For those in the know, it would be easier to criticize anyone else, to their face, than miss an opportunity to offer a simple service to their soul mate. This is not meant as an exaggeration!

Your spouse is the most important person in your life. When you got married, you put all your eggs in one basket, protect that precious basket!

See your marriage (venue) for what it is

Stop the flow of toxicity and replace it with adoration. Experience the dynamic improvements in your relationship that will come from your shift.

None can miss the improvements when you enhance your marriage venue by serving your spouse's needs. This realization happens to all who persevere.

No one can list all the goodies, because there are way too many. Nor is it possible to compare your blossoming marriage with other marriages. There is no "average" marriage. Every flower is different, and so is every marital relationship.

As your awareness of the various venues you take part in begins to click as being distinct venues, and the various venues become more and more definable, and contrasted against your marriage, the abundant and unique opportunities for love, intimacy and deep friendship will slowly, but surely become more dramatically contrasted with the rest of the world's relative pettiness.

Soon you will not be able to miss how no other relationship comes close in comparison to your marriage. You will intentionally treat your spouse poorly ever again.

Marriage has the most possibilities for all kinds of happiness; contentment, self-acceptance, sensual pleasure, intimacy, joyfulness etc.

When you got married, you put all your eggs in one basket. Protect that precious basket

The realization of the importance of your spouse is an awareness that literally grows forever!

Eliminate all toxic flow with determination

The possibilities of marriage will never be realized if you keep squashing them before they have a chance to develop. So controlling your tongue and learning what not to say, and how not to behave in your marriage, is absolutely a must; and we will say it over and over again, it is absolutely not up for discussion.

You have to control your tongue! You also have to control your mind, too! This is not airy fairy! You have to work at this with all your might! Success without effort does not even work out when you are dreaming.

Remember the eclipse effect? Nothing reduces the good feelings from a compliment as surely as an insult or slight that comes afterward. So keep the little digs out, too. They may seem funny to you, or "innocent", but your marriage is not a sitcom. Ending all the abuses you currently extend to your spouse, in every overt or subtle way, complaining or criticizing or whatever; will open the doors wide for all kinds of happiness. You have to stop the misbehaviors!

Please know, without any doubt, that allowing your anger or other degrading inputs, into your marriage, in any overt or passive aggressive way, will slow down the rebuilding process.

Be aware of your attitude and tone in every encounter. Always self-check. What did you sound like, and how did you come across?

Is there any question in your mind of the importance of this warning? So, metaphorically, if we were talking about building a house, the compliments would be the walls and windows, and a snide remark or dirty look would be a wrecking ball hitting the wall you just put up.

Your highest priority must be control your mind and stop your tongue

Sound principles which are undeniably effective in other venues will cause instant tension, disconnection and misunderstanding in your marital relationship.

Your marriage is a venue defined by how visible you are to each other, all the time. So be careful. Little things can get overwhelming in close quarters.

Proving your ideas are better than your co-workers may win praise at work, and maybe even gain you more job security, but will hurt your marriage. Work is competitive, and you get breaks from your co-workers and even change co-workers from time to time. But marriage is always and forever. Proving your idea was better than your spouse's will ruin your plans for a loving evening, with no upside. Useless bragging rights may be your only so-called prize.

The possibilities of marriage will never be realized if you keep squashing them before they have a chance to develop

Will your spouse kiss you and snuggle up when you say "I told you so"? Efforts in some venues will bring benefits, but will create opposite results in your marriage venue.

If you start screaming at or blaming your lover the way you scolded your brother or sister when they took your stuff, or switched channels while you were watching a show, that will not make your spouse feel connected or loved. They will certainly not appreciate you.

Even if you get used to such treatment, it leaves a residue of discomfort which builds and builds. Appreciation is something not immediately important among siblings, but it is a key ingredient of love in your marriage.

Spouses are not your siblings or parents etc., and should not be spoken to the same way. Once again, the same actions have completely different results, all because of the different venue. Even when they are close family venues, they are never going to be close like marriage. Marriage venues have no equal or even proximate.

Be there for your spouse by spending time

The venue of your marriage is designed to be incredibly secure in comparison to other relationships, but you abuse the privilege of being married by assuming you can abuse without a cost.

The venue of your marriage is designed to be incredibly secure in comparison to other relationships

You probably do not even think about how your behavior impacts your spouse. Do not treat your marriage like other relationships, where it is all about what is best for you, where one of you might run just because there are a few misunderstandings. But do not inspire your spouse to run, by judging, blaming or other offenses.

Prioritize your behaviors

Is it really more important to watch a TV show, than attend to your spouse? Is it really more important to exchange jokes, or gossip with friends than to take an evening stroll with your soul-mate?

Obviously, you need to spend time together. Your relationship cannot be nurtured if you are only bumping into each other as you are coming and going, but if you spend time together and just rag on each other, you will damage what little connection is there now.

Make the best use of your venue. Go for the benefits with supportive efforts.

In most cases, the one seeking help is most ready to make the sweeping changes which improve the marriage

When together, do not wait for your turn to be taken care of. Forget yourself in service to your spouse. This is advice for both, but mostly for you who are reading this.

Every professional will tell you that in most cases it is the one seeking help who is most ready to make the sweeping changes which change the marriage.

The acceptable automatic reaction for your marriage is an automatic reaction to accept, forgive, and try to be there for your lover

We need to know how to get along

In other venues, smart people constantly scrutinize (and criticize) the trustworthiness and loyalty of social contacts, even dear old friends, just in case they go sideways (it happens all the time). But your spouse has signed on the bottom line, as you did, to do their best to be your most trusted ally for all your days.

If you are like most people, you are too quick to assume the worst and too quick to blame your spouse (for all sorts of things). That is the habit of reactions. That is the habit of self-protection.

But why are you also so slow to forgive? Why assume it is your spouse who needs to adjust? They stated their intentions to be with you forever right from the start, but you probably wore them out with constant challenges.

Rather than measure their efforts, stay focused only on yours. It gets hairy sometimes and you will want to burst. But keep your cool and stay focused on being amazing, no matter what expectations are put on you.

Acceptance and forgiveness

If there is any acceptable automatic reaction for your marriage, it should be an automatic reaction to accept, forgive, and try to be there for your lover.

Another worthwhile automatic reaction should be to acknowledge your spouse as your loyal companion. The fact that they said they would be there for all time should not be taken for granted, or taken lightly.

Make the most of every moment to give love. But when clouds come, it is wise to remember the sun is still shining, in the form of underlying love and commitment, and all clouds will pass.

In marriage, there are more opportunities to bond, than to unravel

The topics of, and kinds of, communication are very broad in marriage; more so than any other venue. Nor do other venues come close to your marriage in terms of potential benefits, including your ability to fully recover from past mistakes. Your relationship allows for an infinite number of blunders, and is designed to make forgiveness and compassion of your spouse standard fare.

No other venue allows for so many areas of life to be shared openly, so deeply, or intimately. Every imaginable topic can be made relevant to your own lives. Your communication can be serious, about life's issues, or playful, or childlike, or philosophical. You can be chatty, sexual and/or deeply intimate. All formal rules are meaningless, as long as you remain lovingly respectful.

Unfortunately, if you are like most couples, your communication has been disrespectful, ongoingly obliterating the potential for the promised happiness you desire/deserve. Speaking with your spouse as you wish to speak with the most important person in the world is exactly what will work for you both.

Be the spouse of your dreams

Ask yourself if you have been your spouse's greatest friend and champion. You need to be pro-active in holding your behaviors to the highest imaginable standard.

Have you betrayed your spouse's trust? Have you shared their secrets with others? Have you shared their flaws with others? Have you been mean? Have you criticized, condemned, yelled at, or been mad at them? Those are some of the things blocking all the good stuff.

Instead of thinking about your own needs and fears, shift your mind to think of things that will please your spouse and bring them happiness.

When you put your spouse ahead of your needs, big or small, they will reciprocate. It may take a bit of time to be 100%, because most couples get entrenched in their habits, but that will change. If it takes time, no matter how long, keep up your efforts to put them first.

You will see changes in your own awareness and perceptions that will make you feel like a better person. You win in every way.

With all the various venues we encounter, marriage, is in a league all its own

No other venue comes close to your marriage. In marriage, our natural expectations of ourselves and each other are deep, committed and eternal. Intimacy, loyalty, confidentiality, sex, family and everything else all have significantly deeper and more profound meanings in marriage, especially a well cared for marriage.

Please, no useless guilt for past mistakes, please

We discovered, and most successful counselors agree with our conclusions, that neither guilt nor shame can provide individuals any benefits.

People who should feel guilt or shame, based on their premeditated harmful behaviors, do not have enough built-in feelings of social responsibility for guilt to prevent more future abuses anyway. Those people tend to be too selfish to care; while individuals who actually care about others usually did not realize how they impacted others negatively, or what their actions did to their chances of having a good relationship. They were, and are not, bad people.

So all the guilt and shame does for the good folks is undermine their efforts, which would have been better spent improving their perspectives and future efforts.

Everyone makes mistakes. It is part of the life education model. It simply does not make sense to dwell on past mistakes, especially when those mistakes are actually more useful as forceful learning experiences.

Even some religions consider guilt and shame to be a sin, rather than a tool for redemption. They say it is an insult to their souls, which they consider pure of all taints.

Instead of thinking about your own needs and fears, shift your mind to think of things that will please your spouse and bring them happiness

Everyone makes mistakes. It is part of the life education model

We, too, believe guilt and shame to be worse than just a waste of time. They distract individuals from focusing their attention on their needed focused efforts to change. In any case, why dwell on past mistakes when growing your marriage is all you really need to do. When helping living things, it is best to remove the things which are harmful and take better care of them in the future. Your marriage is a living thing.

Pour honey to sweeten your relationship

Positives, compliments and acknowledgments etc, are the things you may have to push yourself to do. Include it all in your marriage venue repertoire, as you begin your new wave of positive efforts. But go ahead, push yourself!

Because you are still learning to work through your own hurt, fears and anger, there will be a tendency for your past habits to resist your new positive efforts. You will not want to push because your feelings are hurt, but do it anyway. Change your feelings. You will gain a lot more ground when you consciously take on your bad habits.

Do not look for "justice", as that is barbaric and absurd in marriage

When you want to act like a spoiled child, admonish the habit, and act like a loving spouse instead. Ask yourself what you have to lose. Ask yourself what the right thing to do is. But do not look for "justice", as that is barbaric and absurd in marriage. Ask what will help you impact your marriage in a positive way. Ask yourself what will best serve your spouse's needs to feel loved.

Everyone has "issues"

We know some people have issues and phobias which make loving communication difficult, and we sympathize with those who get tongue tied etc.

In certain cases, an individual may benefit from working with a coach or therapist. But for most of us, it is only a matter of overcoming the discomfort of revealing our vulnerabilities when we open up, it is shyness.

You may not realize how important your kind and loving words are to your spouse. Try to push yourself a little harder every day towards loving and supportive expressions. Everything in the future will improve if you make the effort today.

In this world, we have to either take control over what happens to us, or our outer, and inner, influences manage to smash us into all sorts of painful obstacles. Learning to control your thoughts, words and deeds is the surest way to happiness and the greatest happiness is within your marriage.

If you wait for the "right" moment, the right moment will never come
You have to push through your anger, fears and expectations

The marriage venue is a world of love and connection, when it is managed as such. Put your attention and energy into making your marriage venue the safety zone of love and intimacy in your lives. As you notice the tensions decrease because you stop the worldly noise at the door of your marriage, there will not be a vacuum as some imagine. You will fill your relationship with a joy that comes from intimate connection based on appreciation and loving actions.

Where all other venues are limited, your marriage venue has no limitations. You can find the infinite love you crave in the heart and arms of your best friend, your soul-mate.

Part 3-The one technique you cannot live without

Slips and recovery

The "I am sorry" method

By now it should be clear there are formulas of cause and effect we can always rely on that look something like

Say mean things (cause) = receive mean things back (effect) or;

Take a hard position (cause) = resentment (effect) or;

Give a compliment (cause) = get a smile (effect) …and so on. You can come up with a million such equations

But what happens if you did not mean to say something, but it just came out, because your habits have not been trained yet? Or, what if you thought about what you were going to say, but for an unknown reason your spouse reacted like you just shot the neighbor's cat.

Hey, we are not perfect, and the words we say may be wrong for the moment, or maybe your spouse may have misunderstood you; or maybe they understood you, but you did not see that what you said was worse than shooting the cat. Whatever might be the cause of for the disturbance in the force, no worries! We have a failsafe solution for just such occasions. It is called the

"I am sorry" diffuser

Saying "I'm sorry" is a way to communicate a truce. It is a clearing method. It does not have to mean you want forgiveness or that you did something you are sorry for. It means there is a misunderstanding and you need to back up, or at least create a new beginning. It means you are saddened, because the conversation has taken a bad turn, and you want your lover back.

This is not to say you cannot mean you are apologetic for stepping on your spouse's toes, but sometimes it is not you who did the stepping, but their feathers are too ruffled for them to know that it was not your fault. You do not have to be right, or be apologized to, for you to want harmony over being acknowledged.

Saying "I'm sorry" is a way to communicate a truce. It is a clearing method. It does not have to mean you want forgiveness or did something you are sorry for

If you insist on making sure they know what happened, there is a chance you will win the argument, not likely, but there is a chance. However, that being said, there is a greater likelihood you will have tension lingering for a much longer period of time. You always have a choice. The thing of it is, you can choose peace, by being loving and supportive, so any other choice is a lesser one.

Some, who are new to this method, think they are pandering to their spouse, and living out of integrity. But it is never out of integrity to be supportive of your spouse. That kind of thinking will, in fact, ruin your month, instead of your five minutes of eating humble pie.

To be there for your spouse is never a mistake by any measure. Sure, you can challenge this advice in extreme hypothetical situations to prove it is "wrong", we have heard it all. But why would you not use a perfectly good tool to quickly get back to what you really want in your marriage.

It is not like it is the first time anyone ever did anything "out of integrity", if that is what the problem is, at some time. But even if you think it takes you out of integrity (and it never does) it will always work. Sure you can write a whole book reviewing and analyzing this, demonstrating the values in one case over another; but we think you should overuse this method and just be thankful for the longer periods of joy which comes as a result of your humility, rather than worry about how you were actually right and had to give in.

Some have experimented by saying they are sorry, and found it worked. Then, after the tensions subside they tell the "truth", that they only wanted to defuse things but knew they were not wrong. It is not hard to know what happens with that one! Admitting to being manipulative is just plain dumb and it is not meant to be used for manipulation anyway.

You are supposed to mean you are sorry, and eat it. If you cannot mean it, you are missing the point and need to review this concept until it makes total sense.

Albert Einstein said if you cannot explain something in simple terms you do not fully understand it. We say you need to understand this works well enough for you to understand that the benefit is that it ends arguments. This is one of those amazing rules for rescue you need to own.

This is not a tradeoff of truth for peace, either. It is a choice you make to give your spouse love in a clear way. You choose to put your spouse ahead of your pride, or you choose to see things their way instead of yours, just because you love them.

It is not your place to point out their flaws, or hold up a mirror so they can see them more clearly. That was the job of their parents. It is your job to love them, honor them, cherish them and prove it in your day to day interactions.

*To be there for your spouse
is never a mistake
by any measure*

It is not your place to point out their flaws, or hold up a mirror so they can see them more clearly. That was the job of their parents. It is your job to love them, honor them, cherish them and prove it in your day to day interactions.

When

Say "I'm sorry" the moment tensions begin to degrade the conversation; better too early than too late, though it is never too late. This tool is amazing! It works so well in so many situations that you should use it (sincerely, of course) even when you are not sure it is appropriate.

The 'I am sorry' method is a power brake that stops runaway words from pouring out of your mouth. Replace the thought, the ugly one that is sitting on the tip of your tongue, with "I am sorry". Insert and reinsert your contrition with the intention of putting on the brakes. Once you catch yourself running away at the mouth, simply say "Honey, I'm sorry."

It is not about begging for mercy, or you admitting you are evil, or anything close. It is about controlling your own stubborn mind in a forceful manner, and giving yourself time to think. You may have to say it several or more times before the situation is defused, but do not go back into an argument, start explaining what you really meant, or anything else, no matter how tempting an opportunity arises.

Saying "I am sorry" is a break off method, so you stop your inevitable spiral into the bottomless pit of arguments. Use it as often as you need to.

Begin changing your ways

Now you understand the principle of communication venues, and how your marriage venue is unique and superior to all other venues.

You always knew the difference between what is toxic and what is like nectar to your relationship. You already know there are many ways you can improve your marriage right now. You can at least begin with ending the attacks, both passive and active. Do not wait for your spouse to "figure out their end", or wait until you read the whole of the lessons before you start applying these simple and powerful ideas.

Make up your mind to be successful. Do not make this another "I'll try "one more thing" to see if it works. Do not be like those who skip from one remedy to another, never giving any philosophy a chance to prove itself.

If what you read here makes logical sense to you, make these ideas your marriage bible, and stick to your efforts, all the way to happiness.

Replace the thought, the ugly one that is sitting on the tip of your tongue, with "I am sorry"

You always knew the difference between what is toxic and what is like nectar to your relationship

You can do this! What it takes to make your marriage work is primarily determination, anyway. If you knew none of what you have just learned, but were passionately determined, you would still succeed. One way or another, you would eventually come to all the realizations found in these lessons.

Later on in the lessons, after you are shown more about marriage, you can build upon what you have learned by studying more proactive communication techniques. You will soon be a marriage expert, too, enjoying the wonderful fruits of a well run marriage.

- Chapter Five -
Marital Materialism

◇◇

Certain behaviors are absolutely going to kill a marriage.
If only one of you overcomes this fear-filled disease of the mind,
your marriage will be allowed to flourish as intended

◇◇

*Entering into marriage as if you are entering into a business deal
is missing the point of marriage. Allowing your marriage to be reduced
to the same expectations you would have for a business deal
creates unhappiness and confusion. You have to recall
your earliest intentions to fill your home with love*

Chapter Five

Marital Materialism

"**W**hat if I do my part, but my spouse doesn't do or is not interested in doing theirs?" This is the question that defines the most deadly and difficult attitude that a couple might ever have to overcome.

If you are the one asking this question, you will, almost certainly, hold back your efforts, and hold back your love. You will react to any perceived indifference by shutting down (at the very least); even though you recognize holding back your efforts will certainly reduce your chances for happiness.

Don't give up

Despite your desire to give up, you need to know for certain that if you reduce the outward flow of your intentionally loving communications and actions of love, you will weaken the foundation of your marriage. It makes no difference that worldly logic forces you to question the wisdom of pouring your heart into your relationship, or not.

When you are pretty sure your spouse is over it, it is hard to regroup and act as if nothing is wrong. How could you feel or do otherwise?! Why should or how could anyone work towards a improving their relationship if their partner is not showing they are interested in contributing? It doesn't matter.

Why kill what you can bring back to life?

Curtailing your efforts, or just giving up on your marriage altogether, does not make the best of sense, as it will halt all relationship building and repair right when you need it the most. But it is easy to understand how giving up seems like the only reasonable thing to do. People in the world give up all the time, although they have much less at stake.

The understandable, although fearful, reaction, to stop most of your effort, will decisively undermine all of your positive efforts to succeed. If you give up but act as if you are still trying, it would be like rowing a boat while the anchor is gripping the bottom. It is a good way to exercise, but you will not move. You cannot make effort, while at the same time, hold back your effort, and expect to progress.

Now, or ever, is not the time to hold back

Your marriage and happiness cannot wait until you are convinced your spouse is on board the same way you are. You cannot wait until you think they want your marriage to work as much as you want it to work. You have to love them unconditionally, to your best ability, and push your efforts even more, regardless of the abuses, or humiliation, you may feel.

Curtailing your efforts, or just giving up on your marriage altogether, does not make the best of sense, as it will halt all relationship building and repair right when you need it the most

Same problem in reverse

Then, there is the other side of the same problem.

When the shoe is on the other foot, if you so much as think your spouse questions your sincerity and commitment to them, it means you do not really believe their heart is into saving your marriage. So, in that case, you will understandably be discouraged from investing your efforts, when you think they are holding back. Every bit of worldly logic backs you up, if you want to hold back.

According to all the natural worldly laws of interaction, your normal expectation is that they should try as hard as you do (it is only fair), to improve your marriage. You think they should at least try to the best of their ability. Isn't that right? Is that not a fair and reasonable expectation? In the world; yes!

Fairness

Fairness, unfortunately, is not only too subjective to be a reliable part of any relationship equation (who can measure the throb of a heart?); but, in case you have not discovered this fact already, fairness is a completely irrelevant concept in the marriage venue. However, in the scenario of questioning each other's intentions, you automatically accept your sense of what is fair as the basis for most of your thinking, because you are not used to adjusting, or shifting, to the marriage mentality of your marriage venue.

Fairness is fickle and misleading in any case, even in the world. You need to see fairness for what it is, because, although it is a factor in every other venue and relationship, it simply has no place in your marriage.

Fairness just does not fit in marriage. Attempting to use fairness in marriage is the very definition of forcing a square peg into a round hole.

In the rest of life, the fairness thing is so crystal clear when you think someone is not fair with you. Your fear of being treated unfairly (humiliating, right?) will discourage you from making a sincere effort in any endeavor. Your boundaries will often be declared with great power, if not resentment, when someone is unfair with you. You will irritably think, "why should I do anything, if they do not care enough to do their part?" You will almost definitely hold back your efforts.

Fairness is cool everywhere but in your marriage

In every other venue of life, the doctrine of fairness comes into play, and always for good reason. Even when circumstances force you to interact with someone who is not fair with you, fairness is not forgotten, just temporarily shelved.

But you never ignore the idea of fairness. It is always a part of all regular human interactions; all, except in harmonious happy marriages.

Fairness is one of those worldly things which will slip into your relationship, but with its only purpose being to destroy your marriage. It just has no positive place at all.

Fairness just does not fit in marriage. Attempting to use fairness in marriage is the very definition of forcing a square peg into a round hole

Fairness is based on identifying what is good for one, in balance with others. It is, at its core, a way of self-protecting even though we say it is for the good of all involved. In every venue of life, it is good for all.

The all involved part is a way to reach an agreement where each person feels like they are protected from each other. It is based on protecting the self. There is no reason to think otherwise. It is selfish, with a small "s", but still selfish. And selfishness is a good thing, in the right context.

In marriage, selfishness is incredibly toxic, like a deadly acid or virile bacteria

No matter how small the selfishness is, or no matter what the situation, the doctrine of fairness is not going to help your marriage grow.

In fact, fairness in marriage is like building a boat, and then drilling holes in the hull. "Honey, I love you, but only as long as you abide by my sense of what is fair, and maybe I will consider what you think is fair, if I am in the mood" is a great way to undermine what marriage is all about.

Any marriage will go down if there is enough selfishness involved. Even arranged business marriages, based on whatever considerations are included, will fail, as a marriage, if selfishness grows unchecked.

Love is selflessness

Love is a selfless energy, if not the energy of selflessness, itself.

Marriage is based on love as the vehicle and goal. So selflessness is the critical component in every successful marriage. Holding back your efforts is another way of admitting to holding back your love. So, obviously, if you restrict your love, for any reason at all, even so-called legitimate reasons, you are holding back your marriage.

If you never held back your love, never expected signs of love in return, and always loved for the sake of loving, you would be very happily married.

Facing fear is the easiest way to overcome fear

Sometimes the discouraging fears about who is, and who is not, working on the marriage are thought about "out loud", but most of the time it is too scary to think about, and even scarier to speak about.

People do not want to entertain the idea of their partner not caring as much as they do, so it remains a hidden killer, creating enormous doubts, sometimes all the way through a divorce. In those cases, it erodes a couple's confidence and security, stealthily acting as the primary, but hidden, reason for their divorce.

You cannot pretend this fear does not exist. You have to face it, or it will eat you up, at least subconsciously.

In marriage, selfishness is incredibly toxic, like a deadly acid or virile bacteria

Marriage is based on love as the vehicle and goal

Almost everyone who encounters relationship troubles entertains the notion of their partner not wanting to succeed as much as they. It is, after all, normal human nature to blame another for your troubles, no matter how improbable the likelihood of someone else being at fault, as is sometimes the case.

And, it may be true that all your marital trouble is entirely your spouse's fault, we do not know. But what we do know is it will not matter if it is their fault, or not. We know it is still on you to love them, and demonstrate your love, with all your heart's intentions, even if they are making zero effort; even if they are working at ending your marriage.

The marriage contract is the securest of all agreements, so trust it

And, by the way, even though we have never heard of one person being solely responsible for a troubled marriage, we have indeed heard of many individuals being responsible for their marriage changing direction without any support from their spouse, and ultimately creating an ideal marriage.

In marriage, you are defined solely by your expressions of love

The one thing (there is only one thing) that inhibits an individual from putting their energy into a troubled marriage, without their spouse proactively participating, is fear.

Fear (or lack of fear) defines us in all the venues of life, save marriage

Worldly fears define us in all the venue of our lives (which makes complete sense), but fears and our reactions only define us in venues of life other than marriage.

In marriage, you are defined solely by your expressions of love

The fear of someone not giving you a fair return or of not contributing equally to your partnership is perfectly reasonable and legitimate in the world.

Nobody can argue the importance of protecting yourself from all the various dangers of the world, or all the treachery waiting around every corner. But marriage is different. Even when you are going through a tough patch, even when the tough patch seems to have gone on from close to the beginning and/or lasts many years, your marriage is still your safe haven.

Marriage is not a balancing act

The marriage venue does not accommodate lines of reasoning which weigh contributions, or obligations, because marriage is not a do for me, and I will do for you, kind of relationship. Marriage is the "I will do for you, do not worry about me" relationship. Bringing worldly behaviors and fears into your sacred space of marriage is a very bad idea.

Almost every form of worldly thinking is an incubator for fear, and discouragement. But worrying about whether your spouse is going to do as much for the relationship as you, only means you do not understand the role of selflessness in marriage, or how secure marriage actually is.

How can you ever have a good marriage if you are always looking out for your individual interests? It is impossible; and until you accept this idea and start looking out exclusively for your spouse, you will never have a happy marriage. Selfishness, expressed in any form, dampens or kills love.

Prove your love during the tough times

When your relationship is rocky, you have to put even more of your efforts to positive, can-do thinking. But that is not so easy when worldly thinking is telling you your marriage is hopeless, because your spouse will not do their part.

It's a good thing worldly thinking is inappropriate for marriage! It's an unfortunate thing this kind of thinking does not come naturally when times are tough or when everyone in the world is telling you to protect yourself.

Equal effort is a destructive expectation in marriage

The bottom line is if you hold back your efforts until you are convinced your partner is on board, at least somewhat, you are unknowingly giving up on one of the most meaningful principles of marriage, and probably your marriage itself; unconditional commitment.

When you entertain any expectations for fairness, you have effectively given up on your marriage, at least the way marriage is meant to be. Putting expectations on your spouse to do their part also means you have rescinded your decision to love them unconditionally.

Why are we, at The Marriage Foundation, so convinced you will lose everything so long as you hold on to the expectation of equal effort? It is because we know equal effort has no place in marriage, no matter what trendy ideas may say, or how strong the arguments for protecting yourself.

Selflessness is a core foundational principle of a happy marriage. No matter how you rephrase any selfish attitude, or demand, it will undermine your efforts to love your spouse in the way you said you would, back when you got married.

Your vows were exchanged, but not as a "deal"

The attitude of selflessly loving your spouse is not more important for one gender or the other. Some, who live in the "old fashioned" way, think a woman must be this way, while a man is free to be an inconsiderate boor, in the name of manliness.

We raise this issue because it is prevalent in some segments of society. There is no universal cure for those who adhere to this perverse way of thinking. If you are a woman who is married to one who thinks like this, it may be your efforts need to be more specialized, but resentment or rationalizing that it is their entire fault is not the answer.

Marriage is a special relationship, which is not based on reciprocal expectations or founded upon selfish individual desires. It is not like a worldly partnership, where one has to do, in order for the other to do back.

Selflessness is a core foundational principle of a happy marriage

Marriage is a special relationship, which is not based on reciprocal expectations or founded upon selfish individual desires

The purpose to learn unconditional love and selflessness

Marriage is a relationship designed for each one to learn to give unconditional love, and your love is hardly unconditional if you expect your partner to "try their best"; no matter how fair and reasonable that seems.

Loving your partner unconditionally means you will try your best to please them, because you choose to love them, regardless of their flaws or mistaken behaviors. It means you choose to love them and support them, even if they may have given up (for now). Unconditional love does not include "why should I work on anything, when they will not do their part".

Overcoming this killer takes self-awareness, and ongoing effort

The first thing you have to do, to get to the other side of this fear of unfairness, is remind yourself that marriage is not like any of the other venues of life.

Overcoming the material marital tendencies takes self-awareness and ongoing effort

Because society does not advertise the differences, along with the unique benefits of marriage, you miss out on most of the clear advantages, so you default, and bring in your worldly expectations.

In fact, the world tells you that your partner cheats you if they are not as serious about fixing themselves and your marriage as you are about you fixing yourself (or them). The worldly ideas of so-called self-love, and self-worth are quite distorted renditions by the time they are filtered through magazines, and daytime TV programs. You cannot count on them as guides.

Instead of promoting the idea of concentrating on loving your spouse, which is the ideal of selflessness, the message from the world is to love yourself, and leave your spouse if they cannot accept you for who you are. No way is that useful or helpful! They appeal to people's weaknesses.

The venues make the difference

The confusion comes from not differentiating the venue of marriage from every other venue, where leaving may actually be very good advice.

Sadly, millions of marriages that could have delivered the benefits which we all yearn for have crashed on the material rocks of selfish expectations. Marriage will not work if it is based on individuals caring for themselves, any more than porcupines will work out for a waterbed.

People mistakenly apply worldly standards and expectations to your marriage without a second thought, out of habit and out of ignorance. If you do not consciously push out worldly protections now, they will stay in your marriage.

If you have vermin in your home, they will remain until you make the effort to exterminate them. Bad ideas and bad habits are the same. You have to push them out, or they will stay.

Your mind will not self-clean. You have to reason out the differences, and reason out the habits, which don't belong in your marriage. You have a lot of work to do, and if you do not do it, your marriage will fail. If you think it is too late, your marriage will fail. If you think you are willing, but your spouse is not; your marriage will fail. If you think this is an interesting approach, but we do not understand the particulars of your marital problems, your marriage will probably fail.

What makes your marriage partnership so different?

The most critical differentiator in marriage is that two of you are defined as being one once you tied the knot.

Every married couple has the distinction of being one by the mere definition of marriage. When two are one, instead of two individuals in a partnership, you do not have sides; you cannot have sides.

Your commitments to each other are seamless, not something that has to be reinvented or reviewed or reestablished at various intervals. You are together through thick and thin, so no matter what temporary doubts may come into your mind, they are not going to impact the foundation of your marriage.

You do not need your spouse to tell you they will stick it out, or they will put in as much effort as they can. They already told you that, when they took their vows.

Marital commitment is not like any other

Even though your head is filled with doubt, you still can accept the dynamics of what marital commitment means, and override your doubts. If your spouse forgets the principles of unity, but you remember it, you are safe.

You have to behave with confidence in your vows. You just have to treat them with love and grace, instead of expectations.

Some make the mistake of using the union to burden their spouse. They tell their spouse "you have to stay with me, you made a promise", as if that will work.

Free will is not just for you

That attitude is selfish and insulting. We say, if you think this is true, you are missing the point of individual will. Yes, your vows keep you together in commitment, but it is your job to treat your spouse with unreserved love and consideration, not hold their vows as leverage against them.

Use the vows as assurance that your loving behavior towards them will be safe.

Understand the power of your vows

Think of a bird. If a bird does not believe its wings will support it in flight, it will not even bother to extend them. The bird, with its wings, has all it will ever need to prevent a fall. Those wings will not only save it from a fall, but allow it to soar in the sky.

The most critical differentiator in marriage is that two of you are defined as being one once you tied the knot

Use the vows as assurance that your loving behaviors towards your spouse are safe

You may not be impressed with the bird having the ability to soar because, duh, having wings is part of being a bird. But if it does not recognize the usefulness of its own wings, it will fall to its death. The same is true for marriage. Commitment is part and parcel of marriage. It is there, and does not have to be looked for, or proven. You can rely on it.

With it, your marriage can soar to heights undreamed of. But if you do not rely on the commitment, if you question it because of this or that, your marriage can crash.

Marriage is not a mere partnership

Your marriage is the highest agreement of unity. It is not a mere partnership. Marital unity is so much more than a partnership. So much so that one cannot even suggest that marriage is an "advanced" partnership. Partnership means something else in marriage.

The word partnership, when thought about, is inadequate for marriage

The word partnership, when thought about, is inadequate for marriage. Marriage is not the same as business or social partnerships, nor can they be understood in usual worldly terms.

The confusion begins in our language. The vernacular of the world at large is the same for marriages, even though the meanings are worlds apart. In business, sports or other social interactions, a partnership has very limited rules, and definitions, when compared to marriage.

Because we are uneducated about the differences, we use the limited definitions we find in other venues to fit into our marriage, and, at best, maybe add a little this, or a little that to embellish, because we intuit that marriage is special.

You have to grasp the meaning, not just a definition

Think of the word flying, where you just cannot compare the flight of a bird to the flight of a spacecraft, but you use the same word.

There are no similarities, really, yet we use the same word, because of the limitations of the language. In the case of flying, there is no confusion whether it is used for spacecraft or birds, because our minds automatically wrap around the differences (and no engineer will want to put wings on a craft meant to "fly" in outer space).

But using the same word, partnership, for marriage, and all other venues, has caused tremendous confusion about what marital unity is.

You still can call your spouse your partner, but the fact that they are your partner does not mean the relationship is anything like a normal worldly partnership. Even though you are forced, by the limitations of language, to use the word partnership, you need to disassociate your understanding of the word from your understanding of your relationship.

Avoid this common pitfall

The differences in meanings for words used in marriage have a disastrous effect, because we should never reduce marriage to a common vernacular. Using the same standards for marriage that are used in lower venues will cheat you out of your treasures.

Part of adapting the mindset of unity with your spouse requires insisting to yourself that your spouse does not have to prove their commitment to the success of your marriage, any more than you do; it is a given.

Understand, it is unreasonable to expect them to prove anything to you. If you cave in to your fears, based on all sorts of rationales that you need to be certain they are on the same page etc. you undermine your marriage with doubt.

You can change everything

If you force your mind to accept the truth of your unity, despite all the so-called evidence that appears to prove otherwise, you will be safe, and successful.

You need to behave with the confidence which comes from that understanding. Your spouse has no power or ability to increase your confidence. Nor can their behavior be blamed if you do not trust the vows. It is all up to you. It is your commitment that counts, not theirs.

What is your commitment? Do *you* take your marriage seriously? Do you want more than just a temporary partnership filled with fear and anxiety? Or do you question the vows you both made?

Have you bought into the ease of divorce? If so you will have to face these fears again, and again, until you realize your power over your own destiny.

You have the power

Your marriage will succeed because of what *you* do, not what your spouse does.

Stomp out any idea that your marriage may be endable. Just because the world says you can end your marriage, it doesn't mean you should. Much of the world says you can kill a child as it is being born, too. Some say it is ok to have a slave, or men should dominate women. There are more crazy ideas than you can count, so you have to be more discriminatory. You get to choose your code of life, not anyone else.

No matter how well a partnership agreement is understood or spelled out in worldly venues, it remains viable only on the good faith and considerations of each. Anyone in business can recount horror stories of partnerships gone awry. They are more common than not.

Each partner has to protect themselves from the potential for losses due to unscrupulous partners, all of whom have probably had sleepless nights due to the fears of uncertainty.

Marriage is unique and special, but you have to trust it at the moment

Marriage is not, by any stretch, a business partnership. If you make it like a business, you will be destroying your chances for the true benefits which are found only in marriage.

If you force your mind to accept the truth of your unity, despite all the so-called evidence that appears to prove otherwise, you will be safe and successful

In marriage, the certainty of the future is based on your vows and determination to stick to marriage principles rather than worldly principles

It is too easy to mistake the conditions within marriage, as being the same as the conditions within all the other venues of life. From the outside, to uninformed persons, it looks the same. Because of this mistaken way of seeing marriage, it's easy to make assumptions which are the opposite of reality. Any assumptions you make, that your spouse has to prove themselves every day, will be disastrous.

Put your marriage ahead of the world's ideas

In other venues of life, each and every action determines the past, not an uncertain future. In marriage, the certainty of the future is based on your vows and determination to stick to marriage principles rather than worldly principles.

You already have the commitment from your spouse. Now is not the time to question them, or give them an out. Now is not the time to give you an out, either. You tied a metaphorical knot. Unless you specifically untie it, the knot remains solid and secure.

Make yourself trusting and trustworthy

It is impossible for two people to meet at the proverbial halfway point

Those who suffer from the desire for fairness must eventually face reality

Desire for fairness comes from insecurity and selfishness, which can never be satisfied! There is never such a thing as fair. Everyone who has a particular point of view filled with all sorts of fears, biases, and prejudice, weighs fairness in their own way.

How can you weigh good and bad deeds, anyway? Who is to say who gives more and when? Even in business, there is not really such thing as true objective fairness (other than exchanging gold for currency). Of all the killers of a loving relationship, this notion of fairness is by far the most crazy-making.

Those who suffer from the desire for fairness must eventually face reality

Once the idea of unfairness takes hold, it develops a veritable army of fear-based reasons in your mind, for you to maintain an eye of examination upon every word, thought, and deed of your spouse.

Your scared mind will find all sorts of clever ways to twist the information you gather, to support your negative point of view and increase the fear. Your judgmental mind will work against your happiness, by fearfully and forcefully insisting on fairness over what seem to be less tangible benefits of expressing selfless love.

This is a very difficult process to overcome once an individual falls into it.

The surest way to avoid this trap of fear is to reverse the spotlight of critical attention.

Start to look at your own speech and behaviors, while you speak and behave. That is correct. Pay attention to your words, as you speak them, and your behaviors, as you act them out.

Be tough on yourself

If you are a tenth as critical of your own thoughts and behaviors as you are of your spouse, you will catch some pretty ugly thoughts. At the same time, be less judgmental. This may be beyond hard to do, and there is no getting around it, but if your desire for fairness is not stopped now, it will follow you until you do something about it. Like rats in your living room, until they are exterminated, they are present.

Correct your own behavior, while you strive to be inwardly appreciative and complimentary of your partner's unique behaviors.

This is a sure path to happiness

When you put goodness into your relationship, without expecting anything in return, you will achieve happiness, no matter how your partner behaves. Your mind may always tell you it isn't fair, or that you are sad. Your also mind tells you that your spouse has the power to make you happy. Reject those thoughts quickly so you are not a victim of them.

Lasting peace and happiness do not come because of external conditions, any more than suffering does

Stop your mind from overemphasizing the illusionary lack. Instead, be appreciative for all you have. Count your blessings instead of pining over what you think you might be missing.

You have the power, through free will, to choose what you see and how to evaluate it. You can choose to see a sunset as no big deal. You can choose to be in awe over a grain of sand. You hold the keys to your happiness.

If you give yourself into your relationship, without expectation of a return, you will soon see a change; a change that will last as long as you keep it up! When you feel taken advantage of or taken for granted, instead of defending your space, offer more of yourself.

The mind is like a little child who cannot be satisfied for long, and gets in the habit of complaining and wanting more. Don't let it ruin your day with justifications for its grumpiness.

You alone can make it work

If only one of you is truly committed to being a real friend and unconditional lover, the odds of divorce or misery are slim. This shift is pretty much an essential. Thank Goodness most people see the truth in this concept and make the effort to make the shift.

Discipline your mind. You will be happy as a giver, instead of as a taker. Fear is the enemy on this one, isn't it?

When you put goodness into your relationship without expecting anything in return, you will achieve happiness

Discipline your mind

The mind tells you that if you change and your spouse remains the same, you will be taken advantage of; and that would be the end of it. Instead of wanting to please your spouse for the sake of love, you have given into the thinking, "what's in it for me," you have given in to the fear of coming up short. Is this how you are?

If not, no worries. But for those who need to hear it, this is important. The idea of a 'balanced fair relationship' is not going to work; but has been the undoing of numerous marriages that could have done well.

If you are committed to rescuing the most important relationship you will ever have, and you are not willing to settle for a mediocre marriage, the wisdom in learning to love without reward from your spouse is what it takes.

If you make the conscious decision to put goodness into your relationship, without expecting anything in return, you will achieve happiness no matter how your partner behaves.

Never give up!
You can do it!
If you refuse to give up, a way will eventually present itself. Don't give up!

Never give up! You can do it! If you refuse to give up, a way will eventually present itself. Don't give up!

If you are determined "nothing but complete success will do," then you will succeed. Never give up! You can do it!

It doesn't work to have expectations of anyone, but yourself. We know this is a drastic concept, because part of being married is getting to be with someone you can "count on"; right?! What's wrong with having that kind of expectation??! Nothing is wrong with it, other than it is imaginative, and unrealistic.

Can you be counted on 100%? Even if someone was 100% sincere, they might let you down for reasons beyond their control, or they may be tempted in ways *nobody* in this world could overcome.

Expectations are a set-up for disappointment

We never met anyone who takes their word lightly. Everyone believes they will do the right thing when they are faced with a difficult choice, or are tempted. But everyone has found, at some time or other, they were too weak to stand up to a temptation, and it got them into trouble.

Of course, we all fail at various things. The problem is that the world is an unreliable place, at its core, and having absolute expectations is an absolute set up.

But failure in marriage is not the same. Marriage is not meant to fail. There are too many built-in safeguards for a marriage to fail easily. It takes a lot of work to kill a marriage.

Keep your marriage safe

In order to have a flourishing marriage, you have to trust your partner to the greatest degree possible; not based on their trustworthiness, but on your ever expanding ability to trust they are doing the best they can.

Cut them slack for any and every error of judgment and make sure you can be trusted to love them enough to love them in spite of their current weaknesses. If you are holding your spouse accountable, like you would someone in business, your marriage will not be relaxed or mutually supportive; it won't work.

In today's world, with our culture egging all of us on in whimsical directions, you need to examine how a selfish attitude cannot possibly work in marriage; stop being fooled by unrealistic expectations. Any and every selfish expectation drives your marriage off track; even little ones, which should be ok in the world.

Imagine how you feel when someone is not doing their part to complete something, when both of you are obligated to work on it. Use a workplace assignment as an example. If there is someone on your team who is not doing their part, that person will be resented by everyone else.

The expectation of everyone pulling their weight is reasonable at work, but it is a killer of marriages

The expectation of everyone pulling their weight is reasonable at work, but it is a killer of marriages. How can an expectation-based relationship lead to happiness? You know how expectations are. Every little desire leads to another bigger one.

How can your love grow if you are always waiting to see if your expectation du jour is met? Let go of yours, no matter if your partner is stuck on this flawed thinking. This is anything but easy! The trouble is there is no other practical way around it.

Expectations make you miserable

We cannot imagine any marriage between any two people working out when expectations get in the way.

Push past your tendencies to withhold love unless your needs are met. For those who are not yet married it is a good idea to know who they are going to marry, but then once decided, it is imperative to let go of any expectations; so called reasonable, or otherwise. Otherwise, there is no way out of the suffering.

Unconditional love is the greatest gift you will ever have

Don't you want to be loved unconditionally? Of course you do! It is the greatest gift you can receive. So make it the one gift you learn how to give.

We know it sounds wrong in today's world and even "feels" wrong to have no expectations of your spouse. Nevertheless, if you think about it in depth and when you read all of the supporting reasons about free will, instincts, drives and how the mind works etc. in the coming chapters, you will get how it is the only way to live; we promise.

The business mentality in marriage doesn't work

The business mentality of waiting to see what your partner is going to do before you are willing to be kind, considerate, loving and proactively build your marriage, is the opposite of what you need to do in order to find happiness.

A lot of people think a business arrangement marriage, as with providing for a "trophy wife", or some other mostly financial arrangement is demeaning (and it is such a waste of time). But it is not nearly as bad as one where a couple really wants a true marital connection, but ends up in a business deal.

In an arrangement where financial security is exchanged for companionship, at least everyone is on the same page in terms of expectations. However, a real marriage transcends any material considerations. Our mission is about showing you what you need to know to experience true connection and intimacy.

Be realistic about your marriage

Pretending you don't fit in the category of a business-deal relationship or that your marriage is "not so bad" can short change you in your life.

It is nearly impossible to be among those who are not tainted by at least some of this disease of the mind and soul, so it's best to take it seriously!

No matter how hard it may be to get out of a hole you have fallen into, it does no good at all to just sit there and sulk, or accept your conditions. Figure out the shortcuts towards connection, and then take them. This book is all about helping you find the shortcuts! Change your attitude from "What's in it for me?" to "What can I do for my lover?" You will see, if you try this method, that it is the way to love, live and succeed.

The difference between success and failure

In the past few decades it has become far too easy to quit a marriage, with the idea that for some reason or another it was just not meant to be. Most people, as you are seeing, usually can save theirs by using even a little of what is shown here. But, in rare cases, quitting is not a choice you get to make, because ending your marriage is a matter of survival, or your spouse is too far gone.

The situations which are, by any standard, physically dangerous, especially to children, do not give couples many options. If you are like the vast majority who don't fall into that category, or if your spouse is long gone but you can't let go, we want you to have hope and not the "wish upon a star" kind of hope.

There is plenty of science behind relationships so when you approach your relationship with scientifically based methods, success will come.

The world will eventually catch up to your potential

The world is evolving. Look back in time and you can see the trend of humankind is moving upwards.

In every area, from material technology to esoteric philosophies, humankind is advancing at a very fast pace. Time and space, for example, are seen completely differently from just one hundred years ago. The barbaric ideas of racial or gender superiority, which were normal only a hundred years ago, are now seen for what they are by most of us.

Medicine, diet, psychology and governing are all evolving. Even studies on human interactions are becoming universally more important. But with all that, the knowledge needed to have a successful marriage is still not commonly known. You are learning what is not commonly known, so you have to grasp it in a way where modern ideas are seen for what they are in order to not get confused.

Your marriage will succeed because you will know what to do, and why, as a result of your personal study and experimentation.

If you are deep in a mess because, until now, you dug your hole, do not despair. Once you change your approach to your spouse, your new direction will take you where you want to go. And, of course; do not give up!

Go beyond just fixing your marriage

The section you just read focused on which behaviors harm your marriage, what you can now do to reduce the tensions, and why it works.

The next section contains what you can use to chart a new and wonderful course, to choose your destination of love and connection. The next section points out the wonderful benefits of marriage, almost completely hidden from the world at large.

You will begin to see your marriage as one of the most wonderful of all the gifts in life.

Our sincere desire is for you to experience the joy you intuitively knew was waiting for you when you said "I do".

- Chapter Six -
Anatomy of Marriage

◇◇◇

When you are able to understand something, anything, as a construct,
you can fortify its pillars and give less time consuming attention to its less important aspects.

Marriage is a real "thing" with real "machinery" and connections.
Nothing is as important as learning about the anatomy of your marriage

◇◇◇

*Marriage is unique and superior when compared to all other relationships.
When you understand its construction and work with the natural laws
which govern it, you will find the treasure you always knew was there.
It will no longer be elusive or mysterious, but rather
wonderful and fulfilling*

Chapter Six

Anatomy of Marriage

The laws of cause and effect are reliable and exact

Anything you experience, in every venue or circumstance, including within your marriage, always, always, always happens as a result of what you thought, said or did.

It is simple and is called cause and effect. *Everything*, without any exceptions and no matter how wonderful or disturbing, small or big, is a precise result of some earlier thought, word or action.

For every action there is an opposite and equal reaction

Nobody can defy physics, physical or human.

Cause and effect is somewhat more observable in material occurrences because our physical eyes can usually see that what goes up will come down. That is not to say there aren't a great many physical occurrences, like in aerodynamics, which are pretty elusive to the eye, but they are still detectable with physical instruments.

Physics are no less real, or precise, in non-physical realms, even though the causes and effects cannot be measured by our intelligence.

Still, as you start to look for signs of this law, you will become more aware of its influence.

**No matter what happened, or happens, you alone,
are the master of your past, your future; your destiny**

No rationalizations, excuses, blaming others or any self-righteous justifications will stop the wheels of cause and effect from turning. As you sow, you reap. It makes absolutely no difference whether you "believe in it", agree with it or not. It is just the way it is, always was, and always will be.

Hope exists for you and your family, because these same laws mean your current situation will improve when you make the right kind of effort, which brings the kind of results you prefer.

If you are smart, you will pay more attention, and then formulate your causal behaviors, which are of course are all of them, to be logical precursors of the effects you desire later.

No more going with the flow or reacting without thinking. Create conscious thoughts, words and actions to gain power over your life. This intelligent approach, of planning your actions, is the best way to create the marriage you always wanted.

Cause and effect rules our world and all our experiences until we use it to bring us to the threshold of love

There are no coincidences

There are no coincidences or random happenings in life, and so, in the absolute sense, there are no accidents. This concept may seem mysterious to some, but it is quite real, even though not always visible, with or without your approval. Life is not as random as it appears.

Some who believe in cause and effect, but still feel victimized, may say "but I didn't know", and they didn't. Most do not recall what they did in some distant past, which causes their current suffering.

Unfortunately, knowing what you did is not vital as the laws of the universe work, whether we know about them or not. But, to be perfectly honest, you probably do not have to look back very far to see which causes you created for your present suffering.

You probably only have to examine yesterday's thoughts, or this morning's! Were they pure? Were they supportive of your spouse? Were they about your spouse's needs? Or, were they about you taking care of you, and your problems? Selfishness always creates suffering.

Your current conditions mirror your past actions

Because of the "laws of cause and effect", current circumstances within your marriage accurately illustrate the past actions of you, and your spouse. And, thank goodness, these same natural laws which determine your future experiences are entirely in your hands.

There is nobody, not any thing, or outside force, you can ultimately blame for whatever uncomfortable circumstances you may find yourself in, as they are your own creation; just as all your welcome successes are the result of your past good thoughts, words and deeds.

All the goodness you enjoy is credited to your past behaviors too, and all your future goodness will come to you for the same reasons.

Both of you steer the marital ship of your life

The actions of one of you, impacts both of you. When it comes to how cause and effect regulates your marriage, you cannot realistically separate your actions from those of your spouse.

As a married couple, you are, in most respects, one entity, like two people in a Kayak. Neither of you can individually shoulder the responsibilities for your current situation.

The healing power of one

As with all of your past actions, the current efforts you make, together,and/or individually, will impact both of you. Ignorance of secret actions by one cannot protect the other from their effects, good or bad. Efforts by both of you, or one of you, determine the results you experience in the near and distant future.

There are no coincidences or random happenings in life. In the absolute sense, there are no accidents

This reality, although it can explain the pain, which for some seems to have come out of nowhere, also gives hope to even the most desperate individuals.

Just as one of you can bring so much suffering into the marriage, so, just one of you can bring in so much relief, and eventual joy.

Those who wonder if their individual efforts, alone, can change their marriage will find great comfort in this equation, because it logically assures them their positive efforts are never wasted. Like a mathematical equation, the rules mean this:

As long as one is really making effort, unless the other is adamant about ending the relationship (very rare, although it can happen for periods of time), the relationship will improve, and then the other, in a less strained environment, will gain hope as well.

If you are the only one who cares to improve the marriage, the odds of success are still overwhelmingly in your favor.

Those who thought it was the end, or heard their case is hopeless from a therapist or coach, can realize through precise logic that the scope of their current problems, although seemingly overwhelming, does not mean the end at all. When knowledge of this reality inspires definite and sustained efforts, it will usually bring success.

On the other hand, a defeatist, go-with-the-flow attitude will bring certain failure. Your individual attitude and efforts alone define your future. Because of this ability of one to tip the scales, we always stress the importance of never giving up.

No matter how great the darkness; never give up.

Because you are in charge of all your thoughts, words and actions, the future will most assuredly improve, as long as you, individually, make the right effort. Those, who defy eroding trends within their marriage by creating positive marriage building habits, inevitably reap the harvest of marital joy.

Get used to the reliability of human physics

If you walk to the edge of a thirty seven foot cliff, you will automatically stop at the edge; you aren't stupid. You accept gravity, and know for sure what will happen if you keep on walking.

No one memorizes "I will stop when I get to the edge of cliffs." Only a fool, or automaton, ignores the laws of cause and effect. Your walks, even when there is a cliff nearby, are safe because of your knowledge of natural physical laws.

It's time to study human physics so you own the knowledge you need to be safely married. When you are on the edge with your spouse, or in any other potentially dangerous situation for that matter, you will stop; just stop. When you study human physics you're in a far better position to recognize and act on potential opportunities. Edges are only a problem if you walk off of them! Knowledge has a way of changing your life.

Just as one of you can bring so much suffering into the marriage, so just one of you can bring in so much relief and eventual joy

Studying a topic which is important to you is not a new idea

People study specialized material sciences all the time, especially when it is part of their vocation for their livelihood. For instance, take the laws of gravity, which play an important role in many fields, as diverse as aeronautics, or construction.

Pilots have to understand gravity in more depth than average people, so they can safely fly higher and faster. Architects, who have completely different agendas, want to build buildings taller and more creatively. In both arenas, the laws of gravity are essential.

It's not just avoiding the bad things

Avoiding deadly repercussions from what might be unlawful ideas is a small part. They also want to squeeze the most benefits out of their efforts; just like you should in your marriage.

Why not go for the best life has to offer, starting at home with your spouse

Of course, everyone needs to keep their efforts within boundaries, as defined by the laws, but also want to get all the good things that are possible. As you become more and more familiar with the governing laws, you hardly even think of the dangers, like going for a walk where there are cliffs. You are able to enjoy the scenery and be inventive, because you know what you know.

Well, you can say your first vocation is your marriage. Nothing is more important to you. So learning the laws which govern the anatomy of marriage is essential. And, by discovering the nuances of the general laws you can do more than first imagined. You will find that most of the laws are obvious, when you look for them closely.

Why stop your education with the "don'ts" of marriage, or in the other venues of life? Why not go for the best life has to offer, starting at home, with your spouse.

Being afraid of the cliffs is not going to get you the marriage of your dreams.

The laws in marriage are obvious when you pay attention

If you are not sure about a law, in any endeavor, you can be sure you will discover its existence the hard way; after some repercussions hit. But go for the good stuff!

In marriage, respectfulness, in inner and outer forms, is basic and critically important. You simply can't have good effects without respectful attitudes, and behavior, nor will you have the experiences you should have, which can be built on the effects of respectfulness. Many happy marriages exist because people discovered how selfless attention inspired loving responses.

But, when you flip the equation from "you will suffer from being curt" to "you will be rewarded for being patient", you can see how, by paying attention to the laws, you can practically turn water into wine. This isn't magic! There are no "secrets"! You only have to get familiar with the laws.

Just because gravity will rudely teach you cannot fly by jumping off a cliff (when you painfully crash on the rocks down below), or you cannot build wings that work out of concrete, none of those crazy experiments mean you cannot fly.

You just have to be mindful of the governing laws, and use them to build a proper flying machine. When you know, and apply the laws, you can fly all over the place. The same is true in marriage.

When you know and apply the laws, you WILL have a phenomenal marriage!

Learn about the laws which govern the construct of marriage

Learning the anatomy of marriage, how a marriage is constructed, and the laws which govern behavior and opportunities, is not merely interesting, it is imperative. By study, you will know what you can do to build your marriage into something extraordinary.

Seeing your marriage as a construct, governed by sure laws, will open new vistas for you. You will be surprised how simple it gets to create a great marriage. You will be very happy. You just need to know how to create it.

Seeing your marriage as a construct governed by sure laws will open new vistas for you

Once again; simply avoiding pain is not what you signed up for when you married. If your lives are lived in an overly defined and cautious fashion, it radically underutilizes marriage, about the same as using a computer as a paperweight! It just doesn't make sense for you to settle for a boring or frustrating marriage, when the only thing missing from yours is a bit of education. Of course, you need to know what you cannot do, but learning what you can do is where all the fun is.

Set your marital goals from the bottom up

You need a vision for your marriage, so you can create a plan to get what you really want. You need to set your life goals. It is not too late. Marriage has special benefits, which are not available in any other venue; but you still need to start with your vision, so you can experience and expand on them.

Needs are the seeds

All visions and all your dreams of achievement grow from particular needs.
Goals typically begin as solutions to problems (how to fulfill a need is what we call a problem, different from a rodent problem, or some other nuisance), and through imagination, they can grow into elaborate and luxurious solutions.

Your need for food, based on pure survival, can easily be satisfied with a simple diet of basic foods. That is what an animal does, and it never misses anything.

But humans are creative and demanding. We take a basic need, like the need for food, and evolve it from nuts and berries into a vision of a beautiful five course meal, served in lavish surroundings and presented on ornate dishes.

But, remember, without the initial primal need, there would not be an expanded vision. Basic solutions are boring for us, not only for meals, but also for marriages.

Marriage satisfies needs

Marriage, as a thing, did not just serendipitously happen. It was created to fulfill some of the core human needs of the vast majority of humankind.

Marriage satisfies the same needs you have, and had, when you decided you wanted to marry someone. Unfortunately, because most people do not isolate their needs (which led them to marry), not enough people imagine the lavish benefits which can grow from them, the visions, or plan a pathway of right behaviors to get them.

The book Jonathan Livingston Seagull is a story about a seagull who wanted more than to just fulfill his needs. He envisioned more, he studied flight, so he could do more than just catch fish, and only do normal seagull stuff. The author wanted to show the human ability. This, desire for more, is what separates humankind from the animal kingdoms. We can, and do, go beyond the mere fulfillment of our needs.

You do not have to settle. You have the circumstances and ability to have it all

We can, and do, envision banquets and palaces, airplanes and luxury cars, instead of remaining content with eating roots, and berries, in a cave. The trouble is, when we become frightened, we run into hiding and hunker down. But now you know how to avoid the trouble, and not let it interfere with the positive trends, when some show up from time to time. You will understand what happened and change instead of react, like a cat in a dog kennel.

Now you can start with needs in your marriage and go further to create the most wonderful environment imaginable. Yes, it will still be called marriage, just as swill is still called food. But you do not have to settle. You can imagine and grow your relationship far beyond one that merely satisfies your basic needs. Isn't that what you want?

But, do you even know why you got married? What was your own motivation to get married? What are the needs you sought to satisfy? What did you do to satisfy those needs, to achieve further benefits?

You might as well have gotten into a car together and drunkenly said, "Yea, baby; let's rock and roll", and then driven nowhere, fast! Neither of you wanted to admit you had no idea where you were going or how to drive your marriage. No wonder you got into trouble and no wonder it seems difficult. It isn't supposed to be either!

Old fashioned marital expectations

Many couples, those who have no ideas of the actual workings or vast potential of marriage, and are scared frozen by the responsibilities and complexities they face, only focus their energy on reducing negative psychological variants which they mistakenly call marital dysfunction.

Connecting marriage to psychology, by looking for psychological flaws as the chief contributor to their suffering, only confuses everything. Making an effort to adjust psychologically and understand their spouse's psychology better is a surefire losing attempt to save their marriage; it doesn't work.

Psychology and marriage are not directly connected

The problem with a narrow psychological approach is, even if you could actually get rid of all your personal psychological flaws, which nobody is able to do; unless you understand marriage as a construct, you will still not know what to do or why.

No matter how psychologically balanced you are, if you are not clued in to what does what (laws of cause and effect), your marital behavior will still mostly be a series of directionless, habitual reactions. You may be able to handle things better, but you will not connect better.

Psychological health is no more connected to successful marriages, than psychological health is connected to building a building. You do not have to become psychologically healthy to build either.

A couple's psychological health is, as far as we have seen, not much of a factor in creating a successful marriage. Sure, if you are clinically depressed or have other deep seated issues, it will possibly (there is no proof) distract you from your marital happiness, and you probably need to get some professional help, mainstream or otherwise. Of course, we agree psychological problems can make your lives more difficult, but your marriage is not supposed to be impacted by diseases of either the body, or mind. Marriage is not designed to be impacted by worldly or material troubles of any kind. It is a venue above the fray.

If psychological soundness were actually a requirement for marital happiness, we doubt if anyone could ever hope for a happy marriage; because, technically, nobody is even close to being truly psychologically balanced. Yes, we have heard many complaints about spouses being bi-polar or narcissistic etc. but could you imagine how few would be eligible for a happy marriage if total sanity or a note from a psychologist was a requirement? We think if you need psychological treatment you should get it, but not as a way to improve your marriage.

We also know of some psychologists who developed some very usefully effective methods for helping married couples. We have seen them and support them. But our approach is all about sharing how marriages work, not drilling down on specifics or some minutia, which some folks may still need professional help with.

Marriage health does not depend on intelligence or psychological health

Isn't everybody a little "crazy" in some way, anyway? Aren't we all dummies compared to an Einstein (who was divorced)? Healthy marriages are simply not dependent on higher intelligence, or sound psychology, but are primarily, if not completely, dependent on adequate marital understanding.

Our mission is to educate, which will help everyone, including psychologists. Many psychologists recommend this information, or similar information, as an adjunct to their therapeutic help. We think you should do whatever it takes.

Besides, pondering why and how you're not perfect is depressing, and it usually wastes precious energy, which would be better spent on thinking of and doing those things which you can do to nurture and grow your marriage.

Psychological problems can make your lives more difficult, but your marriage is not supposed to be impacted by diseases of either the body or mind

Healthy marriages are simply not dependent on higher intelligence or sound psychology, but are primarily, if not completely, dependent on adequate marital understanding

If you really need some personal professional help for deep seated phobias or complexes, you should seek it from one who is known for their abilities in that field, but what you definitely need for a happy marriage is education, pure and simple, and the will to make the right effort.

Knowledge is always needed

Simple information, in understandable form, helps you conceptually understand marriage well enough, so you can achieve marital joy by patiently doing what you can personally see what needs to be done. When you start to understand marriage, you can behave sensibly, because you will know what you did wrong, and what you can do right.

When you understand how your behavior adversely affects your lover, you can begin to change, immediately, and, thus, change the outcomes.

You will no longer stand there, scratching your head, wondering what just happened. You will simply shift into spouse pleasing behavior and not care about what is fair or obvious. You will just care about how you can impact your spouse in a positive way. You can do this!

You can do this

Driving a car is a huge responsibility, too. You are controlling roughly three thousand pounds, moving 70 miles an hour, surrounded by others, inches apart, doing the same thing.

If you looked at it objectively, it would scare the pants off you every time you get in your car! But you know, you know, how to drive. You know how, so you can enjoy driving with all the benefits etc. not wondering about each and every move. You will get that way with your marriage!

The old way of treating couples, as if they are psychologically sick, may still be useful to some. We cannot see it but are open to it. But we share our knowledge, so you can rebuild your marriage in a new light, without so much fear and anxiety.

Begin with…

Again, the logical place to start is with identifying your needs, and desires, because they are what motivated you to get married in the first place.

If marriage did not exist, you would have had to create something very similar on your own in order to fulfill the needs you have. **Needs and desires initiate and launch all our actions** (why don't they teach this principle in school?) **and are seeds in our mental gardens, watered by our imagination, producing our flower visions.**

For example

1) You need to fend off harmful bacteria in order to survive, so

2) Your mind analyzes the need and possible options, including bathing, so

When you understand how your behavior adversely affects your lover, you can begin to change immediately and then change the outcomes

3) Your imagination creates a hot water shower, incorporating other needs for time efficiency, warmth, convenience etc.

4) Then others look for ways to kill the germs which survive bathing, and invent antibiotics

All inventions start with a primal need, and then evolve through imaginative inputs. You could have just used lye soap (or course sand for that matter) and cold stream water, but we are better than that!

Needs compel us to fulfill them

To elaborate further

When you have the need to avoid inclement weather (a cave or side of a tree could work), be safe from predators (could use a club), organize and protect your stuff, have a permanent address, and raise a family etc. (we just skipped from caves and clubs, to present society) you will conclude, through your imagination, that you need a house or apartment; some reasonable form of shelter.

You will use your intelligence to gather more specific details of what you need and like, and try to fulfill more needs "on paper", then you look for, and find, the most suitable domicile, based on all those needs (and your resources); the more details you acquire up front, the better the outcome.

Your needs and desires always determine your next moves (a law in life), unless superseded by a whim or, more often, an instinct driven reaction. If you have a thousand books, as an example, you need to have room for them, so the space you need for them is on your needs list. You can call the room a library, but whatever you call it, needs and desires must be fulfilled.

This same fundamental progression from needs to elaborate fulfillment applies to the needs you had that evolved into getting married. We spell out the instinctive needs and practical desires in more detail later, but the point is you wanted certain things; so even though you probably didn't define them all in the greatest detail, you headed in the direction of satisfying them, which is, in summation, marriage.

But why did you choose the one you married?

You and your spouse had matching lists of desires and needs

You and your spouse individually created your individual "lists" of desires.

Though you were probably unaware of each other's existence, you shared a matching list of needs, which could be met with a particular marriage partner. We are not suggesting you necessarily made a list on paper or gave it enough practical thought. In fact, it is probable your list was not made with enough forethought. But there was a list. That is for sure.

You and your spouse had matching lists of desires and needs

You and your spouse individually created your individual "lists" of desires

If you wanted children and continuing family name, for instance, you needed a suitable biological mate. If you wanted love, friendship, companionship, to avoid loneliness; all these things, plus more, added up to you needing a particular husband or wife.

The details are important. If you are Greek, raised in a traditional Greek family, and you wanted to continue the traditions, your future spouse had to match up; that was on your list. There were some qualities which were very important, and some less important; you probably got what you asked for; most of us do!

Bear in mind that the lists do not usually contain the same traits. A go getter, type-A personality, would probably want one who is more reserved, and vice versa. The lists need to match up, not be identical.

Your actual relationship started as something "outside" of you both in the beginning, but you build it together for you two to share

Then, you met each other. The sought after connection, based on your list, showed itself as a magical moment, when you connected with each other. It doesn't matter whether it was romantic or not, it was your desires manifesting in the form of your spouse-to-be. But it is cool that you are with your choice, and over time you have become even more suitable for each other, despite possible selfishness-driven complaining (we use selfishness in a non-personal way).

The construction begins

At the moment of first mutual contact, your relationship building began; together. More importantly, making yourself appreciate the depth, by recognizing that the two of you began building a brand new, unique entity for only the two of you, will help you recognize how special your relationship is. It is very romantic, practical, and very beautiful.

You live in what you build-cause and effect

Your actual relationship started as something "outside" of you both in the beginning, but you build it together, for you two to share. Your relationship is controlled and enjoyed by (only) the two of you, until it slowly evolves into you, the couple. It is not a partnership, as some think, by common definition. It is an edifice of unity.

Over a period of time, you construct, replenish and reconstruct your marriage a billion times over. It is your home of unity, your Sacred Space. Soon, what you construct is inseparable from you.

If you buy into the current ideas of individual independence within your marriage, you will miss out. Of course, you will still be you as an individual; but in your marriage, you are one with your beloved. That is an unimaginable benefit, once you experience it. You will experience it when you choose it.

Think of your marriage as your home. Eventually, of course, there are natural additions to the initial structure, as you expand your marital entity. Those additions include all your connections; to friends, relatives and pets, and then additions for children. But at first, it is only about the two of you.

Importantly, the innermost part of your marriage, your inner sanctum, is the exclusive heart connection between the two of you, which is accessible by only the two of you. At least that is how it is supposed to happen, and, do not worry if it is not that way, because it is never too late to remodel. At its core, your married life is and always remains about only the two of you. This is a need…this is what you want to plan for and experiment with, building your heart connection.

Making this happen is easier once your behaviors have stopped being (or at least slowed way down) confrontive, defensive and combative. After you relax your protections, you can start to move closer in towards each other. After you stop suspecting and defending, realizing you are in life together for joyful unity, your lives will begin to blend together.

You already have the construction tools

You have to make an effort to overcome the old habits, and you already have the innate tools. You have always used these tools, but not wisely, probably without even knowing you have them. But now you need to use them more consciously, and, when you use them, use them more selflessly.

At its core your married life is and always remains about only the two of you

These tools are sort of like muscles, where you use them all the time without thinking about it. And, like your muscles, when you do use them consciously, you have more control over your life. However, where your muscles are physical tools, these are mental tools. You have other mental tools, of course, but these are the main and most important ones to be aware of and take control over.

Will power and Intention

Your intention tells your will power what to do.

If you think about getting up to go for a glass of water; nothing happens. Then, decide to actually get up and get a glass of water. Once you set your intentions to engage your will, you get up and get going.

How you use your will to set your intentions defines you

Just thinking you are going to do something, without following through, is about as productive as watching a blade of grass grow.

Using your will, by setting your intentions, defines you. It also gets things done. If you think about it, and break it down this way, it makes pretty much anything doable. You just have to

1) Imagine an outcome you would like

2) Define a step-by-step plan of action that will end up with the outcome (anyone can do this)

3) Set your intentions, on one step at a time

4) Do the first step, and then the next, etc.

Your mental tools, when not consciously controlled, or worse, used without thinking, get you into hot water, as they become tools of emotions or whims etc. Why allow your tools to be used by thoughtless reactions, instead of considered thought? When used consciously and constructively, to build your marriage, you get fast positive results.

Not coincidentally, one common denominator among all successful people is they have strong wills, if not always used with the best intentions. You will want to use them to build your happy marriage.

How you shifted your will and intentions to begin your marriage

After you saw the potential, and entertained the idea that the person you were getting to know might be your spouse-to-be, you shifted your energy and will power away from looking for your soul mate, to minor testing of the person you met; to see if they were really who you hoped for.

Usually women put more thought into mate selection

At the same time, you used your will towards laying plans for a new, and expandable, relationship. Then, when you decided they became more likely, you *intentionally*, again, possibly not consciously, moved your will power to another mission. You began directing your will towards investigating, and vetting them. You probably compared notes as part of the vetting, or, as we like to say, compared lists.

You checked out their friends, relatives etc. People want to know as much as they can about the person they will marry.

The feedback we get, as an aside, says that women are much better at doing their research than men. Most men say they went with the flow, and expected to be treated well, just because. Women were more cautious and particular.

But because the vast majority of singles do not have a conscious list, they do not have a conscious process for comparing them. So, they employ their time and energy in largely unscientific, slow and uncertain, evaluations. They watch behaviors, compare them with ideas they have had, and basically put most of their energy into attracting, rather than vetting, the likely candidate for marriage.

Had you done all this with clear intentions, you would have focused your energy, and your will power, with an intensity of purpose. When you focus your energy on one thing in particular, that one thing usually gets accomplished. We go through life fairly evenly, until we really want something; then we go for it. Now it is time to focus on rebuilding!

Will and intention, without wisdom, will not work

There are examples all over the place of individuals, including you, doing things that seemed impossible. It is the focus that brings us closer to fulfilling goals, as long as the effort is correct.

Still, with all the will you muster, and direct, it is impossible to reach a goal, if the actions are incorrect. "Correct" means that the effort is efficient by the governing laws.

The story of the brave knight who went into the cave to "kill" the darkness with his sword, illustrates how people put huge energy into doing something impossible. One little struck match could have saved so much of the knight's energy, and would actually have worked.

Trying to fly with concrete block wings will just never work. You need to know what to do.

Use your will wisely

Now, besides intentionally removing your bad habits, by setting your intentions, you can also put your intention into getting the beneficials from your marriage; which means intentionally doing what works, according to the physics of marriage.

You are in charge. In the case of reclaiming your rights to the marriage you should have, there needs to be a bigger push towards doing what it takes to get the unseen benefits. Remember, the benefits are waiting, even if you cannot see them yet. The first light bulb or flying machines were waiting until the governing laws were discovered. We already know the laws for a blessed marriage.

Your happiness may be over the horizon, but it still awaits you

When I was a teen, I decided to hitch-hike to California from my home in Connecticut. In Connecticut we called anything bigger than a few hundred feet above sea level a mountain, so I had never seen a real mountain.

Long before arriving in Denver, I could see the mountains in front of me, but I had no idea they were just the foot hills. My first ride, from Denver, asked me how far I was going. I said I was going to cross the mountains that afternoon; he didn't say anything. But as we crossed one pass after another, it was pretty clear I had no idea of what all I had gotten myself into or how extensive real mountains are. I kept waiting to pop out of the other side, but no dice. And I certainly was not enjoying the scenery.

It was August, it started to snow, and my ride's car was not going to make it through the growing drifts. Those who have been through a snow storm in the Rockies know how dangerous it is. After three or four hours, it became clear to my ride, he had to turn back.

I got out and stayed in a diner all night, waiting out the storm, finally making it to the other side of the mountains late the next day.

If I had any idea of what was in front of me, I would have done it differently. I would have prepared myself, so I could have enjoyed the beauty instead of setting myself up for a dangerous journey. The bottom line is I could not see what was before me. I should have gotten an education.

Similarly, nobody who gets married has any clue of the potentials for happiness or the dangers in front of them! Of course, you now know about many of the dangers from your own experience and from what you have read. But don't be scared away from trying the logical ideas which can help you avoid them. And, of course, you missed the beauties, because you were distracted and only had a vague idea that there were amazing benefits. At least that was what you thought.

You are in charge of reclaiming your rights to the marriage you should have

People who get married have little clue of the potential for happiness or the dangers in front of them

By sticking to sane marital behavior, without succumbing to the temptations to use worldly solutions, you can begin to explore the unimaginable beauty of deep marital love.

This book is intended to take you above marriage, like when a helicopter takes you above a mountain range, so you will know what is in front of you and what you will need to do to ascend the heights and take in the scenery.

What takes place in a new relationship space

Imagine the two of you in a round room. As you and your spouse kept adding kindness to your new space, the round room, your feelings for each other increased and the relationship progressed.

Do you want to argue in your close quarters by being nitpicky and critical? Or do you want your spouse to be floating in the joy of your adoration, spreading the good vibes all over your now expanded home and life?

During this phase, both of you think "this one is a keeper". As you discover more likable traits in each other and your love grows, picture your space filling with little hearts. The hearts are symbols of love, good feelings etc. Then, when all systems are go, you up the ante to the "OK, let's do this" phase.

While you learn more about each other's needs, you continue your kind and loving inputs, which creates the space/relationship you both want to be in. This is the real beginning. You are building what is meant to be an ever-expanding relationship, your Sacred Space; enjoying what you build together. You begin to appreciate and cherish your relationship and each other.

During this phase, both of you are quick to compliment and quick to ignore communication errors and personality quirks.

It is all rather beautiful, isn't it? The core of your marriage is beautiful, and it always will be. What you put into your space is what your space turns out to be. This is why, even now, you must always think of whether what is momentarily on your mind should be introduced as part of the space.

Do you want to argue in your close quarters by being nitpicky and critical? Or do you want your spouse to be floating in the joy of your adoration, spreading the good vibes all over your now expanded home and life?

The round room is a start

Imagine your marriage as a home in which you live in close proximity. Every action, by either of you, is felt by the other. Smiles spread lightness, sneezes spread germs, and moodiness spreads unhappiness and so forth. Marriage is a non-physical home that encompasses you wherever you may be, physically or in your mind.

Manage your Sacred Space

When each and every thought, feeling, word or deed is preceded by a mental check to make sure your spouse is going to benefit from it, you and your marriage will be filled with joy; guaranteed!

Always ask the question, "Am I doing this for my spouse or for me?" If what you are thinking, or about to say is based on taking care of you, don't rationalize it; change it! No matter how much it hurts (the pain of changing habits is where all the pain comes from), change it!

You both sought to be with each other

When you first met, the building of your marital home started with an unspoken agreement; and affirmative response to the question "Shall we see if we should do this together?"

You started to date, and court. The first period of dating is actually similar to deciding if you will enter into a business relationship (it is not a marriage venue yet, it is a dating venue). Then you did your 'due diligence,' where you test each other's characters, check backgrounds, match values and desires etc.; to be sure your lists really match up.

Once you decided to marry, the intentions and focus of your efforts was supposed to change. Although your opportunity for a change of heart was mostly past, you still had it in the back of your mind that you could be rejected, or you could escape if you had to. But most of your effort was meant to go into destroying your own doubts, criticisms, judgments, and all other ideas which could deter you from your new main mission in life; pleasing your spouse.

What counts now is your future effort

Most couples did not apply too much science (this needs to be taught in high school) to their process of vetting. Just so you are clear, at this point in time, going back in your memory to see how well you did your due diligence really wastes time and creates confusion. The mind is quick to blame and find excuses for failure, so you have to start with where you are now.

Forget past mistakes. By now, the investment of your lives together is so great; both of you have made so many adjustments, you are not the same as you were anyway. Bailing now or switching partners would not make any sense. We have seen how couples succeed when they get back to doing what is good for their marriage, even if they gave up just about all hope.

Your Sacred Space and Sacred Spouse

The step toward marriage, mentioned above, is usually skipped by couples because it is virtually unknown by society; but it is not too late to do it now. This step is when you set aside all doubts and intentionally build your Sacred Space. This is the best!

Simply by calling your marriage a Sacred Space, you give it appropriate significance, as well as validate appropriate boundaries and rules of behaviors. Most importantly, you elevate your spouse above all others and isolate/elevate your new spiritual home. You make your spouse the focal point for your love and good will.

This is the moment in life when you enter into the greatest phase of life, when you choose to love them with unconditional love.

Always ask the question, "Am I doing this for my spouse or for me?"

The mind is too quick to blame and find excuses for failure

This is when you choose to live for them, to do all you can to bring them happiness and contentment. This is when you say to the universe "this is my love and I will never stop, or slow my efforts, to make their life joyous." This is when you vow your loyalty, and you give up any desire for yourself, because that would get in the way of serving them.

This is the first time you have the opportunity to discover true unconditional love

Most of us had no idea of this or believed it to be practical, because we are trained by the world to protect ourselves. But not one person we ever interviewed ever denied they wanted, desperately wanted, exactly this.

When you see your spouse through the eyes of love, you will feel all the love you could ever contain. The love you feel will not be the love coming from your mate. It will flow through you to them, filling you with unending joy and happiness. When you discover this "trick" of life, giving love to get it, you will be among the few who really live.

Your happiness is in your hands

You can choose to build a mansion of tranquility or a prison cell; it is up to you

You can choose to build a mansion of tranquility or a prison cell; it is up to you.

You can share a perpetual honeymoon, or be cell mates instead of soul-mates.

A sacred space means it is valued above all else, but *you have to make it so*. Think about your marriage as your sacred space, your marital sanctuary. Without reservation, think of your spouse as your most sacred treasure, for whom you will do anything to make their lives a joy.

Important note: Marriages are living, so horrors from past mistakes, no matter how devastating they were, will die when cut off and starved. You can build the future with vital and vibrant furnishings of selfless love.

The building blocks of your Sacred Space

Just as a physical house is built from one form or another of wood, concrete and metal, the building material of your sacred space needs to be one form or another of selflessness.

Love, appreciation and gratitude, when properly understood, are all recognized as selfless acts of the heart and mind.

Your efforts are more like seedlings, because they grow

Unlike a material building, which is comprised of material components which age and decay, your relationship is immediately greater than what you just put into it.

Human action is alive, and growing. When you treat your spouse with selflessness, consideration, support and adoration; these improve your lives and expand with a life of their own… But beware, because selfishness, lust, insensitivity and petty demands will erode your marriage with a living darkness.

If all you ever put into your relationship are positive expressions; that is what will be in your relationship space! Like any substance in any container, it is what you put in it that defines it.

If you regularly put sugar in a glass of water, it will be sweeter and sweeter. The flowers you plant in your relationship will bloom and grow, and bloom again, and again.

Protect your Sacred Space, protect your Sacred Spouse

Your marriage starts out as a sealed container, but too many make the disastrous mistake of inviting others into what is supposed to be sealed.

Sharing their private information with others is the biggest mistake made by so many unknowledgeable couples. A sensible rule of loyalty is to keep your space private. Never share anything private about your spouse.

If one is unsure about whether the information is private, it is always better to not say anything. Praise your spouse to others; but without any revealing details; "my Lisa is the most loving person I have ever met, I'm so blessed" or "David is such a good father, I'm so grateful."

Those who share their Sacred Space with others always do so for the wrong reason. They want to complain, compare notes or, sometimes, brag.

From the beginning, or from right now, without explaining to your best friend or confidant, even if your confidant is your therapist (your therapist will understand), do not breathe another word about your spouse. Never speak of their flaws or private attributes. They are your secret treasure. Jealously protect them from any tarnish or views from anyone but you. If you think you have to say something, don't! Remember, no possible good can come from it; only harm.

We know there is no perfect person

Of course, your spouse has flaws, but why would you want to reduce the value of someone in the eyes of others, based on a few flaws? Why would you speak of wonderful secrets about them either? They are your treasure and are not meant to be on display.

If you want to say something very general, it won't hurt. You can say things like "I wouldn't trade him, or her, for anyone" or "my Tommy is the most patient man I ever met" or "I'd never go play golf if Bradley and I could hang, instead."

Thoughts are not you

Any first thought you have or any first urge is not yours yet, so do not get frustrated with them. A first thought or urge is not intentional, so you are not responsible for it.

Until you continue thinking along the lines of a first thought, or until you act on it, it is not yours; it is a passing thought. Until you use your intention to own a thought or feeling, it is not yours; it is passing.

Your marriage starts out as a sealed container, but too many make the disastrous mistake of inviting others in

Your first thought or feeling is neither your will in action, nor a reflection of your feelings or ideas. If there is a thought or feeling that does not belong in your space, due to its inappropriateness, move it out.

If an inappropriate thought or feeling passes in your mind, kick it out. We will discuss this at length later, to combat a generally accepted misconception that your thoughts are you.

Walls and filters do not belong in your Sacred Space

Walls and filters are essential in the world. They protect each of us from the predators, and terrors we confront every day; they are crucial! Yet they are almost completely inappropriate in your sacred space.

Each of us develops unique walls and filters to help get us through life. Usually, they are subconsciously constructed, but they can also be conscious.

It isn't your place to challenge the walls or filters of any other person, because the complexities, of even your own walls and filters, are beyond your scope of understanding.

They must be left at the door of your sacred space. Reminding yourself, at every opportunity, that they serve little positive purpose will help you live in the free air of your Sacred Space. It takes some time, but it is the effort, and effort alone, that will make a difference in your lives.

How your sacred space was first defiled

You probably can't recall the first slip, when one of you said something callous or behaved inconsiderately the very first time, but it happened. It had to have happened; right? There had to be a first time.

And please, don't excuse it with, "We're only human," or "so what, everybody argues." Why would you accept such immature limitations, no matter how common? Mistakes excused by the maker are mistakes multiplied.

This does not mean you should feel guilt or shame, of course. No, never! Mistakes which you catch are excellent reminders that you are growing. They are not scarlet letters.

Never condemn yourself, or your spouse, for making a mistake. One of the greatest errors is to condemn for errors. The other great error is to excuse errors.

The most useful approach is to acknowledge an error when you see it, try to see if it is habitual or if it was just a fluke, and then be mindful in the future so you do not hurt your spouse again.

Mean communication is a mud ball in a sanctuary

Any comment, look or communication that is hurtful is a mud ball. Somebody threw the first one.

Before the first mud ball, your relationship was an untainted temple of love. And though neither of you would ever fashion mud into a mud ball and hurl it, a physical mud ball being thrown by either of you is no more monstrous. Remember, it is only a Sacred Space when you treat it as such.

Of course, you did not want to undermine your relationship or soil your sacred space, but you did not know your space was meant to be so holy.

You were mean; was it because you gave up control over your mind? Was it because you didn't know better, because it is how you treated each other in your family growing up, because nobody corrected you, because your spouse was…? Well, it really doesn't matter! Honestly, it really makes not a whit of difference why!

If you spend your time on analyzing the whys of your bad habits or ignorance, instead of intentionally using your time and effort on learning and doing what is beneficial, the improvement of your marriage will have to wait.

Now is the time to forgive your spouse and forgive yourself. It is time to move forward with practical intentions of building your sacred home. We go over how this happens so you can begin to see how cause and effect plays out in your marriage.

Start thinking in terms of "if I do this, I should expect that", and see if you were right.

The first mud ball

The first mud ball was pretty much unnoticed. It flew from one of you, but because it was so unexpected, the other did not recognize it as an insult; so it went flying out the other side of the space.

When a mud ball goes unnoticed or uncaught, it can't damage anything (if you refuse to acknowledge the insult, you are not insulted, no matter the intention of the insulter). Bad thoughts or attitudes are also mud balls, just more discreet. They have less visible impacts, but they still impact your marriage.

If you throw a mud ball again by mistake, and it goes unmentioned; say you are sorry, maybe only silently, but don't make it a big deal. Instead, shift into focused determination to please.

If you are reeling from some previous insult, take stock. See if there is any truth to the admonition and shift into focused determination to please. Too many people want to get to the bottom of things, so they can get to the other side, but the fastest way to the other side is to focus on what is important; building your love and connection.

How throwing one or two mud balls escalates into cycles of doom

If you do not stop the back and forth, if you allow your habits of insisting on resolution to force you to discuss things, until you have vented out your hurts and pains, you are in a cycle of pain.

If you spend your time on analyzing the whys of your bad habits or ignorance, instead of intentionally using your time and effort on learning and doing what is beneficial, the improvement of your marriage will have to wait

Stopping your reactions and stopping your mind need to be life or death, self-imposed, commandments. But, never suggest this to your spouse! This is what *you* do.

The first one who threw the mud ball, for whatever reason, must have thought it was okay after they did so, because there were no protests, no "don't ever do that again" reactions. The victim (let's be honest, the recipient is a victim) was not even sure if what happened was *real*. The perpetrator, due to a lack of protest, was emboldened. They figured it must be okay to sling another mud ball. After all, it felt good to vent, and there was no obvious cost. So, they were able to repeat the abuse with even less concern of a rebuke.

The trouble is the recipient didn't calmly demand respect for their boundaries with something like "please, never treat me like that again". The recipient, in fact, did the same thing in return, threw a mud ball, perhaps even one upping them.

By the unwritten rules of the world, you both made nasty behavior an 'agreed to' behavior

By the unwritten rules of the world, you both made nasty behavior an 'agreed to' behavior. It is the "what's good for the goose is good for the gander" rule. You both agreed, without realizing the future ramifications, to abuse each other with mud balls for the rest of your lives, which is a very long time.

So, now you can do what over 50% of the Western world does and gets a divorce. Or, you can suck it up like 30-40%, and just live with the tension and misery. Or, you can stop throwing mud balls, which will instantly reduce the number of mud balls by 50%, and eventually as your spouse catches on, by 100%

The unfortunate truth is that you hurt your spouse, and you need to put the brakes on; NOW! That "good" feeling that comes from having the last word, or hearing your friends tell you that you were right, is self-defeating.

It is like taking a drug or getting drunk. It may feel good at the moment, but it slowly destroys you. Don't be OK with those types of feelings. And yes, you can control your feelings! It is your mind.

You can control all of it. It just takes practice, and a bit of knowledge about how your mind works.

Tripping down the steps of the rat hole

What do you do in the rest of the world when someone takes a shot at you; exactly; you put up your walls! In your defensiveness, you angrily move in your offensive artillery, too, just in case you feel like hurling your own insult.

You start finding and categorizing all of the antagonist's flaws. Haven't you seen someone getting really mad, even though they are the ones who began the altercation? They are being defensive; they don't want to take responsibility, so they the turn the tables. You have done that, I have done that, everyone has done that.

Once the first victim realized what just happened, there is a reaction. Sometimes the internal reaction is "they slapped me, so two can play the same game". Then BOOM! You now have one good slap bringing on another.

But this is not a venue in the world. This is not some jerk! This is your spouse, who you want to shower with love and respect…unconditionally!

You must put on the brakes! Don't allow your immediate reactions to control you. Don't attack just because you were attacked, or think you were attacked. Stop the mind from steering you off the cliffs. The mind is not serving you when it is filled with hurt and anger.

You cannot trust your reactive mind at this point. You need to just stop everything, until you gain control and can behave lovingly again.

You became used to the fighting and tensions, but it is not what you want or need. You have to turn your desires 180 degrees to wanting to give love instead of having the last word.

Just stop

Some people become victims and don't overtly retaliate, but all who get nailed manage to retaliate in some fashion.

Who cares whether it is aggressive, passive aggressive or some other form of martyrdom. If you do not attack or attack back in any fashion, the cycle is over. Your marriage is back. So the only thing to do is to not do anything. You will see that if you stop, you will realize how over-reactive you are and how emotional you have allowed yourself to become.

Then, when you are just a little bit more sensible, say, "I'm sorry. I love you. "Please know I'm working on being the best spouse who ever lived. I am truly sorry. I love you"……and mean it!

Keep your space sacred, no matter how much it strains you

You don't want or need mud balls, walls, or filters in your sacred space. You want loving support, sweetness, compassion, and understanding.

However, once the attacks begin, your marriage is just like the rest of the world; no longer a sacred space. Except, with your deep knowledge of each other, you have learned the chinks in each other's walls and make precision hits; with nowhere to run after you strike.

You can see, it is much worse than arguments with a stranger, friend or even a family member. You know everything about your spouse, so your hits are very well placed, and you have to live with the mud all over your mansion of love, all over your walls. So, as soon as you notice what is happening; STOP!

The rule is-   1) Stop   2) Evaluate   3) Behave selflessly

The above describes what happens, but only on the surface! There are more repercussions taking place that are not so obvious. Both of you allow your destructive habits to poison your sacred space. Nobody just happens to one day become violent, harsh, victim,

Don't allow your immediate reactions to control you

Whether it is aggressive, passive aggressive or some other form of martyrdom, if you do not attack or attack back in any fashion, the cycle is over

disrespectful etc. The habits were always there; hiding in dormant form, or simply transferred, until now that you are more comfortable "being yourself".

Your true self, your married self, takes a back seat to worldly inclinations

You are not being your true self when you are less than wonderful to your spouse. You are merely being slaves to your bad habits, which bring about all sorts of bad results.

Although an entire book could be written about all the obvious and hidden repercussions of your bad habits, why bother with such uselessness. Do you actually need to know what repercussions are possible from stepping off a 37 foot cliff? No, when you stop at the edge of a cliff, you do not need to think about a scary bloody fall, cuts and bruises, ruptured organs, broken bones, concussions, missed work etc. to stop yourself from taking the next step. Because you can feel the repercussions physically, they remain a deterrent without having to recall them. Physical stuff is easy to imagine and recall.

But the spiritual connection you have with your spouse is more real, even though unseen, than any worldly, or physical, happiness. You do need to make yourself recall that truth, so you won't be anything but loving, so you will use every opportunity to appreciate your spouse and the sacred space they are in with you.

Every, every, every, communication should be infused with love

It is always best to never treat your spouse in any way that does not intentionally show love, which means it is best to always express love, in some form, at every opportunity.

Perhaps some would say that and follow with a "But" or two, but we do not believe there are any valid exceptions. Unconditional is a big word which we spend our entire married lives trying to live up to. We know people cannot perfect themselves in a heartbeat, or because they can see it is the best way.

But you can turn your intentions towards harmonious unity by making up your mind.

Do not judge how your spouse judges

Filters are our way of seeing things, based on individual understandings of life. If you think about it you will realize not one person sees anything purely objectively, because each person's personal filters puts a spin on whatever they experience.

The easiest way to convey this idea is with an extreme example. A racist will see a person of a different ethnicity from them as flawed no matter how wonderful the person may be. So, where most people will react to a person's character, the racist will react to their ethnicity. The judgment is based on their filter. In structure, a filter is a filter, but in the world a filter can either protect as it is meant, or create drama if it is not rational.

An example of a rational filter would be one that profiles a person who is swaggering around carrying a knife in one hand and an ax in the other. The filter would act as a radar blip for most people, who would become extremely cautious of such a sight.

Each of us has many filters, a few obnoxious, but most of them harmless. Additionally, each person has a unique blend of filters, based on too many reasons, (from upbringing to experiences), to mention. So it should be no surprise when you and your spouse see things differently, sometimes.

It is never a good idea to take your own views so seriously that your spouse's filters would cause you to be critical.

No two people appreciate or are scared of things exactly the same way because of the unique way we filter information. We filter so we can do business in the world without opening ourselves up to continual heartache, so you need to respect, without question, the filters your spouse finds useful.

Never mock your spouse's choices.

Walls are a bigger problem

When you bring your walls and filters into your sacred space, you lose the ability to taste the sweetness you initially created with love. The filters used in the world will naturally fall away over time and be replaced with filters created by *new* actions and reactions. You will see your spouse get mad, because they start to get quiet, for example; so your filter tells you a storm is coming. But it is the erection of walls that causes too many problems.

Walls are hard barriers which protect you from outside attacks, even when the outside attack is not always an attack. It is the reactive part that causes all the trouble. In the vast majority of so-called attacks, it is the perception of an attack which triggers the reaction. In most cases, there is no possibility of harm, just the fear of getting kabashed that sets things in motion. In the world, a similar "attack" would be dangerous, in your Sacred Space, though, not so.

One of the biggies you wanted in your marriage was a trusted and trusting confidant, a best friend; connection. The walls and filters for your day-to-day dealings are harmful to marital relationships. They counter what you are trying to achieve, in terms of trust, and feelings of security.

One cannot condemn those who retain some of the walls and filters; we just encourage a relaxation of your dependence on them, over time.

Try to see around your filters in your sacred space. Try to appreciate your spouse's point of view. Understanding that if the walls and filters your spouse has seem hostile, remember, they are not intended to be aggressive; like yours, they are defensive!

Make it a point to replace your instinctive reaction to their walls and filters, with compassion, so they only fear hurting the one they love. Give your spouse good reason to discard theirs, while you become less reactive to theirs. Make up your mind that no matter how aggressively they act towards you, you will never reciprocate, no matter how much your instincts drive you.

This may seem like a tall order, but in truth it is just what you need to practice.

It is never a good idea to take your own views so seriously that your spouse's filters would cause you to be critical

Make it a point to replace your instinctive reaction to their walls and filters with compassion

You do not have to forgive, but you have to accept

It is always correct to excuse your spouse. Be understanding and patient, but forgiveness is not as important as acceptance.

Sometimes, if you are very hurt, you simply cannot forgive right away, as forgiveness is an ability you have to develop, it has nothing to do with what was done "to you". But, you can always look at what they did and recognize they are victims of their own weakness.

Your spouse isn't perfect. Neither are you, but you can control how you see them, just not how they see you.

When you are hurt by their actions

When you are hurt or offended, take a moment to become aware of your walls going up reactively and analyze them

When you are hurt or offended, take a moment to become aware of your walls going up reactively and analyze them. Were all of them really necessary? Did those reactive walls bring the two of you closer? Did your reactive wall(s) defuse the tension? Did you inspire, or encourage? Are you thinking "they started it, why should I look at my reactions?" If you refuse to look at your reactions to them when you think they crossed (sometimes you make a mistake) your line you will never find peace in the world, much less your marriage.

Reactive walls (the only kind there are) block everything

Walls block love, and your ability to process, along with that which is feared. Walls are a serious problem, but especially when you do not know they are going up, which is most of the time. Awareness of a wall allows you to determine its usefulness, giving you much more power over your life.

Pay attention to your walls

Make it a further point to catch the permanent walls that went up when you weren't looking, and start to remove them. Most of them are psychological antiques, blocking your connection. They went up for some bizarre reason you probably cannot connect to something dangerous.

Love never went away. It just got hidden behind your walls.

Forgiveness is not a prerequisite for wall removal

There is too much to-do about forgiveness with too little explanation of what forgiveness is.

For couples, it is better to not see your spouse as needing your forgiveness. But give it anyway as best you can and always be quick to accept their actions in the light of them learning life through trial and error. If you do poorly on a math test do you need to be forgiven? A marriage filled with expectations will never have a satisfied spouse; not one.

When you see you have become angry or irritated, question if you really should be angry. In many cases, you will find your spouse doesn't need forgiveness at all, but rather you need to recognize your irritation is unwarranted.

But how do you clean up the mess?

You and your spouse's mud balls flew into each other's walls, and that is what your Sacred Space looks like now, a bloody mess. What do you do now? Your sacred space is filled to the bursting point with muddy walls, as their mud balls hit yours, and your mud balls hit theirs.

You can barely feel each other's love, not even sure if there is any. You don't trust each other, or yourselves. How do you reconcile all your differences and accept each other again?

All this stuff sounds good, yes; you are learning; but what if it doesn't work? How do you get a toe hold, so you can get past your mistrust and anger?

Fear not! The work is just begun, but the seeds of love and good will have been waiting to grow.

The sun is still there, even on the darkest days

Love is super powerful and enduring, but mud has buried it. The love is still there, you can feel it if you look past all the aforementioned, but it seems dwarfed by the hurt. Well, you cannot dwarf love, it is too vast.

Think of your love as a giant sun, eclipsed by a small smudge on the window of your mind. So, the idea is to wipe away the smudges of wrong thoughts and enjoy your great love. We know how you feel. It is so overwhelming! The analogy is too simple; right? Kumbaya time; right? Nevertheless, what you can now do works for everyone, without exception.

Take control over your life!

Tear down the partitions of your mistrust. Reject your fears. Reason that if you were to begin a new relationship, all you will do is slowly discover a new vault of flaws, some worse than the ones you are living with now.

Recognize that it is not so much the flaws of your spouse, which is impacting you, but your reactions to them. **Until you recognize that until you are able to control your mind, by accepting the flaws of others, you will never find happiness.** So you might as well work on this right now.

There is no other way, so build your marriage in ways you meant to, before you got distracted. You didn't have a set of plans. Now you do. Use the building materials described; selfless love, kindness, adoration etc. Establish your foundation again; or for the first time, with respectful behavior and selfless thoughts.

Discipline the misery producing thoughts, and attitudes, that are there now, with right intentions, until they are gone forever. Marriage isn't like making a pot of soup. You can't ruin it forever by over spicing it or putting in the wrong ingredients. Your marriage is alive. Your marriage truly is, and it all begins right now, and right now happens every moment of your life. The past will fade into rarely used memories.

You and your spouse's mud balls flew into each other's walls, so your Sacred Space now looks like a bloody mess

Love is super powerful and enduring, but the mud has buried it

Now is the time to begin building your marriage, with enthusiasm, into what you know you will have when you build it correctly.

Make all new construction better than the last

Your energy needs to go into building bridges of loving communication.

Each one of your communications needs to be as described in the lesson on marital communication or better. Don't be afraid of being the first one, even if you have to tell yourself your efforts will never be reciprocated. It does not matter if the bridge between your hearts is built by one of you, or both of you.

Learn to be an unconditional lover

Reaching out is not a business deal, where you say, "Ok, I made the effort, now it is your turn." If you do that, you will fail. You need to strive to be completely selfless, and fearless.

The "deal" mentality does not work; period! It's natural to believe your trust has been betrayed. Many people believe that is a big reason for divorce. "How can I ever trust my spouse again?" But you must remember you have also betrayed the trust of your spouse.

You have too much to lose, so don't consider giving up

Giving up on any level will crush your family.

It makes no difference, which was the bigger jerk. There is no way to measure jerkiness, or figure out who went first. Both of you behaved inappropriately. At the same time, both of you share something in your relationship that is hard to turn your back on. You share the incentive to start fresh with each other, observing the rules that will bring success.

If you have children, you have a billion times the incentive of those who do not, but even those who do not have children need not fail.

The speed of your turn-around is up to you

Most of the current despair, pain, and confusion you are burdened with can be nearly completely gone in less than two weeks, from the time you make up your mind that this is worthy of your efforts, and you decisively shift your intention and redirect your energy.

Decisively is the operative word.

By reminding yourself (never each other), that you are responsible for the mess, and only because you didn't know any better (guilt is not cool), you can start to allow your spouse to be who they are, and move forward. The greater the effort to be sweet, the faster the mind shifts.

Your energy needs to go into building bridges of loving communication

Do not rehash or dwell on the past-it is over…it is over…IT IS OVER

We have seen couples quickly leave gnarly pasts behind them; some instantly! You have to be a masochist to want to go back and relive the pain of past mistakes. That would be like putting the flat tire back on your car. So here is what you can do:

Let the bad stuff go. Absolutely refuse to let the mind reinstall all the fear and pain; just refuse to allow negative thoughts to come in or take root.

Though this is the hardest part, it will begin to work, because you will remember to intelligently use techniques you will learn. Now that you see things are more mechanical than happenstance, you will not rest until you conquer your mind.

You have everything to gain when you make the effort. The foundation of love is still strong. The mud, covering the golden love, must be removed and not reintroduced.

If mud manages to come in again, just dump it again, and refocus on putting in the "ingredients" you want by being complimentary, sweet, gracious, supportive, friendly, and smiling; sincerely and selflessly.

Do your part without expectation. Resist the slightest thought of hoping your spouse does his or her part.

Do your part without expectation

This is a science

The way to transcend the feelings of hurt and betrayal is by first deciding you will. Lessons on controlling the mind with explanations for why the mind clings to harmful feelings will come a bit later. You will learn how you can break negative attachments. You will learn how you can get beyond pesky thoughts and feelings, quickly, by choosing to control your mind.

Don't allow yourself to be a victim-it is up to you

Your happiness is in your own hands

Refuse the temptation to become intoxicated with being a victim, imagining nobody understands your particulars, or you just can't do what you need to for a happy marriage. Of course you can do this! Accepting victim status, so popular among the uninformed, sets you up for repeats of failed relationships (2nd marriages have a higher failure rate than 1st marriages).

The only individuals who give up think controlling the mind is impossible and freak out. Most others grasp the simplicity, and inevitability, of success. At some point, your efforts must begin, or suffering stays.

Your happiness is in your own hands.

An example of a process winning over impossible odds

My, then five year old, son was told to clean up his room. The room looked like it was hit by a hurricane, and he knew what he was ordered to do was impossible. In his mind, my command meant certain death.

He knew what he was told to do could not be done. When I said, "Joey, you need to clean your room," he looked at his room, and promptly burst into tears. I still get a bit teary-eyed just recalling it. Isn't love so cool? It transcends space, and time, instantly, and with so much impact.

I let him cry for a few seconds, and then he grabbed my leg (and my heart), in supplication, for a reprieve. I took his hand, and we stood on his bed. "Joey, I want you to tell me, what is the biggest thing you see on the floor?" which, by the way, wasn't visible under the clutter.

Between sobs, he pointed to his blanky. "Go ahead, fold it up, and put it in the closet." I said this forcefully, to stave off the mental protests (we must be forceful with the mind). After he did this one task, I had him come back onto the bed, and look once more. I repeated, "What is the biggest thing on the floor?" I can't remember what the next object was, or the next, but soon the room was well on its way to being clean.

By breaking the job into manageable parts, and going after, and conquering, the worst first, he soon had his room clean, and life was back to normal.

A clear view of a problem exposes the solution

When you see the problem, so you see the solution, then you see the steps you need to take; it becomes nothing more horrendous than a matter of doing tasks, one after the other, until the mission is accomplished.

This is the same scientific methodology used to accomplish anything, efficiently. Never be deterred by discouragement. Failure is near impossible, if you use what you learn, and, refuse to give up.

You are in charge of your life

It is up to you to stop your own unsavory behavior. It is up to you to invent a marriage you will cherish.

The task of controlling the mind every time it resorts to the unhealthy habits of making a snide comment, giving a dirty look, or dropping into self-pity, is the most worthy effort you will ever make.

Replacing those crazy behaviors with marriage-building selfless, serviceful actions is the trick for matrimonial longevity. It will change your life in all areas. In the meantime, though, seeing as we are human beings and not exactly perfect, even though we may know better, there are techniques we can use that will help us over the humps.

There will be momentary slips no matter how hard you try-they won't matter

Over the course of time, momentary issues inevitably pop up, but they will be as nothing compared to your overall state of happiness when you are focused on relationship building.

It is up to you to stop your own unsavory behavior.
It is up to you to invent a marriage you will cherish

The little pebbles won't seem like the end of the world anymore, because you will see them correctly, as external aberrations instead of as a part of your marriage. No matter what you may have to go through due to some past mistakes, when you focus on building your marriage, those inevitable repercussions will be like a few fruit flies that got into your vast mansion of marital harmony.

Slipping is not a big deal when you are working towards bliss

As unthinkable as it is to pour water into your car's gas tank, because you know it will ruin it, neither will you intentionally pour anything into your marriage just because "it feels ok".

You will know, by your own knowledge, what is and is not beneficial. Sure, you may slip at times or make a mistake as you learn through trial and error. But at the same time, by knowing ways to proactively improve your marital connection, you will intentionally include thoughts, words and actions that work towards marital bliss.

You can't be building up and tearing down at the same time

The fact is, when you put your energy into creating an ideal relationship with your husband or wife, you will screw up much less as you keep pouring joy into your lives.

Who does things on purpose that they know hurt them?! In marriage, when you err, because mistakes are made all the time, you can back up and try something else, knowing you will ultimately be successful. It becomes less complicated and easier as you experiment.

Just like any topic you study, you keep learning from the results of your mistakes, and applied ingenuity.

Think about anything you have ever begun from scratch, and practiced, till you got good at it. The first strums on a guitar, or the first attempts at writing your name; all began with repeated attempts, and plenty of mistakes.

Relax about the mistakes, yours and your spouse's. Everything improves in the future, if you make the effort now. Look how much you have already learned!

Look how much more aware you are, and how much more you will control your behavior!

Your marriage is improving already, just by your shift in intentions.

We are mortal . . . when we express love; then we are Divine

There is a Hungarian saying, "Everyone wants you to have bread, but nobody wants you to have butter." The saying rises out of observations of how people are in the world. And we all know there is, sadly, too much truth to it. In order to avoid either jealousy, or criticism and the like from curious friends and family, keep your Sacred Space and everything within it a secret.

You will know, by your own knowledge, what is and is not beneficial

Just like any topic you study, you keep learning from the results of your mistakes and applied ingenuity

We are mortal . . . until we express love; then we are Divine

Visualize your marriage as an edifice

Marriage has no materially tangible form. So using analogies, metaphors and examples helps form a picture of marriage in your mind. A marriage is a thing, yes, but you cannot see it with your eyes or touch it with your fingers, but that doesn't matter. You can experience marriage as the most tangible thing in your life!

The foundation of your Sacred Space is a mixture of love, respect, understanding, and wanting your spouse to flourish. The most important ingredient is selflessness. Your sacred mansion of love will grow without boundaries by merely following the dual prescription of

1) Keep out the destructive thoughts, attitudes, speech and behaviors, and

2) Put in the binding and connecting ingredients of respect and selflessness

The grand cathedral of your marriage comes in the form of intimacy; which you will learn about in the last chapter. You are cautioned to not skip ahead. If you do, there is too much that will not make enough sense about intimacy for the attainment of true intimacy to be practical.

You need to get more of an understanding of foundational principles first.

- Your spouse is of such high value that nothing compares; never abuse

- Make your behavior nothing short of reverent

- Be so humble with your spouse that you could never feel abused

- Selflessness and gratitude will improve your life

Keeping your relationship sacred in a world that wants to destroy love is an effort worthy of your efforts

You have learned the sacred space concept, which separates your marriage from the rest of the world; as it should be. You have learned about walls and filters, the concept of controlling the mind, and better ways to communicate within your marriage. You now have enough tools and concepts to apply to your marriage to have some great leaps forward.

Many people think they have enough education at this point where you have now arrived to stop poisoning their marriage and are ready to apply their new found knowledge to being a good spouse and to show their love and loyalty; as they should have from the beginning. Then they went on, learning more, and succeeded with faith born of knowledge.

The idea of giving up on their relationship was no longer a consideration. They learned any problem could be solved, as long as they knew why it was a problem. They also got that giving up is the worst possible choice. You, too, will succeed.

Begin applying what you have learned with intensity of purpose. Never give up!

- Chapter Seven -
The Hidden Survival Drive

◇◇

*Becoming aware of what drives your behaviors and why, changes you from
an automaton to a free willed human being. You will never see life the way you do now,
because you will realize the difference between being a victim or
a master is completely in your hands.*

◇◇

The key to understanding psychology is understanding how the survival drive controls the mind. The key to understanding the superior psychology of humans is by recognizing that anything not prompting selflessness is initiated by the drive to survive

Chapter Seven

The Hidden Survival Drive

You will soon understand the underlying reasons people are the way they are, and why they behave the way they do.

In this chapter, we reveal more than just the biologically produced differences between men and women, but the very origins and primal causes, called innate drives (science has not labeled them as such, yet, so we have), for virtually all behaviors.

You will soon see how gender differences and superficial psychological influences tell only a small part of your behavioral story.

Drives are the 'Rosetta Stone' of all behaviors

It is fascinating how these primal drives adapt themselves, according to gender and environment, so they stealthily, and steadily, retain control. When you finally see that everyone is imprisoned by the exact same core innate drives, tailored by various conditions including gender, you will be able to follow the chain of influences from drives, to actions, to reactions, which make you and your spouse do what you do.

You will see why you and your spouse sometimes act emotionally. You will see how you can stop misguided behaviors, and even backtrack, because you have the right to reclaim control. You will see that all your relationship troubles can be traced back to two drives, even though you didn't even know they are there.

Literally, all the mysteries of human behaviors will be revealed as we illustrate examples that demonstrate the incredible power and ever-present influence of the drives. You will learn to view all behavior as influenced by the drives.

You can follow every behavior of every person back to two simple imperatives. With your new insights, you will be able to change your perspectives and judgments. You will understand, and appreciate, your past experiences within your marriage. Then, you can better navigate your future, and your life.

You can make your marriage as wonderful as possible, by avoiding the drive created pitfalls. This knowledge, all by itself, will give you greater power over your life than you ever dreamed possible.

Innate drives are the catalysts of, and underlie, all desires and instincts

Every person needs to know about the forces that drive them and the nature of those forces. In the future, this science will be explicitly taught in every school.
But for now, learning about the innate drives will give you an upper hand over your impulses. You will understand what "temptation" is and where it comes from, not in

Gender differences and superficial psychological influences tell only a small part of your behavioral story

Nearly every behavior of every person can be traced back to two simple psychophysiological imperatives

contradiction to religious doctrine, as those doctrines are born of truth and provide great value to many people, but as a cognizable scientific outcome of cause and effect.

You will see that what people refer to as "evil" is usually, in fact, the result of the compulsive drives, which go unchecked by human wisdom (not to say real evil does not exist).

If you are a religious person, you will see how deeply the other side has corrupted life, even down to the individual cells. If you are a non-religious person, you will marvel at the simplicity of the unimpeachable science. Either way, you will know what you and your spouse (and everyone else) are up against.

Like turning the lights on to see what you kept stepping on

Identifying gender differences may be entertaining, but it is harmful when used as an excuse

By incorporating this information into your day to day thinking, you will have numerous new insights, which will come in greater and greater revelations. They will not only help you with your attitudes towards others, but will evoke an evolving compassion for yourself and others who err, especially for your spouse, so you can stop feeling anger toward them.

You will see how drives compel you to trust your ideas over your spouse's, even when theirs make more sense. You will see why you overreact to their demands for their ideas to be honored, even if they are not as good as yours, even when the differences are ultimately negligible. You will see your defensiveness, and over-reactive reactions, for what they really are, in the context of the drives; efforts to save your life.

You will begin to understand anger, fear, jealousy greed, lust; and all malicious behaviors which spring from them, in a new light of understanding.

You will see how forgiveness of yourself and your spouse (and others) can be based on educated reason as well as personal good will. When you objectively understand what drives people, to do what they do, to see how they are victimized by their behaviors, it will help you see offenses impersonally, even when it feels very personal.

You will see evildoers as wretched prisoners of their own evildoings (we would never suggest you overreact to your newfound knowledge and become a martyr to another's selfish intentions; but you will understand why they are cruel, instead of blaming yourself for their misguided actions).

Identifying gender differences may be entertaining, but it is harmful as an excuse

We are not saying to ignore gender differences (as if it were possible). But knowing about them, without knowing what actually cause them, will not provide you help or protection in your relationship. That leads to excuses.

Blaming gender differences, for what you misunderstand makes matters worse, by legitimizing all kinds of troublesome rationalizations, with excuses and judgments. You can see that.

It's easy to ignore an actual communication weakness or impatience if you write it off to "oh, you know how men/women are". Blaming a gender trait because you didn't understand your spouse or because you disagree with how they see something, minimizes what is important to them, and makes you apathetic to their needs, non-supportive, and you may even tune them out. Care and support are vital expressions of love, so you want ways to enhance them, not reduce them, nor accidentally insult your true love.

Focusing on gender differences, without awareness of the causes of those differences, won't help you increase intimate connection with your spouse, your primary goal. Writing off a communication, or a point of view, to a gender idiosyncrasy, is insulting.

Nobody wants to be categorized and written off

Do you want to feel like your opinion is minimized because you are being categorized as a man, or woman?

How can you create connection with your spouse if they just fit into some derogatory stereotype? If what they feel, or think, is devalued by an assumed perspective, instead of appreciated, you cannot connect. You may not be able to fully understand your spouse all the time, nobody does, but you still have to do all you can to appreciate their individual well thought-out point of view.

Listing gender differences and all the variable comedic or tragic scenarios, without understanding their origins, minimizes the other half of the population.

No matter which gender, your inability to understand them is a problem for you, not a reflection on them, so try to remember that.

It is easy to put down what we don't understand.

Don't allow your mind to reduce the most important person in your life, to a cliché!

Enhance your connection

When you recognize the source, and true motivation of what is driving your spouse's actions, you can put yourself in their place.

Putting yourself in the place of your spouse, feeling their frustration or helplessness, will allow you to be there for them instead of being critical of them. It is not too much to ask of you, who committed unconditional love.

It just makes sense that you have to know how the drives, coupled with environmental and biological conditions, instigate what you see, and how you respond.

Understanding life through your spouse's eyes enables you to make their life more joyful, by pleasing them in ways you know is meaningful.

Focusing on gender differences without awareness of the causes of those differences won't help you increase intimate connection with your spouse

Understanding life through the eyes of your spouse enables you to make their life more joyful

People expend more effort pleasing their pets than they do their spouse, and take more time trying to understand their pet.

Learn about your spouse's tickle points, not just their trigger points. But don't think yea, they never put themselves in my place. Keep your efforts focused on changing yourself instead of finding their faults.

Understanding something takes more than illustrative comparisons

You cannot understand genders by knowing the differences. Nor could you avoid inserting a bias if you start comparing, and obviously, leaning towards your gender.

Saying men are often abrupt and women are more nurturing, though maybe true, does not give you enough insight into either, because without knowing the cause of the differences with the relevant context, the information is immaterial.

It also leads to comparing you to your spouse, which makes no sense. Of course you are different. You want to be different, and enjoy the differences.

Never write off genders, as is so popular

Dwelling on gender traits distracts you from the actual person in front of you, the person you married because of their unique individual qualities

Dwelling on gender traits distracts you from the actual person in front of you, the person you married because of their unique individual qualities.

Stay focused on your spouse as a unique individual, even though they have gender qualities. See their traits as unique, in the context of who they are, at least until you can note differences with gratitude instead of frustration.

Those of you who have read "the Little Prince" would recall how his flower was unique in all the universe.

Happy couples are glad for the ability to blend and contribute to each other. They complement one another, and praise each other for the traits they admire and see in each other.

Too many people look at gender differences as obstacles to harmony, and happiness, because when they get into trouble, they fall back on stereotypes to excuse themselves, rather than seek more understanding. At those times they forget how exciting those gender differences are, in the right context.

When the fear of the unknown is penetrated, you will be able to leverage those differences to your advantages, to create a much deeper connection through mutual support.

Gender differences make more sense when seen as channels for and of innate drives

You don't blame man-eating Tigers for being cruel, because you understand they are built to be killing machines. You see the true cause of their ferocity. It's how they survive, so you don't hate them.

Of course, you wouldn't like it if they kill one of your own, but you understand they are driven by instinct, so you understand hatred toward the animal is useless.

Knowing why, about anything, gives you the opportunity to observe it with dispassionate understanding, and thus compassion, when needed, or, at the very least, with a non-judgmental or non-emotional perspective.

When your observations are dispassionate, they are much more useful, in that you can decide what to do without being controlled by those passions and emotions.

This is exactly what you need to do when your spouse offends you. First, stop your thoughts from drowning you in sorrow and confusion. You need to see how you are tweaked, tweaked because of your habitual perceptions and judgments, not because of the offense. No matter how hurtful the offenses are, refuse to take it personally, even when insults are meant to be personal.

Look past your emotional reactions, and theirs, so you can see their untamed drives are what are causing them to be so awful. You need to also see how your drives cause you to perceive their behavior as threatening.

Is controlling your mind unnatural? NO!

Some think shifting the mind is controlled, and therefore unnatural. No, it works to make your marriage work, same as unnatural airplanes allow you to fly. So don't think of it as unnatural.

Of course it is natural, in fact, to control your mind and emotions; or you would not have the ability to do so. Just because it isn't usual does not make it unnatural.

When you feel forces pushing both of you in antagonistic directions, it's time to react by pushing yourself into loving and supportive thoughts and behaviors. You need to create the right kind of reactions within your mind.

Most people generally want retribution when someone does something horrible to them, or their family. But, if they discover the perpetrator is mentally deranged, they calm down, and are glad to just get them off the streets, so others are not harmed.

The cause of a person's offensive behavior is important to normal people, because they want to decide what is right, even when their own desire for revenge, or other fairness based desires, must be put aside.

Recognizing your behaviors are driven by unseen forces gives you the ability to get beyond the offenses. It is not always easy, but it is always profitable to recall you are being driven to survive and your mind is confused by past misconceptions which formulated your reactions.

Look past your emotional reactions, and theirs, so you can see their untamed drives are what are causing them to be so awful

It keeps things in perspective to recall you are being driven to survive

You will know about emotions, and remove their power over you

Everyone has had the experience of screwing up when they acted without due consideration, and everyone has seen a person close to them seriously blunder because they couldn't shake emotions, temptations or compulsions that were driving them.

You will see how **temptations and emotions are not innate**, as many believe, but the result of drive driven instincts.

Emotions and instincts can be removed, or replaced. Most people think they cannot be changed, that those are who you are, but it is not true. If it were, you could never improve yourself.

You are not your emotions, not by any stretch. You have never been taught the nature of emotions, instincts and compulsions, or about the drives which precede them, so you have been their slave.

Temptations and emotions are not innate as many believe, but result from drive-driven instincts

You will learn to identify the power that feeds these personality drivers, so you can be rational, no matter what the situation.

The drives are a force, like electricity, which can be channeled. And, although the drives have a specific purpose, they still allow us choices about how to fulfill those purposes.

Instead of going along for the ride, you should intelligently and consciously choose the means of your survival, and decide for yourselves when your life is actually at risk, rather than leave the controls over your actions on automatic.

What drives a person to behave badly makes a difference

The drives, which are hidden commanders, tell you your life depends on do-or-die actions of self-protection.

When you see that the directives which compel your behaviors, originate from innate drives, that escalate everything you face into "life and death" choices, you can dissect to sift the fear (fear is survival based) out of the compulsions. Then and only then, you can act with wisdom.

You submit to the blind drives because you always have, and don't see how to take control over your life. Nobody ever showed you the way you react, so you are an unknowing slave. But, no more! You can change everything!

None of us like to think of ourselves as pushovers, much less as slaves. Yet, you automatically submit to the drives, and their consequent instincts, all the time. You allow yourself to be at the mercy of an unseen force, and forces.

You are not a slave to your "true" self (the self is pure, untainted), as some say, nor are you victim of your passions, which are merely intermediaries.

The drive to survive is at the top, or at the bottom of your biological self, it is what you are a slave of.

It is immediately valuable to recognize the cause of a trait

What makes tigers fearsome predators, and some people merciless competitors, and others world class manipulators is the same; the ubiquitous innate drive for survival.

That same drive is at the root of all behaviors and is found, in fact, in every single living cell, every living thing, and everyone. There is no exception.

We are slaves, but we don't know it

"I freed a thousand slaves. I could have freed a thousand more if only they knew they were slaves." This poignant quote by Hariet Tubman, a courageous freer of slaves in the 1800's, defines exactly how we should see ourselves; as oblivious slaves to unseen masters.

How could it be otherwise? It's time for you to free yourself!

You are a slave to the drives to survive and procreate, but do not see the invisible shackles unless you specifically look for them. Then, once you see them, you cannot ignore them anymore! See the shackles, though once invisible; and you can undo them.

Drive to survive

The strongest innate drive is the drive for survival, which will single-mindedly force you to do anything and everything, for individual existence; first for you as an individual organism, and secondly for your family (species) of which you are part, but barely for others.

Survival drive is above the procreative drive, because procreation protects individual survival by recreating, and, when possible, expanding protective community.

But, it is always, always, about individual survival

It is ALWAYS all about individual survival! Everyone knows this already, but although the drive is omnipresent, hardly anyone considers why or in how many ways it impacts us, so it remains hidden.

As soon as you start to look behind the curtain you will find the drive hiding in everything! Not almost everything, but actually in everything.

Start by looking in your marital interactions

Think about any difficult interaction between you and your spouse. You will always find an element of fear that drove it.

There is always something your mind, or theirs, found threatening, which caused defensiveness and retaliation. You do not typically think of offenses as threatening, but if you think about it you can see how it is true.

You are a slave to the drives to survive and procreate, but do not see the invisible shackles

The drive for survival will single-mindedly force you to do anything and everything for individual existence

Perhaps you were treated disrespectfully. That threatens your security or your status. Bear in mind, a threat does not have to be a direct threat to your life, and in fact that is the point. It is the drive driven mind which misinterprets little things as threats, which cause you to overreact.

Why would you overreact to a mere insult? You wouldn't if the mind didn't tell you it was important. You would hear insults only as your spouse's problem, if it was not somehow also perceived as a threat.

Why you react so strongly to such little threats is understandable, when you understand more about how the drive creates instincts.

Or, maybe your spouse didn't say or do anything at that moment, but you are generally afraid your marriage is in trouble.

Fear of death is the underlying unseen catalyst

Every little thing would then be like a sharp needle in a raw wound. Your buried fear will be enflamed, and you will react, not with thought out intentional words meant to heal (as you should react), but with clawing survival actions, like a drowning swimmer who grabs at their rescuer.

Fear of death is the unseen catalyst

Reactions are amped up because when you trace fear, in any form, back to its origin, you will find at its root a subconscious fear of annihilation (death).

Of course, you cannot be annihilated by an insult, but the psychophysiological auto responses, or habitual instincts, do not know that! Fear is not rational, it is a force. So when the mind hears a threat, it reacts as if your life is at stake. Once instinct takes over, once you allow it to dictate your next moves, it protects you (your body, actually), but it does so ruthlessly and indiscriminately.

Fear, instincts and emotions do not reason. They only react. Your mind does not suggest a possibility of danger when it is triggered by something scary, with the intention that you assess and work out appropriate solutions.

It just reacts, based on unthinking instincts, which push you; as if your life depends on it. This is why things get out of hand so quickly. Both of you, without realizing it, are unknowingly fighting for your lives.

Check your state of mind to gauge your status

If you are calm, cool and collected, you will not be reactive. Your state of mind will tell you when you have turned your life over to a dumb instinct, or some emotion. It is very simple;

If you are not calm, you are not in charge
.
If you are internally calm, you are in charge of your mind.

Never forget this!

Being reactive means being over-reactive

The rule of thumb; any automatic reaction is going to be padded with protection, just in case.

An automatic reaction is useless if it doesn't cover any size emergency, so it reacts without any evaluation. Therefore, every reaction will be an over-reaction, allowing you, the thinking mind, to jump in and take control of the situation, after the initial jolt.

But because of habitual complacency, you keep on running with your reactions, without evaluating, and then you add more drama, by reacting to your spouse's reaction to your first reaction.

You were had by the instincts which scared you.

The drive to survive, fine for the jungles, invaded your Sacred Space, and you unthinkingly allowed it in.

Rule for married life

Never blame your spouse for how you feel, or for making you act in a certain way.

It is always, not most of the time, but, *always* up to you, to control your state of mind, and behave accordingly.

You can stop the madness anywhere along the way, no matter how deep in the muck of conflict you are in. If you allow the thought "it isn't my fault" to slip in, to any degree, the reactions and counter reactions will bounce back and forth, until one of you is exhausted.

All the way to the very core level of your biology, survival is all anything is ever about

Single-cell organisms strive to survive. In fact, it is pretty much all they do. They come into existence adhered to a protective community, which protects them; no thinking of any kind motivates them, it is purely driven to eat (loosely speaking). The other thing a single-cell organism does to survive is make more single-cell organisms…*kind of sums up most people's lives, doesn't it?*

The drive in every individual single cell is exactly the same, and is always there, in every plant, ameba, fish, bird, elephant etc, as it is within you, and every other living organism.

Differences are in numbers and arrangements

The biological difference in species, and how the drive manifests, is determined by the number of cells, and their arrangement, nothing more. Your body has trillions of cells, all working together to survive.

This reality means the drives dictate your actions, almost exclusively, almost without any input from you. Until you decide to take charge, and stay in charge, the drives-created instincts run your whole life.

Because they are unthinking, every reaction will be an over-reaction

Until you decide to take charge, the drives dictate your actions without any input from you

The errant, emotional, or drive-driven thoughts which drive your behavior against your morality are what you need be concerned about

Trace your outer behaviors to confirm you are driven

How much of your life is devoted to personal survival?

How serious is earning a living, staying healthy and making sure you fit in? All those have to do with survival, and are good results of the drive. But the drive shows up in small, not so good ways, too.

How often do you put your own needs ahead of others, even when you know it isn't the fairest thing to do? Be honest about your evaluations.

This is not a challenge of your character. There is no question about whether you are more or less driven than the next person. You are not bad, you are a victim. This is a fact of life, which you can ignore at a high cost. The price is nothing less than your marital happiness.

Trace the drive when you are in a calm state of mind. *If you wait for exploding emotions before you trace your patterns, you will have a hard time seeing it, as your mind will be clouded with the emotions* (emotions distract you from the ability to process information).

But, as you become better at uncovering the drives, you should begin to trace them when you are agitated, too. So you become the master over your instincts, no matter how explosive they are. What will happen is the emotions will step aside when your mind is determined.

Taking stock, is not self-criticism

The errant, emotional, or drive-driven thoughts which drive your behavior against your morality or best interests are what you need be concerned about. When you compromise your values to this drive, you need to introspect and think about changes you need to make.

In your Sacred Space, the drive needs to protect you and your spouse as one entity. How many times do you see people compromising basic values in any given day? Not just like in crazy stories in the news, but in your own day. How often do your friends cheat, "just a little"? It is the drive to survive which convinces you to behave like children stealing cookies. But if you cheat your spouse "a little", it undermines trust and security.

Taking over your mind is a worthwhile challenge that cannot be ignored

You can control only yourself. If your spouse is cheating you, or on you, you can remind them (not self-righteously, but humbly) that you will never intentionally betray them (but expect a defensive reaction, and don't react to their reaction).

This is not meant as a license to call anybody on anything. There is no benefit for anyone if you point out each other's mistakes. This is meant to expose the true culprit in conflicts, which relentlessly and secretly drives you; so you can override it, and expose it.

Of course, you are ultimately responsible for your behavior, but you need to learn what has been pushing you all your life, and patiently take control; without shame!

None of us try to be liars, or cheaters, or try to be petty thieves. But look around, if not in the mirror. Have you never been deceptive in order to save some personal skin? It is normal, and it is the drive to survive, in action.

But, see how it has invaded your marriage, how the same fears, laced with expectations, break the cycle of love from expanding.

Survival drive is taken for granted, so you miss its ramifications

How many universal sayings, which we all take for granted, demonstrate the imperative to survive is greater than the need be moral and decent?

- It's a dog eat dog world

-Better he than me

-All is fair in love and war

-You have to look out for your own

-Losers weepers, finders, keepers

-As long as you don't get caught

And so forth. Everything is about individual survival. It's the way of the world. However, the drive to survive is not supposed to control the way you think, or especially act, within your Sacred Space!

Those sayings should never apply within your Sacred Space!

There are those who try to completely overcome the drives; not just in their marriage. Some fiercely independent people hate being controlled by anything, ever.

Gandhi, who strived to make India independent, was shot. As he went down, he looked at and blessed his assailant. He did an amazing job of overcoming his fear of death; but you? Let the great ones set examples, sure. You, though, just have to make sure you don't mistake your spouse for an assailant.

Keep the drives under your control in your Sacred Space

You can always spot the drives by their obnoxious manifestations. As soon as you see yourself being less than kind or feeling irritated, you have to put your brakes on. Or when you see your spouse is caught by the drive, you have to put the brakes on your reactions not theirs.

You are ultimately responsible for your behavior, but you need to learn what has been pushing you all your life

Everything is about individual survival. It's the way of the world

We do not care so much how you navigate the treacherous waterways of the world, or what you think you have do to get ahead or not be left behind; that is your business. How much gold you have to put away to feel secure or how much you mistrust people; it is your business. It is none of our business if you smile so people don't know you are scared or if you are a lawyer who looks a judge in the eye as you lie through your teeth.

We do not condemn you for faking your expense account, or telling a ticket seller you're kids are younger than they are, or if you sneak candy into the theater to save a couple of bucks. It is none of our business if you are a professional con artist, a fifth grade teacher, do accounting, or work in high tech.

We know there is no end to the ways the drive shows up in your life, and everyone else's, no matter what your life is like. We know you are doing the best you can to improve your life at your best rate. We admire you and care for you. We just want you to know that you can change your married life into something wonderful. And we want you to do it with as much efficiency as possible.

You can change your married life into something wonderful

None of how you survive in the world matters to us. But where your spouse is concerned, in thoughts, attitudes, words or deeds, we want you to control your mind, rather than let your self-preserving instincts control you. We want you to treat your spouse with love and feel blessed to have them. Confide your love to them, trust them and care for them. You cannot do that if you act on the same fears you feel in the world.

When your mind tells you to lie to them, don't! When your mind tells you to take the bigger piece, or better seat, or softer pillow...don't! When your mind tells you it is their turn to do the dishes, or your turn to pick the movie, or they are not doing their part, remember, at those 'driven to be selfish' moments, it is your drive to survive calling the shots, not your love-based desire to please your spouse unconditionally.

We want you to experience unconditional love. If you do not learn to control your drives and instincts, and study and practice ways to override their commands, we know you will never experience unconditional love. You can do this, so don't be discouraged!

Channel your drive to serve your higher, human needs

Why let your biological drives steal the most coveted of all human prizes?

When you agree with the common sense logic. that you actually gain more by putting your spouse's needs ahead of your own. and start to act on it, you will not necessarily become a master at defying the drives, as that is almost impossible for most of us; but you will be introducing wisdom into the equations, satisfying the drive in a way or ways which you, the you who is above the drives, believe are better for you, based on your evaluations. You will choose between your bodily cells winning, or your soul and mind winning.

Eventually, although your drives will still push you to create instincts and habits, they will more and more be designed with your approval, and wisdom. As you progress in scrapping the old ones, replacing them with beneficial automatic reactions, you will literally feel peace most of the time, instead of anxiety, fear or strain.

Override your instincts, think things through with the intentions to please your spouse, and your lives will change.

Let's be really honest

Generally, people who discover this scientific explanation are of two broad types.

One kind enthusiastically embraces what they learned, and start to mentally note all of their reactions, not just in their marriage, but in every venue. They begin to see how they have been puppets of their habits and instincts, and so start to modify their reactions. They begin the sometimes painful process of objectively evaluating their actual needs and evaluate their current typical reactions towards them. They begin to tone things down, paying more and more attention, changing their reactive behaviors, challenging ancient hardcore instinct habits, which have been running their life.

Those people, who at last see how their free will is mitigated by habits and instincts, always improve themselves, because they can see what needs to be done more clearly, with practice, and they do it.

They begin to make their new efforts in their marriage, first, where it is most important. They ignore any of their spouse's negative attitudes towards them, and choose to love, without compromise, even if they are not receiving love from their spouse. They put incredible effort into reducing their hostile reactions to their spouse, quickly changing from spouse antagonists, to spouse supporters. **Of course their marriages improve, and it happens quickly.**

They stop the guilt trips, screaming, comparing, complaining, condemning, controlling, criticizing, judging, nagging, accusing, silence, demanding, retaliating, professing…are we missing anything? They focus on self-improvement and honoring their spouse. **Of course their lives improve!**

The other group, which we make every effort to reduce, in size, through education, blames their spouse and the world in general, for all their troubles and sorrows, in spite of the logic of this marital science. They may concede a bit, say they see how they did "their part" to hurt their marriage, but they always rationalize, if only their spouse would change, everything would improve…so sad.

They try to "share" blame, and responsibility; even thinking themselves noble when they imagine they may be "mostly" responsible. But it still does not work, and cannot work. Somehow they miss the point of giving unconditional love, still insisting they will give "unconditional" love, if their spouse will.

They do not realize their greatest enemy is fear, which makes them unable to see what marriage can be, if only they would separate it from the rest of life's perilous venues. These folks are like those who will not jump into a safety net from a burning building.

Is that you? Do you think you are fine, but your spouse needs to change, or at least meet you halfway? Do you think our insistence you learn to love your spouse, without wanting anything in return, is just not fair? If so, we promise you, your desire for fairness, as reasonable as it sounds on paper, will just not work.

Override your instincts, think things through with the intentions to please your spouse, and your lives will change

Your greatest enemy is fear, which makes you unable to see what your marriage can be

So, we want to give you as much evidence as possible, until you can see for yourself how the drive to survive has taken you over, how you need to break free by not caring about fairness in order to be happy. We want you to realize how only you can ever be responsible for your happiness, and, as importantly, the process of creating happiness for yourself and spouse is methodical. We want you to also know the results are certain, when you work with physics, material or psychological.

If you believe us, but cannot find the strength, enlist the aid of a competent coach, or express your dilemma to your spouse. Perhaps, in your situation, you can help each other learn to trust each other.

The pecking order of survival

Survival, as a protective drive, creates a hierarchy; putting you, and then close associates, in prioritized order

Survival, as a protective drive, creates a hierarchy; putting you, and then close associates, in prioritized order.

A close look will quickly reveal a practical and ruthless system. Because the pecking order is bio-based (no human considerations), it is savage in its approach. Your self-preservation is always going to be first (until you have children), unless you consistently manage the drives and instincts. Next, in line of priorities are your family members (trust through familiarity), then your community, your nation, and so on down the line.

But, did you think about and plan this order of importance? Was all the information carefully sorted, and then reasoned out? Did you sit with your choices, and struggle with some of your ideas? No, of course not; the system was dictated by the innate drive, as seen through the filters of biological necessity and unique education from your family and community, which combined with tiny residues of information from your personal experiences. You pretty much had no say in any of it.

The drives secretly control us all, without any personal conscious input of reason; until we recognize what we are doing; and how it is operating on its own, making almost all of your decisions for you; many of which are counter to your best human, and marital, interests. You have been a slave, without ever knowing it!

Enslavement, or love and connection-choose

The biggest problem for you who are married is the drives pit you against your spouse, making them out to be another competitor in the battles for survival. You do not see it happening that way, of course. You do not think there is a need to be at odds with your spouse for survival, but it drives you anyway, as if they are competitors.

Because the instincts for survival are the same ones you use in the world and have been in place since birth, they make your choices for you, based on worldly threats. You do not discern the need for protection does not belong in your Sacred Space. So you do not modify them accordingly. You do not recognize it is overriding your higher human needs for love and connection.

The same triggers of the world, which elicit fear, hit the same buttons your spouse hits in your sacred space, which create the same internal reactions such as anger.

In the world, people modify their external reaction somewhat so they don't go to jail or something for aggravated assault, or lose their job for chewing out their boss.

In the world, you modify your reactions so the person you are interacting with does not know how you truly feel. But, in your marriage, because of over-familiarity, you unceremoniously blast your spouse with all your fear-driven might.

Isn't this ironic? The one who should never feel your wrath is the one your mind tells you it is ok to scream at.

The obvious best practice for marriage is to protect your spouse from abuse. But it is not so easy if all you try to do is stop the behaviors you know are destructive, when they arise. In fact, if you just fight the behaviors when they come up, you will fight the same internal battle over and over, until you give up.

No, that will not work for you in the long run. You have to redirect the driver of destructive outer reactions, so the tendency to strike is changed to a tendency to express love. You also need to see your spouse and you as one.

Just as cells work together to protect the organism they belong to, just as organisms work together to protect their intimate community, so you and your spouse need to put your relationship ahead of your individual selves.

When you do so, as only humans can do so intentionally, you will act out of unconditional love.

Rework your instincts for your Sacred Space

Divert the drive's power to a reconfigured instinct, one you create.

You cannot get rid of the drive; it is innate, but you can channel it into an instinctive reaction which still fulfills its mission, but also fulfill yours.

Remember, your body, due to the drives, has a mind of its own, one not interested in your desire to connect for love. It only wants you to connect to make babies. Until you take charge, the body pretty much controls your mind.

In a good marriage, a spouse does everything in their power to override, and change their instincts, to make them conform to more appropriate survival scenarios, ones that puts your spouse ahead of self. Putting your spouse ahead of your own needs is absolutely logical, but only if you want to have love.

If love is not a goal, your spouse's feelings are irrelevant

If you just want a business partnership with someone, it makes no difference whether you carry over the survival instincts into your marriage, or not. But, know, it is not possible to grow your relationship into a good marriage if you do not commit to a 100% effort. If you hold back your efforts to put your spouse first, you will fail, until you, at last, shift to what works.

Because of over-familiarity, you unceremoniously blast your spouse with all your fear-driven might

You cannot get rid of the drive; it is innate, but you can channel it into an instinctive reaction which still fulfills its mission

Halfway is no way

Some think they will give this "philosophy" a little try, but just a little at a time, not realizing it is not a philosophy, anymore than gravity is a philosophy, but rather a system which works with the laws of human physics.

This is science; and miniscule changes (regardless of your sincerity), like not being quite as much of a jerk to your spouse as you have been, will not give you tangible desired results. Of course, slowing the pollution you put into a river will reduce the toxicity, but it won't make it drinkable. You have to make a sincere effort, but the right kind of effort, to reverse your approach.

Put your spouse first and your life will change

A wise spouse puts their soul-mate first, ahead of themselves and even their children

A wise spouse puts their sou-mate first, ahead of themselves and even their children ("love" for your children is not pure, because instincts force you to put them first-but you chose your spouse). Use wisdom to redefine and realign your instincts, even though the instincts are telling you to wait and see or encouraging some other halfhearted strategy.

Some say they do put their spouse first, but fool themselves by expecting their spouse to appreciate their efforts, even though their efforts do not match what their spouse wants or needs, jut what they think their spouse "should" want.

The key is effort, to the best of your ability, as that is the physics of it.

Use triggers to your advantage

Each time you feel anger, in any of its forms, is an opportunity to redo the internal mechanisms (instincts). As soon as you realize you are losing it, see it as a way to train the mind to build or support a new, connection building, instinct.

When the mind feels threatened or questions fairness, the wise spouse stops their mind, calmly evaluates the circumstances, and acknowledges the influence of the drive, putting them first, so they can then, unambiguously (look out for unconscious holdouts), change the instincts of self-protection to instincts of loving service. You cannot change the drive, but you can change the instincts which come from the drive.

The smart spouse quickly and powerfully puts aside their anger, even if they cannot trace it back to the drive at the moment, and shoves the new command, to love their spouse, down their own throat, so to speak. Not only can it be done, it must be done. Otherwise, you remain a slave, and an unhappy one at that. You have to be strong, as you are fighting lifetime habits of selfishness.

Realize at that moment, or later, that your reaction is/was an overreaction, and you need to train your instinctive reaction to be a loving one. If you want to yell, walk out, point out their flaw, tell them they are jerks, blame their family or etc…stop!

Stop your mind. Tell your mind you are not going to be a victim of anger, and you will now take over control of your emotions. Tell your spoiled mind to go to its room until it is user friendly again. Then, tell your spouse you are sorry. Tell them you love them, and want to please them, even as your mind is screaming at you that you're in the right etc.

It is not enough to only stop being angry. If it is the best you can do at the moment, you have to extend the moment, until you can proactively improve your connection by expressing love to your spouse.

Until you are on the lookout, with the intention of scrutinizing your thoughts, to see the survival drive in your thoughts and actions, you will not see how this drive impacts so many of your thoughts and behaviors, or how the drive, which has no intelligence, which does not care for you as a human, only your biological survival, manipulates your intelligence to do things which challenge basic common sense.

Remember, the drive prefers to remain hidden from you, so it hides sensible thoughts behind the curtain of fear and anger.

It is not like your instincts are "evil"

The drive instigates instincts, which are mechanical mechanisms, to react instantly.

Instincts would not be effective if they reacted a split second later, so they shield themselves from scrutiny of the mind, which otherwise might want to evaluate, and delay the launch. Instincts do not want your last minute interference, because you may hesitate, and thus die from the hesitation. Does this make sense?

But, as humans, we have the unique ability to observe our thoughts, so catch the reactive behaviors, often in mid flight.

Remember the prize fighter who got flak for saying he did not realize he bit off his opponents ear? The instinct does not want to be stopped, so you need to change the instincts. As soon as you see a trigger, make it a trigger for a positive act of love. You can train your mind to do that!

Once you see the triggering mechanism and how it drives a reaction, you can alter the biological instinct, which, in civilized human beings, is not intended to be driven by the challenges of the jungle. But you have to be very serious because the muscles to do this have gone unused for so long.

The drive to procreate, reproduce…have sex

In every living cell, from the most primitive single cell, which survives through community, and self-divides for procreation, to the various birds and mammals, with countless elaborate and sophisticated mating dances, to human love with subsequent marriage-sanctioned family-building; the survival-driven drive to procreate is at the bottom of it all. Survival controls the world, and controls us.

The smart spouse quickly and powerfully puts aside their anger, even if they cannot trace it back to the drive at the moment

It is not enough to only stop being angry

Making babies is all about survival, isn't it? The myriad mating rituals, which distract our attention from the underlying purpose of procreation, are performed without awareness that their act will produce offspring, (except in humans). Nor is mating associated with love, except for (not all of us, by any stretch) humans.

Drives tempt us to self-deceive to get their way

Sexual reproduction is unquestionably a mechanism for species survival, and although it is pleasurable, sex is instinct driven, to serve the drive to survive.

The drive to procreate is single-mindedly ruthless and does not care how it gets its organism to comply. This is where we see temptation enter our lives, not just sexual temptation, but temptations which are offshoots of the procreative drive. The drive will tell us whatever works, to get us to make babies (and improve the gene pool).

We can see how human minds compromise with the drive, by introducing the idea of sexual pleasure, even though in males the actual physical pleasure is barely enough (this is not a study of human sexuality so the information is narrowed to make certain points) compared to the effort made, to have sexual pleasure.

Pursuit of sexual connection by men, with all its numerous travails, is usually a lifetime frustrating effort

Yet, the pursuit of sexual connection by men, with all its numerous travails, is usually a lifetime frustrating effort; all for the idea of fleeting pleasure.

In fact, the idea of pleasure has captivated us all, females too, but rarely delivers pleasure in proportion to the effort or the advertising. Much worse, it distracts us from something far more satisfying; psychological and spiritual connection.

We can make sex work for us, too

When we understand the big picture, we can use sex to bridge our minds and souls. That is the real prize of human sexuality. Humans lower themselves when they use their powerful minds to concoct great imaginative ways to, basically, satisfy their biological drive. It is sad, when you think about it, to trade off pleasing our minds and souls in order to be vassals of our bodies.

Sex is biological

Have you ever seen a pair of animals walk away from mating with smiles on their faces? No, the act is a biological one, with a simple biological purpose. Humans, disregarding their psychological and spiritual potential, made the act something it isn't, trying to make physical pleasure the grand reward for their efforts. But, that is a losing proposition.

Humans have much grander opportunities than to be slaves to the drives. We are special. We are beyond animals, in capabilities and awareness.

We, like all our animal cousins, use sex as a way to create offspring, yes, but we also, uniquely, use sex to express our love to each other, by using intimate physical contact as a way to be closer, emotionally, and spiritually. In that case it is not a trade off at all.

The trouble we run into, however, comes from not consciously separating our biological lust, which is instinct- driven, from the uplifting human intention to connect.

Animals, even dogs, do not think, "Wow, I would love to share my deepest feelings with that puppy". Only humans have so grand an opportunity for expressing and enjoying unconditional love.

The how's, and understanding the pitfalls etc, for getting the most from human love making, is not complicated. But it is involved. So, because it is incredibly important, we will put off the discussion, to later, when we address it in detail.

The evolution of instincts

If you understand the simple science of drives, instincts, emotions etc, well enough to share it, you can be sure it will stay with you, and help you remember what you have to during times of need. Try explaining these principles to another, or to a mirror.

Instincts do not just show up. They are not innate, like the drives. They are intelligently devised, and subconsciously, or intentionally, installed. The complexity of an organism determines how they are installed.

Drives are the catalyst for instincts, emotions etc. In primitive organisms, where an organism is a cluster of cells, it has a simple nervous system, and instincts are established in a simple fashion. Instincts, in those, unify the organism, so the individual cells serve the needs of the entire organism.

Reactions to stimulants are organized. Every cell cares for the community of cells, rather than just for itself. The drives are ever there, but they filter through organisms, regardless of complexity.

Instincts protect whole organisms rather than individual cells, providing automatic responses to food opportunities, or threats. In organized cell colonies, the single cell has given up its independence, and lives for the sake of the whole organism, which competes with other organisms.

A good example of an advanced lower life form, with a simple, non-brain, nervous system, is a plant. In a tree, the cells, and cell collectives, form to make distinct parts, like roots, leaves or bark. They work in harmony, to defend the tree from predators of all sorts, and, collect nutrients from air and soil.

There is no brain or central command center. The actions and reactions are not thought about, even in the most sophisticatedly simple (hardly simple, we know) or brainless organisms. All its actions are instinctively organized, not intelligently considered and conceived. Plants cannot think about storing water or reproducing. It is all instinctive reactive behavior.

Only humans have so grand an opportunity for expressing and enjoying unconditional love

The drives are ever there, but they filter through organisms, regardless of complexity

Human brains, though not significantly physically different from "higher" animals, have hidden differences which dramatically set it apart

Brains are unique to higher life forms

In more evolved organisms, when there is a more evolved nervous system, instincts are found within, and are dispersed by, a centralized command center, called a brain. The brain evaluates and computes its responses to survival needs, and formulates reactions, and non-emergency responses, threats, or opportunity.

Brains are a big step in terms of evolutionary development. Information is organized by the brain, which determines the best function of each of its various cells, as well as its body parts. (Although libraries of books are written on this topic, we hope to provide you more than enough for you to get the picture).

Because it has a brain a fish sees some food and swims towards it, opens its mouth etc, without any thought. Its reactions to sustenance are instinctive. Computations, memories etc. occurs within the brain, but the physical reactions take place in all the other parts of the fish's body in a coordinated, efficient manner, by the brain.

Organisms with a brain have a psychology, which means it intelligently processes and considers information. In lower forms, where there is no central command center, or brain, there is no psychology. The psychology of creatures with brains ranges from the very simple, as found in insects and other little creatures, to very complex, as in mammals and birds.

Human brains are incredible

Human brains, though not significantly physically different from "higher" animals, have hidden differences, which dramatically set it apart.

Above all other life forms, in so many ways, humans enjoy added abilities such as abstract thinking, and can make moral judgments, experience love as a spiritual experience, etc. It has nothing to do with difference in complexity, weight to body ratios, or any other physical consideration.

Objectively, we know there are huge difference between humans and animals. Some individuals minimize the differences, or look for a "missing link", because biologically there are so many similarities. We should not be fooled into thinking we are just "smarter" animals. Humans are extraordinary!

All living things demand survival

In all cases, from most primitive, to human, the nervous system unifies the cells into a living survival machine.

The number one priority for every living thing is to survive. From a material objective point of view, that is pretty much all any organism does with its time and energy. Some do it obviously with simple active, reactive efforts, while others do it with more flair. But there is no question that life on Earth is always struggling to survive. And, when the struggle ends, the organism, whether it is a single cell, or a human being, finds that its biological life is over.

These are the two parts to survival we see in every life form, feed and defend. We see that we, as humans, also do this, but, as described before, with our advanced imagination, we do it with finesse, and in luxury. But, still, we give ourselves sustenance, and defend ourselves from predators, for the purpose of survival.

If you count up how much of your waking hours go into survival related activities, with all their nuances, you will be amazed!

Humans are incredible

The gap between a human mind and the mind of the highest animals; dogs, horses, elephants, certain apes, and some say dolphins and cats, is profound. Our human mind can

1) Come up with all sorts of varying solutions to various problems, along with predicting future events

2) Discern, and include, moral considerations

3) Weigh things in the abstract, to consider more than just what is in front of us, or what is physical

4) Humans can do what no animal can do.

We can completely override our instincts, and the drives which inspired them, based on ideas, not just events.

This is an amazing multifaceted, and liberating, attribute

Humankind can also conceive of, and connect to their spiritual origins, which, for purposes of teaching principles required for a healthy marriage, we need not discuss at any length, just touch upon later.

The ability to override or install an instinct, based on abstract considerations, is unique to humankind

You, as a human, can evaluate any of your instincts for its usefulness and value. You can, and must, literally, change the ones you do not think help, you.

You can consciously implant instincts you desire.

You can imagine new instincts, and implant them.

Humans have unlimited potential to reason. You can manipulate triggers, and reactions

The gap between a human mind and the mind of the highest animals; dogs, horses, elephants, certain apes, and some say dolphins and cats, is profound

Humans have unlimited potential to reason

How to make an instinct

Make things you encounter every day into triggers, or reminders, for positive use. This idea works very well when it is done with some planning, and self-checking.

You may decide, for instance, that every time you look at your watch it will trigger you to think of a positive trait of your spouse, or it can remind you to send them a beam of love from your heart.

Or, maybe every time you hear a bird, you will be triggered to close your eyes, and imagine kissing your love.

Use practical methods to self-train

Using your will and intention, you are able to imagine and create a future you prefer

If you keep a small card or notebook, you can hourly, or every three hours, track your progress in remembering to implement your new instinct.

If you stick with it, your new instinct will take root as quickly as in a week or so. When your habit is securely imbedded and your reactions are automatic, you can add more. Each time one good habit is lodged, you can install another, and then another. Soon, your mind will be filled with positive reminders…You have to do this. This is not a novel!

Using your will, and intention, you are able to imagine, and create, a future you prefer. Make yourself behave in ways needed to achieve your vision.

This is not to say there are redo buttons in life. You cannot go back, and change the course of events by "taking it back". But, hopefully, that is not a problem.

You learn from your mistakes, when you don't like the results of your mistakes. You can change your attitudes, and behaviors, to improve your future, creating future happiness.

Your self-designed future will soon overwhelm your past mistakes, and, what now seems like an impossible circumstance will very likely shift. Over time, your lives will go from despair, if it is that bad at the moment, to ever expanding love and connection.

Train your instincts

You can train your reactions, making them all positive. You can choose to be endearing and supportive etc, by ignoring, or overriding old instinctive mental reactions. If you are currently tweaked by a certain mannerism, it is up to you, and you have the power, to change the tweak into a good feeling.

Perhaps your spouse coughs every time they are about to speak, and it drives you crazy. Little things like that are not uncommon, and it does not matter if you imagine your reaction is just a way for you to express your displeasure of them in general, or if it is because some adult from your childhood neighborhood had that trait, and you hated them. You need to get over your negative reaction to your spouse, even if it is only inside.

Remember all your tweaks have to do with your stuff, not theirs. You can imagine a way to reframe the cough. Maybe tell yourself it hurts them, so from now on you can feel sympathy when they cough. Or maybe you can start to hear the cough say, "I love you, and I would throw down my life for you."

You have that much power over your mind!

Redefine your interactions by implanting user friendly instincts into your mind

You currently instinctively interact with your spouse. You aren't working with wisdom and the self-control of a human being.

An animal's mind does not evaluate situations, based on moral principles, or forethought, nor do animals employ wisdom in their decisions. They are 100% instinct driven (except for your dog, of course). But the human mind is incredibly designed to minutely evaluate past, present and future experiences and opportunities, and then intelligently plan imaginative responses.

You can imagine outcomes, and plan courses of actions based on individual preferences and tastes

Uniquely, at your human, disposal, are conscience, wisdom and free will. The human mind is a superior alternative to lower minds relying on instincts. The human mind is above instinct! Even an animal mind will learn from instinct driven mistakes, and change its behaviors, but you can go much further, and reason complex problems, with multifaceted ramifications; even the lowliest of us have that power.

What typically happens, though, is a person's instinct misreads some event as life-threatening, based on habitual misreading or misunderstandings. A panic may be triggered by the termination of a job, or an insult from an important person in your life. Even though these are not life threatening, they still trigger all the bodily and psychological kneejerk reactions normally reserved for real threats.

Your reactions may include anything from lies and evasions to avoid perceived "death" traps, to threatening someone away who is merely being a jerk. If someone is being a jerk in a way that scares you for some buried psychological reason, your instincts kick in.

Misclassification is the cause of distress, and ongoing stress. It ignores 'human sense' and, when unmonitored, ignites reaction.

When you react without a clear evaluation of what you are facing, your mind always gives in to your most primal behavior. Over time, you eliminate a lot of those threats as triggers, because you subconsciously reclassify them; but imagine the power of reclassification when it is done consciously!

That is the better way. If your first reaction of fight or flight is suppressed; put it aside long enough to evaluate, that is the way to go! Catching the reactions, by making those reactions reminders for you to stop, evaluate and behave appropriately; that is the way to go.

The human mind is incredibly designed to minutely evaluate past, present and future experiences and opportunities, then intelligently plan imaginative responses

When the drive for survival is unregulated and responds to the uncontrolled imagination's interpretation of danger, it is freak-out city

Methods such as deep, slow breathing, which pushes more oxygen into the brain and slows the heart rate, will stop automatic processes dead in their tracks.

Speak to yourself (your mind), about how silly its reaction is. Even if your mind seems so out of control that you can't think of a technique at the moment, remember you must ultimately gain control; there is no other way.

It is your mind and body, and it is your responsibility to control them. Don't be satisfied with a little temporary relief. Take a walk, take a cold shower, go to the gym; whatever you do, try your best to betray the instinct. Pay attention! Slow down the movie! Own your destiny!

You can reason, you can will, and you can act. Use your reason, will, and actions to create harmony and connection. Feel true intimacy with your spouse.

Take survival out of your sexual encounters

There is a direct link between survival of the individual, and survival of a particular species.

Sex is not some casual, fun thing discovered because mankind had time on their hands. Biologically, sex was imposed upon us by the drive to survive. It is a reactive, reproductive survival instinct.

The drive to strive to have sex, or behave in other ways which culminate in sex, and off-spring, completely controls you, until you override it.

Current societal thinking hurts

Because, as a society, we sought to understand sex in the context of recreation, we became slaves, who, despite all the associated difficulties, sincerely believe we're enjoying ourselves.

Imagining sex, as an "ultimate" pleasure device, reduces us to the equivalent of six year olds, coloring on top of Da Vinci's Last Supper.

Sex between biological organisms is not a turn on. Yet we have astonishingly turned orgasms, a physiological message that the sperm is delivered, into a goal of goals.

We are no better than physical creatures when we are used by lust or physical desire. When we succumb to biological needs to the point of forgetting our mental and spiritual selves we are missing the point. In fact, many people become intoxicated in order to shut out human thoughts and feelings. Talk about getting it backwards!

It defies common sense that humankind, which has so much mental and spiritual capacity, has reduced itself to imagining sex is only, or primarily, for the purpose of sensual pleasure and occasionally for making babies. No wonder there is so much frustration!

When the drive for survival is unregulated and responds to the uncontrolled imagination's interpretation of danger, it is freak-out city

The sex for pleasure idea is embellished and exaggerated by human imagination. Of course, sexual pleasure is a gift of and for our advanced awareness and not a problem when kept in proper proportion and context.

Of course you should have sex for pleasure and be as creative as you wish. But why be a slave of your survival instincts and procreative drive. Utilize sex as a means to connect, so you are not just being used by your instincts.

Sexual intimacy is not mere sexual satisfaction

Sexual intimacy is an important part of a fulfilling marriage, but first understand how powerful the influences are and why and how it makes you act. Enjoy the benefits of sexual pleasure, but as a byproduct. Focus, rather, on using it as a bridge between your souls.

Many women intuitively understand the true purpose of marital sex, but they get side-tracked because the concept of a spiritual connection is not supported by our male-based societal perspective.

When sex is used only for physical gratification or pleasure, it wears out the nervous system, and eventually becomes more boring than pleasurable. Does that make sense considering how society comes up with new ways to "bring excitement back into your sex life"?

For many, sex is the only thing they have left in their marriage, and for others sex is not even part of their marriage anymore. Either way, it is due to lack of knowledge. Own what sex is, or sex will own you. Use sex as a way to create, and delve into your soul's connection.

From infidelity to inability to perform, sex is a topic which has to be addressed without fear. But we need to give it the time it deserves, so we discuss this simple, but extensive topic, in depth, later.

Influences of drives on genders

Men and women are driven differently, by the same core drives. But the drives show up differently, tailored by two genders, creating misunderstanding and resentment.

You do not have to submit to your body

People do not know that biological influences of gender are not absolute in their persuasiveness. They are so driven that they believe there is nothing to do but submit, or be frustrated.

Religious or martial arts monks, use willpower to stop the drives from pushing them around; and homosexuals, who do not strictly behave according to their gender, ignore their body's call for reproduction. We think those who almost completely override their instinctive demands are somehow different from us. But they are biologically the same, and have the same core drive to survive.

The sex for pleasure idea is embellished and exaggerated by human imagination

Sexual intimacy is not mere sexual satisfaction

Although the drive to procreate is a heavyweight, the above examples demonstrate the power of the drives is not absolute. They are not your master when you choose to choose.

On the other hand, we advocate a healthy sex life, but you need to learn how to have your cake and eat it too (the one area of life when it's ok). Rather than begin the last chapter, on intimacy, now, we will address the pragmatic biological drives.

Sexual desire is mutually misunderstood by both genders

Women are not driven by the procreative drive to have daily (or hourly) sex the way men are.

The psychophysiological imperative for women to have sex for procreation occurs once a cycle, only for a number of hours, only when there is a suitable mate.

It is the opportunity for fertilization that triggers the pressure to have (reproductive) sex, which is biologically driven sex (there is, of course, psychological lust, but there is no need to delve into that topic, for these purposes). Because it takes a cycle to grow a viable egg, having sex when the egg is not viable, is, biologically, a waste of resources.

The monthly urge is the closest a woman comes to experiencing what a man experiences 24-7. Men, constantly driven, cannot grasp why women are not like them, and vice versa. But the answer is embarrassingly simple. Men have to be ready to fertilize whenever the egg is ready. The timing is controlled by biology.

Ladies, do not blame your husband for being creatures of lust, who only love you for your body, because you will learn, in the last chapter, how to shift their attention. Men, do not blame your wife for being cold and uninterested. You have been sold a bill of goods by practitioners of French ticklers and "sure ways" to entice her. Just don't go the last chapter yet! There is still foundational knowledge you need before you can execute what you will learn.

Men, appreciate your wives for what they endure

Women are biologically designed to rotate eggs (with all the hormonal craziness we are all familiar with) conceive and carry a child until it is ready to leave the womb.

They are designed to breast feed, nurture and care for their child until it is ready for an independent life. Complex human children cannot be birthed and left to their own devices. The woman's role in procreation is undeniably more complex and far more demanding than that of her husband.

Women are not driven by the procreative drive to have daily (or hourly) sex the way men are

There are other factors which prompt a woman to crave sex, and we discuss the uniquely human drives, but everyone will agree the bio drives, if they were the only ones in play, are a bummer for men.

Men do not have the same physical and psychological requirements to sustain their off-spring, so they have no idea, other than intellectually, what it feels like to be in a woman's body, driven by the biological survival instincts, and specialized procreative drives.

All a man's body is going through is pressure to spot, fight for, and fertilize. Obviously, the biological drives are tailored by societies, but that only forces men to sublimate (until properly educated).

Thank God we are evolved enough so as not to be locked into the spousal roles these instincts would "naturally" drive us towards. We need to know about them, but we should not be controlled by them.

Honor your spouse

When your spouse reacts to something, it is wise and kind to make a mental note of his or her area of sensitivity so you can avoid striking the nerve that sends a message of danger. That makes sense, right? If someone has a sprained wrist, you wouldn't ask that person to help move a piano, would you?

Neither do you have a right to point out their weaknesses, or how you see them trapped by their psychological stuff; you do not. Keep it to yourself; only use the intimate information you have to bring them more comfort. The reasons you don't let them know what you see are

1) It is intrusive; like pointing out a pimple or weight gain

2) They can only handle self-improvement at the rate they are improving, or not

3) being attentive to their weaknesses distracts you from noticing your own

Be aware of your own reactions

On the other side, it is smart to make note of your own automatic reactions to your spouse's reactions, so you can recalibrate your sensitivities to calmer and proactively positive responses.

All a man's body is going through is pressure to spot, fight for, and fertilize

It is smart to make note of your own automatic reactions to your spouse's reactions, so you can recalibrate your sensitivities

If you fly off the handle because your spouse didn't ask for your help in the way you expected, it is a good idea to stop your reactive explosion dead in its tracks. Watch how crazy you are. If you pay attention with an objective open mind, you will be amazed at your own behaviors.

Reactions become hotter as triggers are repeatedly hit, like a nerve getting more and more sensitive; or an open wound being touched. So, if you are the accidental hitter, back off when you see your spouse getting caught in a psychological trap (even if it appears so easy for them to overcome it from your safe perspective); you are not there for that.

Alternately, when you are the hittee, step back from yourself, and explain to yourself that you are actually safe, and don't have to be defensive. Remember, be only your own teacher, never your spouse's.

Our free will is hijacked by instincts in every area of our lives; this is not an exaggeration

If you reverse the equation, you see that letting things go, when your spouse is getting their buttons pushed, allows the buttons to heal over. They may get calm enough to where they see it themselves. This way you can be a good spouse, by giving them the space they need to heal; without comment!

Defensiveness

Our free will is hijacked by instincts in every area of our lives; this is not an exaggeration.

It is so easy to miss our instinctive defensiveness that we often find ourselves in a pickle, without having seen it coming.

No matter how you feel, no matter how frustrated you are, no matter how much you want to "share" or how many ways you think it is ok; it isn't OK.

There is never an excuse to complain to your spouse about how they are, behave or see things or anything else.

Your goal in marriage is love. Don't allow your mouth to open when meanness is about to come out

Misreading signals creates all sorts of harmful reactions for both.

How often do you misjudge what is really going on, and do the opposite of what is called for? Maybe your wife commented on your receding hairline, thinking you look sexy; but you instantly take it as a put down, because of having unsettling thoughts; so you assume she is getting on you.

This happens because

a) You misunderstood what was intended (defensiveness causes you to imagine the worst)

AND

b) You don't ask your spouse if what you imagine was what they intended; again; your defensiveness convinces you they cannot be trusted, so you assume.

The idea that suffering comes from external events, like an off-handed comment, is simply inaccurate. No matter what is happening, there are an infinite number of ways to see it. It is how you see it that causes pain or pleasure; everything that happens is more or less neutral.

Be indifferent to your spouse's imperfections and misunderstandings; never taking their communications or their momentary misguided intentions personally.

Instincts create pitfalls because of biological attractions

"A man and a woman can never just be friends" should be taken as a strong warning.

Any who imagine friendship outside of appropriate group venues, such as work, church or clubs, when unavoidable, is defying forces that will undermine your marriage. Instincts will win in the end.

A closed friendship between a married person, and someone of the other gender, married or no, is going to create a future problem; it almost always will. Most (no statistics, just a lot of revelations in sessions), so-called innocent friendships defy the best initial, and well meaning, intentions, as these friendships usually evolve beyond what is appropriate.

Wisdom and knowledge end suffering

Never be a doormat or victim of circumstance. For the most part, victims are self-created, and attract those who wish to have power over them.

Because they do not control their minds, most people react to life like a frog caught in a fast current. They fearfully kick, in reaction to an immediate danger, or they jump for a bug meal, when they can and should. Instead, aim for the highest goals, especially of intimate connection, never realizing they can navigate life's journey, with the powers they already have.

You got married without knowing about what drives you, or your spouse, and without knowing your capabilities. Until you are familiar with the pitfalls and your counterbalancing assets, you are in big trouble. But once you see the vision of a superior marriage, the pitfalls and the safe pathways, you can succeed in ways that will bring you joy beyond belief.

Everything in life produces more and better fruit when it is understood, just like gardens, when you can take care according to its needs rather than your imagination!

A wise gardener learns what they need in order to get the most they possibly can. Your marriage, too, will bear the most abundant and best fruit when you are knowledgeable about all that makes it work. Most successful couples keep this book handy; reading parts every evening, until it is how they think.

- Chapter Eight -
The Reason You Got Married

◇◇◇

When you understand the relationship between "you" and your body/mind,
you will also understand the actual reasons for your life decisions.
Then you can make your needs and desires actual goals to work towards,
synchronizing your efforts with your actual beneficial desires.
Happiness will be what you work towards, instead of merely hope for.

◇◇◇

The reason or reasons you got married are very important, even though some of them are obscured from your own sight. Your reasons are purposes, which keep you pushing through the tough spots (life is filled with tough spots) so you can enjoy your good goals. The more clarity you have about what you are doing, the easier it will be for you. We want to help you find the easier and most fulfilling paths of marriage

Chapter Eight

The Reason You Got Married

When you put all the reasons to be married side by side and measure them against your desire to be loved unconditionally, there is simply no contest. The need for unconditional love is paramount!

Though rarely thought about as the reason to marry or a purpose of marriage, wanting to be unconditionally loved is still the number one reason; always. It is the primary purpose of marriage.

Your need for love is as much a powerful a drive as it is a great reason to marry. The underlying and most compelling purpose for marriage is to fulfill the innate human need for unconditional love. You will soon agree that designing your lives around this golden goal of life, to intentionally bring unconditional love, tangibly, into your marriage, your home and your Sacred Space, is the most vital effort you can make in your life.

You have always had all the resources you will ever need to achieve marital bliss (a term rarely used any more). Those who commit to achieving unconditional love never regret it. When they see their spouse as the one to love unconditionally they cannot lose.

Superb marriages are achieved by couples using this scientific approach, making unconditional love their life's goal. Their marriages stand as unassailable testimony, to the fact that joyful marriage is as marriage is intended.

As a married person, your unique opportunity for unconditional love is too good to ignore and too precious to not strive for, at whatever cost of pride, ego and effort. What better reason could one ever imagine as incentive to work on their selves, than to improve the most important relationship you will ever have? What better goal to strive towards, than unconditional love?!

Those who make unconditional love their primary effort in life, those who put more effort into pleasing their spouse, than themselves, are never disappointed.

The usual reasons for marriage are alright, but don't stop there

Getting married and raising a family is an inevitable part of life for most of us, isn't it? Everyone, usually from early childhood, looks forward to marriage and raising children, which brings with it the personal, social and psychological benefits we are all familiar with.

It is a shame there is so little education in our schools, which should teach basic knowledge for a basic marriage. But the focus in education will change to what is important in life, over time, as it has already changed for you.

Your need for unconditional love is paramount!

As a married person, your unique opportunity for unconditional love is too good to ignore and too precious to not strive for

There are three main purposes for marriage

1) Regulate procreation- which satisfies the needs of community

2) Learn how to get along with others- which satisfies the needs of society, the family and couple

3) Learn how to give unconditional love- which satisfies the human requirement for love

Usual reasons for getting married

No doubt you will find your original reasons among the typical reasons people marry, listed here in no particular order

Learn how to give unconditional love- which satisfies the human requirement for love

- Companionship

- Children

- Social acceptance

- Sexual bonding

- Emotional bonding

- Financial security

- Family security

- Sense of belonging

- Romance

- Tradition

- Economical efficiency

- Trusted spouse

When you marry for one or more of the above, and lovingly interact within positive behavioral guardrails (cause and effect), as described in the first chapters, you will lead a calm, happy and fulfilling family life.

However, if you look back to your courting days, you will probably note that few, if any, of these basic marital goals were discussed with your spouse very much, if at all. Most people just wing it.

Fix the basics, but, at the same time, strive for the highest ideals of marriage

These days, most marriages, at least in the West, begin with an attraction based on chemistry. Then some evolve with some friendship building, but most relationships evolve primarily with romance building; at least until soon after the wedding.

People live with their assumption that all the sought after benefits just sort of magically happen, because it is what you want.

Your desires get ahead of your efforts to produce even modest results. You didn't realize it is you, who has to do what is necessary to achieve goals, either humble or grand. Nothing of value "just happens".

For reasons, based on a lack of education, and too many fairy tales and movies, you assumed good marriages just happen, without knowledge, planning or effort. After all, you reasoned, its "natural".

You didn't think to compare your ideas of natural marriage relationships, with other things you think of as natural, like vegetable gardens or orchards, which also need systematic nurturing, and cultivation.

As illogical as fairy dust, you readily bought into the happily ever after notions; it seems to be the easiest path, at least until trouble hits.

Mediocre is acceptable to those who are in pain

Typically, after a fairly short time of "natural" desultory (aimless) married life, most people would be quite satisfied with a little less natural and would gladly accept a mediocre marriage. Especially after a period of lingering war, when most uneducated couples (who remain married through it all) learn to avoid the bigger insults, and learn how to stay out of each other's way.

Mediocre, which you do not need to accept, is a big step up for most couples. If you had a look behind the curtains of marriages you think are doing pretty well, you would discover most would be thrilled with a marriage that causes less stress.

Everyone always thinks they have it worse than others, but doing things wrong creates unhappy marriages, all for different reasons.

On the other hand, couples who knows what they are doing keep their marriage happy, no matter how miserable others are.

You don't have to settle

We vehemently disagree with the idea of accepting mediocrity. Based on what we know is attainable, by making a little of the right effort, we don't think anybody should have anything but happiness within their marriage.

The divorce rate is sending society a strong message. Would you think things were fine with airplanes, if half of them crashed?

People live with an assumption that all sought after benefits just sort of magically happen

The divorce rate is sending society a strong message. Would you think things were fine with airplanes, if half of them crashed?

Our social response would be schools and standards, advanced training, laws and regulations. Our social response to the divorce rate is obscene. We have more courts, child psychologists, divorce lawyers and neglected children, every year. But we still have no coordinated effort to learn about marriage, itself (The Marriage Foundation is intent on changing that).

Comprehensive understanding of marriage is absolutely essential. It is pretty crazy to think you can excel at something you don't study… and, fortunately, it is equally unimaginable to think you will not do well at something you understand well, like marriage.

Always keep the innate drives in mind

As you learned in the previous chapter, the innate drives for survival (and procreation) are always in the background, which until you learn to control, are constantly forcing you to overreact to every little misunderstanding, perceived as a threat. Among other inane reactions, the drive makes you judge your spouse, based on fear-based perceptions.

To have a sound marriage, you have to take control over your instincts, and remove the fears caused by the drive(s). Fear and lust distract you from love (and pretty much everything else).

On the other hand, expecting perfection from your spouse, or yourself, will make you a very anxious person! In fact, we easily could have listed "expectations" as the fourth killer, as it delivers all sorts of things, but never what one expects.

You will win

When you work with the drives (you cannot subdue them), by beginning the work of training their manifestations (instincts and reactions), which you *are supposed to* subdue and retrain, you will no longer be a slave.

Always look for their nefarious hidden prodding. When you understand it is their nature to sound alarms at the slightest provocation, you can learn to tune them out, and quiet or calm them. Or, at the very least, you can adjust your responses. Instead of being an unthinking reactive automaton, which instantly reacts to every hint of trouble you will control your happiness.

Living the good life of a married couple based on the normal reasons for marriage and appropriate behaviors, is not enough.

Had you been maritally educated, things would be different; but still

Had you been given a scientific education for relationships, and marriage (not including unconditional love), you would have prudently identified your goals, spent a lot of time distinguishing and prioritizing your needs and desires, and then you would have created a plan, to meet the person who came closest to fitting the qualities most important to you.

Comprehensive understanding of marriage is absolutely essential. It is pretty crazy to think you can excel at something you don't study… and equally unimaginable to think you will not do well at something you understand well

Then (in this hypothetical scenario), after you met the right person, and were sure about each other's qualities, (character surprises are not much fun), you would have used what you learned about marriage to systematically coordinate your lives.

You would have lived within your family, in such a way that would have superbly fulfilled your stated desires. But, even with all of that good effort, there still might, would be something missing.

Life would have been pretty good…But not good enough. And, of course, there is no time like the present to start behaving like you ought to!

If you did everything you were supposed to do in terms of thoughts, words and behaviors, there would still be something missing. Not romantic love, (psychological and physical) which is sweet and fun, or the reliable home life with routines and consideration, but something much more necessary.

Your marriage would still be missing unconditional love, the ecstatic connection between your hearts. Unconditional love is the missing ingredient, and is desperately craved, in every troubled marriage.

Unconditional love is the grand prize of life

Our approach to marriage is anything but airy-fairy. So, this is not the section where we ask you to blindly walk off the cliff and step on a cloud of bliss with faith. How would that help anyone?

We don't want to, nor do we want you, to "believe" in order to succeed. We want you to know where you are going; the steps needed to get there, the obstacles you may run into along the way, and the requirements for unmitigated achievement.

We would not bring up unconditional love if it were not a practical goal which you reach by taking practical steps.

Our approach to love is pragmatic, methodical and practical; it works

Follow tried and true paths to take you where you want to go with as efficient processes as is humanly possible.

Our "belief" is in the laws of cause and effect, and intentional effort. When you do what works based on material or human physics, it works every time (sometimes a nuance is important in a particular circumstance, and you learn those as you experiment).

We don't mind ignoring or dispelling myths, no matter how entrenched, and neither should you. Just because an idea is endorsed by cultural tradition or flowery anecdotes, or are guild approved "teachings"; if it doesn't work, we're not interested.

Our approach to marriage is anything but airy-fairy. This is not where we ask you to blindly walk off the cliff and step on a cloud of bliss, with faith. How would that help anyone?

The idea of unconditional love is true and usable

Love makes you feel whole regardless of your physical or emotional state

We endorse what we know to be true and usable

The idea of unconditional love is true and usable. In society's academic world, which thinks biology and psychology are one and the same, the crucial idea of unconditional love is too readily denigrated as wishful thinking.

The worldly attitude towards love, that it's only an emotion, is sad, but the limitations are self-imposed and unnatural. Don't bring that into your Sacred Space.

In your Sacred Space, you can do whatever you want, so you might as well do what brings you and your spouse the greatest happiness.

Attaining unconditional love is the epitome of success for anyone

In all the venues of life, individuals strive for venue-specific goals. In politics, it is power. In business, it is money. In health, it is physical soundness. In art, it is a recognized masterpiece, and so on. But life, itself, is a venue, too, which transcends all of life's subordinate venues, and its simple goal is happiness. All we want is to be happy.

We look for it everywhere, but always find happiness to be fleeting, at best, in any, and all, of the achievements of life, save one; unconditional love.

Love causes happiness

True and lasting happiness is never lacking for those who feel love, whether with family, friend, pet or someone who you randomly connected with, perchance, even for a moment. Love and happiness are inseparable.

Of course those who confuse love, with selfish desire (sex or security), may think they suffered because of love, but that is impossible, and those ideas of connecting suffering with love are examples of how biological drives and instincts easily pervert the meaning of love...

Love is completely different from life's material gains. Because love is not physical, emotional or material, it is impossible to define or measure love by

The senses, which measures everything

Or ideas, which quantifies "things"

Or time, which limits with boundaries of time

Love makes you feel whole, regardless of your physical or emotional state

Even though it cannot be adequately described by common words or concepts, the experience of love is undeniable, and the goal of experiencing unconditional love, which means unrestricted happiness, is absolutely achievable.

Is it not odd that the one thing every single human being craves, unconditional love, is not even mentioned in any text book, in any school?

The one true equalizer

The attainment of unconditional love is peerless, without a close second, yet no individual is prevented from having it, in as great a measure as is available to anyone else.

Is it not ironic, that when it comes to unconditional love, those who conquer nations, build mega corporations, or have the greatest personalities and sexiest look, still have no greater advantage over the most humble among us?

Money, power, health and popularity are, ultimately, empty rewards. They only last a short time. They do not self-generate nor last beyond waking, or the final breath. The ordinary goals of life, as much as they may beckon you, give no lasting satisfaction, other than what the mind attributes to it. But love, love is different.

Love is perfect

These ideals are attainable by any individual, not just when they are a couple; but they are especially there for you, who are married. All we have done is present a commonsense observation, of the true nature of marriage, as it's intended.

Unconditional marriage

We did not invent or discover unconditional love, nor the frameworks we describe. We discovered what others discovered, in other, esoteric, venues. These are proven methods, adjusted for your marriage.

Pure friendships and pure discipleships are the most obvious model venues for noble expression of unconditional love. But the greatest, most well-constructed models available to us all, for expressions of unconditional love, are pure, unconditional marriages.

That the ideals of selfless love, and service, fit within the necessities of the marriage venue perfectly is not a coincidence. What venue of life is more suited than marriage, to give individuals the security they need to progressively open their hearts to another, without worldly risk?

The marriage venue is ideally suited to express uninhibited selfless love

Despite any fears of commitment, a married couple agreed to be bound together, by the powers of contract, community acceptance, religious confirmation and mutual responsibilities.

The dynamics of any of the above, each on their own, would be enough to make each feel secure enough (if not for the counter balancing of the drives), that their relationship will last a lifetime.

.

Pure friendships and pure discipleships are the most obvious model venues for noble expression of unconditional love. But the greatest, most well-constructed models available to us all, for expressions of unconditional love, are pure, unconditional marriages

With awareness and acceptance of such powerful commitments, the opportunities to experiment with unconditional love are literally endless. Then, the connection becomes so real and so powerful that the contracts between the individuals are seen as tiny stepping-stones to what marriage is really all about; ever expanding intimate connection.

It is only sad that couples have not been given the tools to get along as you have, or they could take their relationship to the higher levels of love.

When you are not all the time wondering if he or she meant this or that, you can put all your intention on loving your spouse, whatever might be their or your latest error or temporary flaw.

Neither the past nor can common ideas can hold you back

Be assured, no matter how much your current scenario may have improved by following the "rules" in the first section the way is paved, and you will soon have a marriage where it is all about love.

We know what we present works, and when you use it, you will know too

We know what we present works, and when you use it, you will know too. When you ignore fears which you no longer need, your heart will soon soar in love. It is a process to get there for most, yes, of course. The mind has to be brought under your control. But it is a journey filled with great rewards all along the way.

It is of great value to become solid in your feelings and knowledge about what love is. Ideas of love are best grounded in reality.

Unconditional love is not an abstract concept or verb

Love may be 'accepted' by the worldly authorities, but, only as an abstract thought, or verbs (look it up in the dictionary and you will be surprised).

Unconditional love is not an abstract concept or verb

Material minds trained in biological/psychological sciences, believe if something cannot be measured, quantified and qualified, it may still be real. But they use real, in a vague sort of way, not being able to categorize it as more than an emotion, or an abstract idea.

A few, who are a bit too self-assured by their particular training, use "real" as a way to patronize us uneducated folks, but it is not real to them, as it is to us.

Calling love abstract is a disturbing distinction, which comes from those who do not consider the possibility of souls, and the like. Those good folks have been in charge of defining love? We disagree with them.

Maybe we might go along if the word 'abstract' did not reduce love's actual value, or if their intent was to allow for what they do not know, but their skepticism has taken root. We need to be honest about how this distinction impacts us.

Love is not a product of the mind

Allowing the suggestion that love is just a product of the mind, and then combining that with distrusting your intuition (instinctual biological defenses make us wary of our feelings), the idea of love being identified as abstract drastically diminishes its value, all the way down to an intangible pipe dream. It creates doubt about what you felt when you said "I do".

So, ultimately, you will start to distrust love, even though you have experienced it a billion times. This problem is serious.

Now is the time to bring forth your will and choose to trust what you feel, over what you heard from those who wish to bring you down to a loveless land, where no man or woman can survive as they should.

Have you ever felt love? Did you doubt it when you felt it? Trust your intuition!

We are taught to distrust love

Society's ideas of love are skeptical, and absurdly insecure.

You do not trust love, or what you have seen in the form of love's broken promises (when you blame the other person for not doing what you did not do either).

A common expression is "love is not enough". Or you think of love in silly little ways with not so silly deep expressions, which go on greeting cards, or in demonstrative binding ways like, "he's my brother, so I know he has my back." But you miss the unconditional love, which your soul craves, when you put love into those various little boxes, even though you have felt the real thing.

To make matters worse; and this is a huge consideration, calling love abstract, means love is the product of the mind, or thought. In other words, love is not equal to, or above the mind.

Love, when only seen as a thought, is not a stand alone, perceived and experienced by you, but according to these inadequate "safe" definitions, love only exists because your mind is able to create its existence.

Most scientists claim love is a product of the mind; they think it is subordinate to the mind. Ha!

That is crazy, and we all know it! Love does, absolutely does, exist on its own!

Love, in fact, is the highest, most tangible, and therefore, most reliable, reality

Just because one cannot "prove" its existence in a test tube, or with measured electrical charges, doesn't mean you are obligated to reduce it to a hallucination, or "wonder" if you should put trust in it.

Society's ideas of love are skeptical and absurdly insecure

Love is the highest, most tangible, and therefore, most reliable reality

If you agree with the scientists who follow the thinking that love is subordinate to the mind, maybe you still can have a very good marriage… maybe… by applying the laws we have shared with you thus far… maybe… We know the laws of right behavior work, but we do not have faith in marriages which are not based on unconditional love, but… but, maybe it can work for you.

Or, journey with us, into the higher science of unconditional love, and enjoy unconditional love, which is your marital right.

Love is not material, so it cannot be perceived by biological senses, or material science; so what!

Because physical senses cannot see, feel, hear, taste or smell love; that does not mean it is not there.

It only means you have to trust your intuition, your sixth sense; the reliable, though invisible, instrument of detection, which is the only sense that can know love.

Of course, we will continue to trust material science to explain material things, but it would be foolish to trust them to explain unconditional love. A scale detects gravity, a lens detects light, a thermometer detects temperature and your sixth sense detects love. You have to use the correct gauge to detect what you are looking for.

Would you deny the existence of unconditional love? Would you seriously believe it is only some figment of your imagination? Or, maybe you are willing to deprive yourself, by just saying you feel it, yes, but there is no reason to go beyond that.

Maybe you believe it is merely an emotion (which, we agree, emotions are of the mind), and you know how emotions are.

We want you to be blessed with the kind of marriage you would never trade for anything. We want you to look at your spouse and feel such joy and love, that you cannot wipe the smile off your face.

We want you to know because you know, not because you were told

You can learn how love and unconditional love works,. Everyone can, and we implore you; do not be satisfied until you really understand how to bring unconditional love into your life. If you learn nothing else, in your entire life, we affirm you should learn to love, unconditionally!

PLEASE, do not be satisfied with, 'kind of', getting this

Begin with who you are; a soul. As a soul you have a unique innate drive, just as the biological body does. Its innate drive is for love.

The soul's innate drive is to find, and live in, unconditional love, and this drive is every bit as powerful as the biological drive to survive. You, as a soul, *must have* unconditional love. And, not coincidentally, it is what you sought, and still seek, from your spouse.

Love is not material, so it cannot be perceived by biological senses or material science; so what!

You can learn how love and unconditional love works. Everyone can, and we implore you; do not be satisfied until you really understand how to bring unconditional love into your life.

You got married because you thought they would love you…unconditionally. And, don't forget, they married you, because in their mind, you were going to love them unconditionally. True? You know the answer!

Stronger than the drive to survive is the drive to feel unconditional love

Awareness of the drive to survive was probably obvious to you very quickly, because you have enough experiences, both vicariously and personally. You see it manifesting all the time. So, you are able to translate those experiences widely, and trace your behaviors to the drive.

Exposing the drive for unconditional love is just as simple

Our essence is love. Whereas the biological body we own, its essence is survival, is constantly prodding the mind to survive, the soul is constantly alluring its love. (Don't confuse love with biologically driven sex!).

The big difference is that the body, with all its demands, is annoying. The essence of all, love, is patiently waiting. So we are distracted.

Love is everything

Love, real love, is the ultimate panacea. It is always beneficial, and *all* satisfying. This is not an exaggeration, we mean all satisfying.

You never feel deprived, or insecure, when you feel love, nobody can. You cannot feel fear while you feel love. You would never trade love away; not for more money, a bigger house, a greater intellect or better reputation; nothing is superior.

When understood, by *feeling it*, love gives you the ability to move closer to it, move into it, and get more benefits from it. This it is what everyone wants, and you will not be happy until you have it, and you will not be happy until you give it.

Marriages (we mention this as a side note) do not dissolve because of mundane, material problems, like money or family troubles. Those are outer conditions, byproducts which spring from our biological drives and subsequent psychological instincts. Marriages only dissolve because love is lost to couples, unfelt because of a selfish focus on fear-instilling dilemmas. There is no circumstance that weighs in, which compares to love. When you have unconditional love, you can work through anything, and everything; not almost anything, but actually everything.

Decide; "I will have unconditional love", we will show you how

You know love is real and know it's what you want, and you know that you want it in unconditional form. You just need to know how.

First we will tell you how to get unconditional love in broad-brush terms too simple to use. Then, we will explain why it works. Then we explain how you can do what you need in order to have unconditional love in your marriage.

Prepare for internal battles

There is one itty bitty problem.

As soon as you begin to wrest control from your instincts, the drive to survive will go directly into panic mode. Just the thought of what you will do, from the body's point of view, is completely unacceptable.

Like a stubborn old person, set in their way, the drive controlled mind will absolutely flip out, because you are about to introduce the number one fear inducer, perceived as the greatest threat to life and limb; change!

Change is scary, because to an instinct enslaved mind, routine creates security. Routine is very positive, yes, but only for those who are in control and stay in control over their habits. For those in control, routine is a real time saver; but for an enslaved mind, it is a prison without an outside view.

But, not to worry! The mind will eventually see how the new arrangements you impose upon it, actually reduce risk to the biological body. Then all your current instincts can be reworked, or removed (a lifelong vocation).

The reason your body is not on your side is because it does not have a soul. You are the soul who inhabits it. Think of it as a machine you drive around in. It has all its little computers so it looks "smart", but it isn't.

Receive unconditional love, by *giving* unconditional love

When you give love, you receive love, **but it isn't like you think!** *Most who read this think, from their experiences in life, that this is another* cause and effect *equation, as exists in physics, physical and human, but it is not.* You cannot use the material laws of cause and effect to impact love.

Or, they think it is some kum-ba-ya kind of thing, like we tell our six year old kids about the "spirit" of the Easter bunny, but it is not that either.

This is, absolutely, an actual equation, that works like mathematics. The science behind this equation is real and, although it is probably new thinking for you, it is very important for you to really understand it.

And remember, your mind is going to look for every loose nail, and possible reason, to deny this, so keep your mind's resistance at bay. Think it through, until it clicks; it will definitely click!

Love is immediately experienced by the one giving love

The above is worth repeating, and adding a new part. Love is immediately experienced by the giver of love, and *barely felt (if at all)* by the intended recipient.

Those who have children know very well the experience of love, when they clearly experience how their love, flowing out, is far more evident than love coming to them.

While a parent looks upon a sleeping child, who because they are asleep, is obviously not giving love in return, the parent's heart is filled with incomparable love. Logic dictates what the instinct protected mind would like to distort; **it is the outward flow of love which gives us the true experience of love.**

It is the outward flow of love, which is the true experience of love

Yes, it is true, all of us wish to feel we are loved, but our "need" to be loved is caused by the drive to survive.

The survival drive's instincts want to keep its organism surrounded by those who will provide protection i.e. those who love us.

But you miss the point of how to actually feel love when you take orders, in the form of compulsions, from an organism which only has an agenda of physical survival. You cannot really feel love when it comes to you. You can only think you are loved by the other's behaviors.

Your walls won't let love in, from anyone

You are not capable of feeling any more than a trickle of love when it comes from someone. Your walls and filters, no matter how much you may try to be open, do not open up past the point where your instincts warn of too much exposure, vulnerability.

It is the rarest of moments when you feel anything near perfect love from another (it will happen for you more and more as you progress), because then the mind freaks out, and shuts it off.

You can, on the other hand, love another, with as much intensity as you choose, to the point where you feel all of the outward flow, just as you do with your kids, because it is very safe.

The mind is threat averse

When your mind determines there is no threat, as with your children, the outward flow of your love is both constant, and powerful, so you say, "I cannot believe how much I love my child." You do not stop to figure out what is really happening, as above, or why. But the point is clear, and simple; you can only feel love to your personal degree of comfort, and only when you give it.

When someone loves you, you may or may not even know they love you. Of course, you can surmise love coming from another by their actions, as a child knows love from their parent by their protection and selfless nurturing; but the actual feeling of love, you produce that with your giving.

Those who speak unkindly of others, blaming them for not being vulnerable, are fooling themselves. They do not realize they cannot really feel love either, at least not as recipients.

It is the outward flow of love, which is the true experience of love

It is the rarest of moments when you feel anything near perfect love from another

They blame their lover for not loving them enough, not recognizing the impossibility of what they ask for.

The following is probable, if not authoritative

Love is not a thought, or feeling, or any kind of product of the mind. Based on simple logic, we are certain of this. Love is; it just is. And though detectible in countless ways, by far, the easiest way to feel love is by loving another. And this is where and how it all comes together. The equation looks like this

The love you give to your spouse, whether they consciously feel it or not, will be detectable by you, in greater measure than you give. The only way you can feel unconditional love, the only way, is when you give it unconditionally.

Then, when your spouse's heart is aroused by your sincere effort, they will (probably) be inspired to open their heart to you.

Why?

Without pinpointing the ultimate source of love, we are sure of one thing; individual minds do not create love. Love just is, and is drawn from a source (mostly), as well as from a reservoir of love residing within our hearts.

Although it is fascinating that individuals take credit for things they had no direct impact upon, such as looks or intelligence, it is even funnier that we take credit for our children; as if we had any idea of the time of conception, much less any details about who will enter our family!

But the goofiest, is thinking we create love. We cannot even define it; how can we imagine we can create it?

Love is, we know that, and we also know we can give it. So, we should work with what we know.

Here is what we know. We know we can give love, and we will talk later about the unconditional part, and we know we can express love in two main ways, both of which are important.

You can express love with your heart, and you can express love with your behaviors, including thoughts, words and deeds.

Hearts love

The heart we describe is not the physical heart, but is the soul's heart (where you feel love, is physically in the same place as your physical heart). Every single human being has felt love and felt it in their heart.

Imagine your heart with an opening in the front, like the opening of a water hose or pipe. Direct (as in mentally push) love towards your soul-mate or to others.

We cannot define love; how can we imagine we create it?

Directing your love takes will power and is, by far, the absolute best use of it. Directing love towards your spouse is always the wisest choice you can ever make, no matter what else you can choose from. For the "what-if-ers" out there, you will discover we are not exaggerating when you make the effort we describe.

Will is the valve which opens, closes or directs the flow of love

You choose whom you love, you choose with how much intensity you love with, and you choose how long you focus your love on the recipient, your spouse.

The operative is free will, will power. None can ever be compelled to love. What happens within; that is your business; and only yours.

Nor, because of free will, can you be told when or who not to love, not even by your drive-driven mind. It is your will and your will alone, which determines who will receive your love and to what degree. You are about to discover something. Try this exercise.

Tapping the source of love

Visualize an opening in the back of your heart (or the top of your head) to be an inlet. Use your imagination to feel it as an opening which only receives pure love, maybe from an unlimited reservoir, which you picture in the vast sky. Imagine liquid love flowing into the receiving gates of your heart and mind.

Visualize the liquid love, and feel it, feel it fill your heart, and bubble up into your mind, and all of you. Feel it oozing out of your eyes, your ears your pores, and surrounding you. Feel it as warmth, protecting and embracing.

Now, visualize a vast gate on the front of your heart, which grows to a size much greater than your body. Your heart, in your mind's eye will grow to any size, as love is without end, and unrestrained by anything physical.

Love will grow within you and never burst you, because your heart grows with it. Now use your will.

Open the gates of your heart toward your soul mate. Pour the love all over them. Picture them in your mind's eye, maybe with your eyes closed, being bathed in your love.

Pour your heart's love all over your soul mate, in greater and greater volume. Push it through your heart, with internal words of caring and encouragement.

Tell them, in your mind, that you do not wish to judge them, no matter what. Tell them with tenderness that you do not wish to criticize them or point out their flaws; but you love them no matter what, even if they hurt you.

Will is the valve which opens, closes or directs the flow of love

Love will grow within you and never burst you, because your heart grows with it

Pour out your love to them

Send silent messages of good will, devotion and loyalty to your best friend and lover.

Fill the mental spaces with words of praise and kindness, While at the same time feel your heart expand, as the love flows out in greater and greater volume, as your heart becomes you, and you become the love. Keep this up, until your heart is all you feel, gushing with love for them.

Do your best to not allow the inevitable errant thoughts to ruin your experience, even though they will try; maybe not the first time, but soon after, because, as you must always recall, the instinct enslaved mind does not like you becoming vulnerable.

When doubts and anger surface, do your best to calm your mind. Speak to your mind as you would a child; that works sometimes. Tell your mind "everything will be better if we take this new tack", you can live in joyous love when you realign with the love pouring through the gates of the heart.

Over time, your mind will adjust to this superior tact. It will be won over

Don't be discouraged by the difficulty, or persistence of the resistance.

You have been building walls for so long. Your fears are shallow, but your instincts are trained for life or death, and not on your side. It takes time.

You have been building walls for so long. Your fears are shallow, but your instincts are trained for life or death, and not on your side. It takes time.

It takes less time then you may imagine, after you first experience the intensity, but when you hear all the complaining in your head, all the resistance from the drive-produced instincts, it may seem impossible at times, but it does not matter. You really have no choice but to battle your own mind.

Technically, of course you have a choice. But, if you have been paying attention you gather that if you do not get control over your mind, but choose to come up with justifications for anger and blame, you will just have to face the same moments of challenge someday in the future. It doesn't get any easier later on. The choice is to get your mind under control now, or you can keep on suffering until you do.

FAQ's

How often should I do this practice? At least a few times a day, especially practice this visualization during sex. Otherwise increase the frequency, until you discover your heart is constantly open, and the love is constantly flowing to your spouse

For how long should I do it? Rather than a time, think about three stages

a) feel the flow of love, then

b) feel it take over, then

c) enjoy as long as you can

What if I'm angry? Override those unhealthy thoughts, reminding yourself they are your instincts trying to protect the body, then flood your heart with love, even as you are segregating out the anger

What if my spouse is mad at me? Experiment, and you will see, when you are sincere in your effort, this effort will heal your relationship faster than anything else you can say or do; it is like prayer. Don't try to pander or confront

Do I stop when things are getting better? No way! You want to do this forever, with deeper, and deeper concentration

What if we are not living together? This effort does not require physical contact. It heals both of you, mostly the one doing it, but is also felt as peace by the receiver (though they cannot detect where it comes from).

What does unconditional love mean?

Unconditional love means you love your spouse with all your heart, mind and soul. It means you do not taint your love with thoughts which pollute love, such as anger, apathy, argumentative, bossy, critical, complaining, corrosive, condemning, deceptive, harmful, judgmental, mean, nasty, ridiculing, sarcastic, vexatious etc.

It means you accept your spouse for who they are, not who you think you want them to be, at the moment. It means you continuously and consciously renew your vows, over and over, and disallow your mind to entertain any kind of expectations.

Accept your spouse for who they are, not who you think you want them to be at the moment

Completely eliminate ideas of reciprocation, appreciation or anything which reduces your love to a business arrangement; and you to a beggar.

Learn to love because you want to love, not because something will come back to you for the love you give.

If your spouse notes your change and thanks you, don't receive thanks. After all, what you are doing is working for you more than them. Instead, be thankful they feel loved, because all you want is for them to be happy. Be thankful they are in your life.

The second part is training your mind

The above is the way of the heart, and the way of the mind is just as important. Neither should be neglected.

Your spouse should see, by your behavior, that your desire to please them is sincere

Train your mind. Do for your spouse out of love, and infuse your words and behaviors with your heart's love. Never miss an opportunity to praise and uplift.

Your spouse should see, by your behavior, that your desire to please them is sincere and without expectation. If you do not get positive feedback of any kind, remind yourself you should not care, but will redouble your efforts until your mind is no longer complaining.

Your mind only complains because it is worried that you, the body, will die, but you will not die by loving your spouse without getting anything in return.

Your mind will do all it can to "protect" you. It is ill-mannered and ruthless. It is up to you to discipline your mind and behave with human grace and contentment. When the results come, your mind will tell you it is okay now, time to get something out of this program for you. Don't fall for it! Never cease being the giver.

Nor is this a competition. Some think they will show their spouse how noble they are. If you do that, you will have tainted your love.

Your mind will always try to trick you out of being a lover

As you practice this, you will see how incredibly devious the mind is, and how it comes up with all kinds of excuses to stop, some of which are very "reasonable".

It is up to you to discipline your mind and behave with human grace and contentment

You have to be on constant mind patrol. Listen for reactions which tell you when you are not being sincere. This is not an overnight thing. It begins with a transition time, and then the good habits begin to take over for you. But they are always challenged by the body, which is paranoid and greedy. There are stages many go through

1) Some make some half-hearted efforts (no matter how strong you think they are)

2) They begin to feel irked by their spouse's insensitivity, and question if it will work

3) They will commit to a self-prescribed trial period-Doomed!

4) They will read this all again, and start to consider it more seriously

Or, you can go for it and save a lot of time and suffering

Love is different, and cannot be relegated to, or circumscribed by, material laws

Remember, love is not circumscribed by material rules of any kind. All the equations used in physical (which includes verbal communications) venues do not apply to love. But, the equations in the science of love are just as solid.

Your effort will determine the results

Notice how we say you can observe the equations, in practice?

If your efforts did not produce results or only promised far-off results, we would not call this scientific. Scientific means if you follow the same prescribed conduct, you will get the same results.

You will have the same experience of results, when you correctly do your part, as we, and anyone else has. This is not a promise, anymore than telling you what goes up will come down is a promise; it is just a fact.

Don't expect outer results. The inner ones are the ones that count

Giving love does not mean the person you give love to will love you back. Nor does it mean the love you give will come back to you from some unanticipated source, sometime in the future.

Of course, all your acts, whether good, bad or indifferent, will most definitely come back to you in some form, but there is a universal intelligence which does those infinite calculations. It is a waste of time for us or you to try to understand the grand equation of cause and effect for purposes of improving your marriage because love laws transcend material laws.

Besides, the "what goes around comes around" crowd usually, conveniently forgets that what has just come around is something they initiated. But that doesn't matter, because love doesn't travel like that.

Begin with the basics

Unconditional love is, by definition, not dependent on anything given in return. Love just is, remember. So if the blocks of love are removed, love is all that is left.

You can give love, even if you do not fully understand it, by setting some ground rules for yourself, many of which you, hopefully, already have begun to re-infuse into your relationship. The first lines of action are loving words, inflections and behaviors.

Force yourself, in the beginning. When you face your bad habits, you have to force yourself, or you will just do what you have always done. Force yourself to speak only words of loving kindness. Force yourself to behave in ways which communicate love. Force yourself to smile at your spouse, tell them how much you appreciate them.

The second line of action is to rearrange your thoughts. Thoughts create words and actions, so you have to stop those thoughts of resentment and vindictiveness from dragging you lower and lower.

But don't just stop the marriage-destructive thoughts, reverse them. Replace habitual thoughts of misery with habitual thoughts of praise, support and admiration.

Be strong! Never give in to thoughts or ideas which take you off track. You will not perish by holding your tongue, even if your tongue is filled with venom, but it is better to perish from holding it, than letting it rip into your spouse and pull your marriage into the streets.

Practice until you become competent, then proficient, then expert

For the vast majority of us, when we got married, learning about marriage was no different than your older cousin throwing you off the boat to teach you how to swim. Not many world class swimmers started their swimming lessons that way!

All your acts, whether good, bad or indifferent, will most definitely come back to you in some form, but there is a universal intelligence which does those infinite calculations

Be strong! Never give in to thoughts or ideas which take you off track

Those who do well in any avocation have to start with the basics, slowly perfecting their skills through practice, and then when they are proficient, they push themselves into un-chartered territory of expertise.

When you got married, you had less than no training. You were given terrible advice. Now, the first thing to do is stop doing what hurts your spouse; get back to the basics. But, it doesn't mean you have to wait until you are a competent married person before you go for the grand prize. Unconditional love is yours, as soon as you turn your energies towards experiencing it.

You want love

Most of us just want to be loved. All of us want to be loved without being judged. You want to be loved no matter what you say, do, think or believe. You want to be loved simply because you exist, and you believed you found that in the institution of marriage. Well, you did.

All of us want to be loved without being judged. You want to be loved no matter what you say, do, think or believe

You came to the right place when you got married, but you need to go in the right direction, with the right knowledge, so you can have what you wanted in the first place; unconditional love.

The shift is an about-face in expectation. You need to stop wanting to receive love from your spouse. We know, for some, that seems preposterous, but it is accurate. Go back and read again if you do not understand, or contact us. Get unstuck, so you can have the love you want.

Direct all your effort towards loving your spouse. Ask yourself, ask them, what will make them feel loved; off-the-charts loved. This is the new you. Put all your effort into making your spouse feel loved.

Every time you feel doubt, like you might "go too far", push yourself, regardless of how much it humiliates your drives-controlled mind.

Your obstacles will fall away

The difficulties you encounter, in spite of your legitimate quest for love, are driven by the selfishness rooted in the body's needs. It is literally a war between the bodily drives, and the soul, that causes all the trouble.

On one hand, the body is demanding you put all of your mind's attention on keeping it alive and procreating. The drives of the body are relentlessly compelling and demanding. On the other hand, the soul is seeking unfoldment, in your expression of selfless love; but only as an invitation. The drive for unconditional love is less a drive, but more of a golden invitation.

It is an epic struggle

The mind is pulled by the allure of love while being assailed by a body, which is afraid it won't be taken care of. The internal conflict never ceases!

It is up to each individual to choose between the sides. The choices, when not made intentionally, are already made for you, by the habits of satisfying the bodily instincts.

It never becomes completely intuitive to go with selfless love. The choice for love has to be made over and over, because the soul is silent, while the bodily demands are boisterous.

The most important purpose of marriage is to learn how to give and receive love; how to experience love by choosing the allure of love over the screams of the body.

This science of love is worth learning

To imagine ways to give unconditional love, you only need to ask yourself what would make you think someone was giving you unconditional love; then do those things you think of. The list of things will include all sorts of things

> Be interested in what they think, and what is important to them, and show your interest by asking questions, and trying to really see things the way they do

> Appreciate them, for who they are, and show it, by not trying to correct them or prove you know a better way

> Listen to them, with full attention, when they speak

> Admire their taste in clothes, food, art, music and other of their observations, and show it by acknowledging them; even when their taste is different than yours

Make a vow to yourself that you will do this and then stick with it. Start with a short time span, like twenty-four hours, so you can renew your vow again and again, until your mind gives way to your heart, and you are again living in joyful matrimony.

Forget the adages about not going to sleep without making up—don't get in a fight. Treat your spouse in ways that make her, or him, want you forever. Never give cause for an altercation.

The effort required to do the right thing, no matter how great, produces miniscule suffering when you compare it to the suffering that comes from not doing (or trying to do) the right thing.

It never becomes completely intuitive to go with selfless love

The effort required to do the right thing, no matter how great, produces miniscule suffering when you compare it to the suffering that comes from not doing (or trying to do) the right thing

Always treat your spouse as the most important person in your life

Everything will be fine, for you, when you remember to love your spouse with all you have and show it in ever more creative ways.

Remember

Earth will always be Earth; but if you behave like an angel, you will have heaven on Earth.

Earth will always be Earth; but if you behave like an angel, you will have heaven on Earth

© *The Marriage Foundation*

- Chapter Nine -
Control Your Mind

⬥⬥⬥

Recognizing your mind as a wonderful tool that belongs to you
will change your life and how you live it. You will see how either you control it,
or your drive driven mind will continue to control you.

⬥⬥⬥

"Control yourself" is a phrase each child is familiar with. But what if children are told "control your mind"? This distinction is far more loaded than one may first imagine. It is a distinction which gives you the power to really change your life. You will learn how the mind works and that you are not it, but rather its owner and master.

Chapter Nine

Control Your Mind

A venerable and essential principle each of us has to recognize and accept in order to have a successful marriage, or a successful anything else for that matter, is that your mind is controllable and, more importantly, you have to learn how to control it… but never attempt to control anyone else's.

You *have to* learn how to control your mind

No matter how difficult you find it to be (and, admittedly, it's the greatest of all challenges), there is no way around this imperative of life. Without the ability to control your mind any possible success will be serendipitous, random, and temporary; at best.

You *have to* stop trying to control your spouse, and their mind

This life-saving rule ranks at the very top. No matter how many ways you spin it or try to justify with whatever rationales you or anyone else come up with; any and every thought or effort, subtle or overt, to control your spouse will, as a matter of cold hard fact, undermine all your other efforts for the deep connection and meaningful relationship you seek.

If you are thinking about ways your spouse can change to meet your expectations you are not thinking about how wonderful they are, nor feeling your love flow from your heart to theirs.

Honor your spouse, by honoring their free will

As you stick with your intentions to honor your spouse you will see how the drives relentlessly try to undermine your efforts by trying to get them to see things your way; which is nothing but a bit more subtle way to control their mind and put you in power. The drives put your survival ahead of what is right.

Your spouse was not born so they could live up to your standards of correctness, your ideas of morality or your personal perspective of wisdom. Each person has the innate right to choose their ways, big and small. It's also your innate right to choose yours. It is immature to expect conformance from your spouse.

Further, it is not your right to point out their flaws or their possibilities for improvement (unless requested). But it is your obligation, as a matter of common decency, to hold your tongue, and replace any negativity or judgment with kindness and support.

It is your obligation to make every possible effort, to do the very best you can to control your mind so you can find happiness. Make the effort without ugly strain. Positive strain is fine; the same kind of strain you might exert while playing a sport you enjoy, or gain a higher proficiency in something you enjoy, like music.

You have to learn how to control your mind

Your spouse was not born so they could live up to your standards of correctness, your ideas of morality or your personal perspective of wisdom

Effort to control your mind is the most beneficial effort you will ever make, so make it with enthusiasm. Be proud of catching your mind before it gets you in trouble. Be vigilant. Listen to your words, always checking them for hints of crossing the line.

Go further

It isn't enough to stop doing those things which undermine your relationship. Removing a dilapidated shack doesn't do anything constructive for the neighborhood. You have to *replace* your old bad habits with the most beautiful behaviors you can imagine.

What do you imagine is the number one thing your spouse would appreciate? Do it, then. Purposeful correct actions are the only things that bring you to desired results.

Your right efforts will bring your desired results

Too many of you think are doing the best you can. You cannot imagine why you are not appreciated.

This world is brutal when it comes to making demands upon you. If you allow your mind to put you in the "I can't win so I might as well give up" box, your suffering will continue.

This world is brutal when it comes to making demands upon you. If you allow your mind to put you in the "I can't win so I might as well give up" box your suffering will continue. The reason you are learning is so you know what to do to improve, not so you can feel like a toad for everything you have ever done wrong.

Please, do not miss the point. Take credit for wanting to make the right kind of effort that will change everything. But, at the same time you simply cannot take responsibility for not doing in the past what you did not know anything about…Your life begins with every new moment. The past is gone. When you do the best you can you will change your future.

What your mind is

Ultimately your mind is quite an amazing tool which is at your disposal; that is your mind is at YOUR disposal, while your spouse's mind is at THEIR disposal.

Many correctly think their spouse has no right to impose their thoughts and feelings on them. However, usually for some contrived subjective reasons which are only important to them they have no problem intruding on their spouse. You have the right to object to intrusions upon you, but you also have the obligation to not intrude.

Yes, of course it is easier to give advice to another rather than yourself, but it is a huge waste of time and that is not the end of the trouble it causes. Intrusion aggravates the communication problems you have with your spouse. Nobody wants to be controlled. But everyone still wants to be heard.

Uncontrolled minds, or minds used unwisely, are destructive

Minds are the ultimate two-edged sword. When used properly yours can be utilized to bring you all the happiness you will ever desire, along with great friendships and love in great abundance.

But, if you continue to let yours be completely run by drives and their subsequent instincts, so that it is effectively running on auto-pilot; or, if you entrust it to others out of fear, or an attempt to get along with a group or because of laziness; you will suffer.

The mind is a tool, your tool. Yours will serve you when you take control over it.

Is there any question about whether you should, or not?

Use your mind to take you in directions of your choice

It is fascinating, really; your uncontrolled mind is the cause of your greatest suffering while your mind is supposed to be the cause of your greatest freedom. You choose, in every instance, which it will be by your deliberate actions or dumb laziness.

The idea is to gain control over your mind to the point where it becomes useful to you and your marriage; rather than let it do its own thing.

Utilize anything, including mental tricks, courses in mind control, meditation or anything else that helps you gain progressively more control over your mind so you can bring a progressively better "you" to your lover and your marriage.

But, at the very least become aware of what is going on with your mind.

We have consistently seen people's lives improve disproportionately to their efforts. Your marriage will gradually become what you want it to become, as you gain more and better control over your mind.

Just thinking about this is not enough

Only reading about change will not change you. **There is no chance for improvement without specific effort.** You have to commit yourself to escalating efforts. But even a little effort will change your life, so don't allow fear or discouragement to beat you back.

You can do this! Anyone can do this!

You would be surprised to hear some of the success stories from people who everyone gave up on. Some initially thought controlling their mind was hopeless but they made the effort anyway, and now they have incredible marriages (and much better lives). They couldn't stand to suffer any more and finally understood it was not their spouse, but rather their misunderstanding that caused all their pain.

Education about the mind is vital for your success

It always was vital and it always will be. It is not that you have to be a psychologist to be happily married or that it would be enough, by itself, to give you what you need.

You have to know how your mind does things so you can make it work for you!

The mind is a tool, your tool. Yours will serve you when you take control over it

Education about the mind is vital for your success

Neglecting to control your mind by leaving it on auto-pilot is a sloppy and dangerous way to live

You can choose to go on without learning about your mind or not do anything with what you learn, and you will continue suffering; or, you can start to take control.

If you think you can succeed or find happiness without controlling your mind you are wrong

Of course, you can influence your mind just enough to get by if that is the best you can do. Or you can work towards outright control over it; the choice is yours. But admit you are far too often a victim of moods, urges and unhealthy desires.

When you see gnarly traits in someone else which you will see in yourself (when you look), you are critical of them. You expect them to change.

The terrible traits are terrible in you, too! So, of course you need to know *how* to control your mind, because it is impossible to improve anything in your life if you don't. Taking control is a choice which requires intention, and then action.

You have to do something. Just intention, alone, will not work.

This is simplicity itself

You need to understand the reasons you 'automatically' see things in certain ways and then learn how you can shift your perspective by taking your mind off of auto-pilot.

It means a better life for you when you do so.

One of the many benefits that come from making the effort to control your mind is you will develop a deeper appreciation for what everyone else is going through. So a cool byproduct is you become less judgmental. Not surprisingly, being judgmental is always a hidden symptom of a hurting marriage.

Seeing your mind as a "possession" is a profound philosophical distinction

Recognize your mind is not you but a possession which, because of your neglect, acts more like your boss and a crazy troublemaker. Your mind is supposed to be your disciplined servant!

But making the point that "you" control your mind automatically brings up a potentially controversial philosophical point. Though getting sidetracked into any type of controversy is a waste of time, we have to explain this principle in a way which defines "who" is in charge in a way that is both crystal clear, and visual.

At this juncture being politically correct would be a great disservice, so if you don't believe in souls please don't give in to being offended. Maybe it would help if you substitute the term "higher self-consciousness".

Are you a mind… or a soul? This should be obvious!

Most nonsectarian academicians try to avoid the concept of souls, etc. (very wise choice actually, considering the infinite number of concepts, and how personal each one is to the beholder), and settles for considering "you" to be a mind/body…At least that's the best we ever find as a descriptor.

But we, and we are also categorically non-sectarian (no religious affiliations), as do many others, believe you are a soul, irrespective of religion, or no religion; who has a mind, and has a body.

We need to digress

But before we address the issue of "who" is responsible to control your mind and how that is done; there is an individually based societal problem we must first address that stems from individual widespread misunderstandings.

Drugs and alcohol

True euphoria comes from the singular experience of love

The ability to experience sexual pleasure or experience more open-heartedness is only falsely enhanced by using mind altering substances.

The so-called euphoria which substances induce is a misinterpretation of what is actually happening.

You just can't justify calling biological and mental destruction "euphoria" no matter how much it appears to mimic some of the manifestations. True euphoria is nothing like drunkenness or little buzzes that come from substance abuse.

Intoxicants' side effects are costly

The physical destruction of brain stuff which causes the highs reduces your ability to enjoy much greater experiences!

It is hard enough to wrest control from instincts and habits! When you indulge you are effectively turning your mind over to poisons which, even for short periods (not talking tiny indulgences like occasional wine) mitigate your efforts to control your mind.

The mind has incredible powers which you have not yet explored, so it's best to not give away your control. When you use intoxicants you are both reducing your experience of the moment and your potential to enjoy the moment.

People don't realize the power they have to turn every moment into a euphoric experience without outer stimulation because it is not taught. If they knew they would never trade off the power to attain true happiness by killing brain cells.

True euphoria comes from the singular experience of love

People don't realize the power they have to turn every moment into a euphoric experience, without outer stimulation, because it is not taught

Even the so-called "harmless" drugs are devious

Substances don't contribute to creativity or intelligence as falsely claimed by users (a clue is that only users are the ones who say it). When not prescribed they reduce will power, which is like draining gas from your fuel tank.

Happiness depends on properly using your will power! Will power is your most precious gift!

Additionally, your intelligence suffers from substance abuse as you brain cells perish and synapses collapse.

The "positives" never materialize; they are lies

People think intoxicants open them up. They don't understand the walls and instincts which need to come down in marriage need to come down by building trust and intimacy, not by drugging the mind. Nobody taught us these ideas, or how to build bridges of love but we intuitively know they are realistic.

If you used a lot of drugs or alcohol (why are they different??) and currently have some addictions you will need to regain your self-control. It may be difficult, but you have to start sometime.

Don't confuse medication with drugs

A doctor prescribes medication for the purpose of providing a temporary (could be a long time) crutch so an individual can regain their strength. That's not using drugs.

There is nothing wrong with sensible usage of drugs when prescribed by competent physicians. They help the mind and body heal by fighting off an attacker or fortifying a weakened physiology. Prescribed drugs are a blessing

There is nothing wrong with sensible usage of drugs when prescribed by competent physicians. They help the mind and body heal by fighting off an attacker or fortifying a weakened physiology. Prescribed drugs are a blessing.

But using substances for other reasons is almost always detrimental. Temporary feelings from abuse are the result of electrical short circuits, usually caused by physiological brain destruction or chemical rerouting which weakens the will.

Sexual enhancement will come from love, not wine

Drinking wine, spirits or smoking pot before sex creates more problems for people who are already disconnected from their heart or afraid to be connected, or pretend they are connected by being passionate when they're stoned.

People need to find authentic soul love, not get sidetracked

In other words there is no benefit derived from drug use. On the contrary, the physiological and mental impacts of substances (when not used for medical purposes) upon the brain are universally detrimental.

The use of un-prescribed drugs including alcohol is a road of and towards suffering. Those who imagine they are in control of the drugs or alcohol are deluded. The use of substances always moves the victim towards increase until they finally make the effort to stop. It may not be easy to quit even for those who only have a glass of wine a day, but they should try.

Habitual users need to do all they can to break their addictions or dependencies. If you read this as being preachy rather than as non-judgmental information; well, you probably have a problem.

The solution is to find love; and it is very simple for you (though the mind will "pooh-pooh" it) who are married. **Learn to love your spouse unconditionally.** Make that your most important mission in life. Put their needs, no matter how petty or unfair they seem, ahead of any other desire.

Why people use intoxicants

The use of substances, we surmise, is a futile attempt to escape the loneliness and desperation of feeling unloved. People who experience love never want to reduce or cloud those real feelings.

Although some young people who use drugs may insist they know they are loved they are intellectualizing. There's no reason to experiment with drugs if you actually feel love, the ultimate panacea. Young people need to be taught to give love so they can experience the real thing.

The trouble is not only do substances not work so the experimenter keeps increasing their dosage; but they incrementally reduce their will power, thus reducing their ability to make the necessary changes that would bring love into their life.

Usage pushes the individual further from their need. Self-pity, other's pity, condemnation by self and others; or running away from current circumstances never gains one the love they crave.

The only cure for loneliness and all other vexations is to learn to love. There is no other cure because the drive for love must eventually be satisfied in the only way it can be; by loving another.

Wanting to be loved won't bring you love

Most people seek love by becoming attractive or otherwise useful to another, hoping they will please them and so be loved in return. They are always disappointed.

Although those efforts may create some dependency, it won't produce the kind of love you seek and need. The kind of love every one of us needs to seek can only be experienced by being the unattached giver of love, as described in the previous chapter.

Only the giver of unconditional love can know unconditional love.

The solution is to find love; and it is very simple for you (though the mind will "poohpooh" it) who are married

Only the giver of unconditional love can know unconditional love

Looking everywhere for love (when it is within you)

We absolutely do not condemn anyone who is in pain, even when they try to ease their pain with harmful attempts such as with the use of intoxicants or other forms of escape. So please do not take our words as finger pointing. It is only information.

We clearly recognize the tremendous burden of loneliness, even in marriages, so we never condone condemnation. We seek for you the only panacea, which is learning to love <u>unconditionally</u>.

Because of the overuse and nearly universal social acceptance of alcohol and drugs it is worth identifying the real underlying reason for so much addiction. Thankfully, your marriage can very well be the way to experience the cure - love is all you will ever need. Those, and there are many who found what they are looking for within their marriage, do not have to swear off anything as they are fulfilled by the love they give their spouse. It is then that suppressed and depressing desires to run away through intoxication typically simply fall away.

Because of the overuse and nearly universal social acceptance of alcohol and drugs, it is worth identifying the real underlying reason for so much addiction

≈

Now, back to the topic we were on, about who is in charge of and controlling your mind

≈

Distinguishing your mind, from "you" will be the most beneficial thing you will ever do

Have you ever thought of your mind as being some "thing" that you as a user can control?

As you develop a human/servant relationship with your mind you will see how much power it gives you to gain this sense of division.

Your mind is exquisitely elaborate. But despite its complexity it's still designed in a way where anyone can control their own. The fundamental controls are simple.

What you are learning now will eventually be taught in school, from early childhood, so future generations don't face the same challenges we do. All things are assimilated more easily by youthful minds. But because this is so logical anyone can learn it at any age. Still, change is always a tricky thing.

Imagine yourself as being apart from and above your mind

Visualize you at a control panel controlling your brain.

Your mind is a user-friendly supercomputer. Logic dictates that some "one" must be ultimately in charge. Some "one "outside of the computer has to monitor and control your mind.

There are two possibilities

a) Either the mind controls itself… or

b) You, a soul, are the "one", the "You" who controls the mind.

This isn't complex when you realize that you are a soul

You are in charge of your mind. In fact, there can't be a logical explanation of how a mind can control itself.

It is the soul who has the free will, not the mind. And, as a bonus this premise means you and your spouse are soul-mates, not mind-mates.

Visualize a computer in your head which you control with intention and will power
It is scientifically known that your liver, heart, and lungs, are all regulated by your mind, as are all the other organs, and all the processes of your body.

You the soul master your mind, and enjoy your life as *master* of your life, not live as a passenger or victim of fate.

You can question invisible radio waves too if you wish

The concept of a soul is questioned by those who have to see test tube experiments. But just because science cannot measure something does not mean it isn't there. If that kind of thinking was accurate light waves would not have existed until they were discovered and "proven".

The proof that the soul exists and is in charge of your mind can be experienced. That is how we know it is accurate. When you do as we suggest you will see for yourself that the mind is your possession. That when you tell it to think of a sunny beach, it will.

We don't care whether you call your actual self a soul or use some other term. We only insist that your mind is controllable, and you won't have power over your life until you learn to control it.

You can experience what controls your mind every time you control it

You use thought impulses, your original creations, to control your mind.

Most of your thoughts are currently tainted with fears and instincts. But you are able to change your thoughts from those of being enslaved by fears and instincts to constructive joy-producing thoughts.

The final authority over your thoughts is you, soul. When you pay attention you will see the taints and remove them.

You are in charge of your mind. In fact, there can't be a logical explanation of how a mind can control itself

We don't care whether you call your actual self a soul or use some other term. We only insist that your mind is controllable

Even though you may not fully understand the actual mechanics of how software works within your computer, similarly your mind is *your* personal possession and will do what you want even though you cannot build one. You only have to learn which buttons do what.

Don't be intimidated by having to learn something new, this is too important.

The mind has incredible processing power with infinite memory and storage. It is a great tool.

There are numerous default and hidden programs working behind the scenes giving you nearly limitless power, waiting for you to discover them.

Seeing yourself as a soul is more of a practical than a religious thing

When you are at the controls of your mind, when you start getting some idea of how it works, you will feel safer than if you go with the natural flow of life.

"Going with the flow" actually means allowing instincts, habits and whims to run things. You should be in charge of your life. That is how it is set up, and meant to be!

As the king soul you can benefit from a practical detachment which allows you to make decisions with objectivity. You can try different solutions to your challenges, experimenting until you find what works best.

It's your mind so it has to obey you. As you gain a deeper awareness of the separation between you and your mind you will see the power it gives you. It is truly incomparable.

You are used to being a slave of your habits and instincts

It's only because you are used to the current arrangement with your mind that it seems normal to do its bidding; but it isn't "normal" for your mind to be in charge of you. You will see.

As you question your instinctive decisions and start to see the survival roots of your bad traits like greed, fear, lust, power, etc., you will see how your mind cheats you. In many situations you do things you aren't happy with, even as you do it.

When you see you are not your mind you won't have to take everything personally or react to fears, lusts or whatever; you will have choices.

When you make a mistake because you got caught by entrenched habits or instincts you can recognize it as a mistake (in the beginning you must learn how to monitor your mind) of the mind rather than yours. You can change the course of your life very quickly, when you so choose.

When you are at the controls of your mind, when you start getting some idea of how it works, you will feel safer than if you go with the natural flow of life

It's ok to move on from your mistakes

Detachment from errors is not a built-in excuse for mistakes and shouldn't be used as one, thinking it will get you off the hook. Unfortunately, once you act it causes repercussions in accordance with human physics no matter what.

But you will see that your instincts drove your ways. Then you can make plans to not get caught in the future by triggers that 'got you' that time.

Your intention is supposed to guide your life. You are not meant to be a slave of blind instincts.

It is very interesting. As you progress you will see the effects, the karmic repercussions that you should have paid fly by you, as you are no longer the person who did those deeds. You will, through the power of mind control, change who you are.

How you deal with mental mistakes defines your power

Mistakes occur when the mind misses information or miscalculates a proper response based on the information it has.

If you don't hang on to mistakes as though they mean the end of the world (or get emotionally derailed), but instead use your energy to find the cause of an error, you can learn something from it. That is how you reduce future mistakes. This ability is a power, but only when you use it.

Usually you can also reduce hurt reactions you cause your spouse by your mistaken misbehaviors. When you admit to an error and are able to define it well enough that your spouse knows you are not just trying to get out of trouble they will more easily let it go; no promises, but usually.

The ability to reason and then correct your future course, is another power; but only when you use it.

Changing the future

Most mistakes happen (ed) because the mind didn't calculate *at all*.

It's not only that it miscalculated but it unthinkingly and spontaneously reacted, like a cat running up a tree when it sees a dog.

So, when you recognize some old reactive habit pop up, refuse to think "oh what an evil person I am". Or refuse to add to your mistake by justifying or excusing like some big shot lawyer, or politician, caught in a lie; only then you can use your time and energy to diagnose a false calculation.

You can isolate the culprit reaction, which is some spring-loaded instinct or other, and you can work to remove or replace it. The ability to use this process is a power; but only when you use it.

Detachment from errors is not a built-in excuse for mistakes and shouldn't be used as one, thinking it will get you off the hook

Most mistakes happen(ed) because the mind didn't calculate at all

When you see your mind as a high performance tool and not as "you", you can responsibly manage it with the noble intention to improve its performance. This is another power; but only when you use it.

Being responsible for your behavior not only means being responsible to keep learning, but it also means you can make necessary adjustments and changes to your instincts and habits. Use your power wisely.

Not using your power with the purpose to improve your life and marriage makes no sense. Nothing is more important!

Is it better to zone out in front of the TV or computer? Just because it may be difficult to take charge over your mind does not mean you will somehow stop suffering if you choose to ignore this obvious responsibility.

Don't be a passenger, be the captain of your life

The expense of effort is nothing when you compare it to the pain of enduring your life as a perpetual victim.

Be careful about holding others accountable

Remember we are all in the same boat. Those who intentionally (we are not talking about your spouse) do evil are not easily rescued from their delusion.

You and they, and all of us, were not born knowing everything, so cut yourself some slack. If you berate yourself when you err you will spend more time in self-pity than in self-improvement.

Learn what you can from paying attention and move forward. In the meantime have compassion for others as you realize they too are suffering.

Don't be a passenger, be the captain of your life

When people get a new app, or program, they play with it to see if they can figure it out; without reading the documentation. But they usually get frustrated as they feel they are not getting the promised results and finally break down, and read the instructions.

Don't take anything too seriously

The more you know about the workings of anything the more control you will have. You don't have to get freaked out when the controls don't work as you think they were supposed to. You can try different things without thinking you will break the whole computer. Everything works in accordance with physics so you will know you just did something wrong. You didn't kill it.

As you learn, you can still enjoy.

Almost everything is fixable to some degree, or completely. Because you are in your marriage and you are just learning about marriage you cannot really trust your own evaluations as to where your marriage stands. But what you can trust are your evaluations about your own efforts to control your mind.

You can work on your self-improvement and that is what you need to do.

Work on improving your mind, and your marriage will improve. That should be obvious.

Your mind does it all, so, learn how it works

Your mind directs all the traffic, all the goings on in your body including repair and maintenance of internal organs, rate of breath and heartbeats, assimilation, elimination… all of it, and also your outer life; making constant adjustments while simultaneously interpreting everything going on within, and around you.

It records…it analyzes… projects… considers… monitors… imagines, etc. The enormity of its functions and capabilities are beyond remarkable, and although it may be fun to start listing everything it is sufficient to know the mind is everything.

Your mind efficiently performs all of the above and more with *or without* your participation

As you can imagine, the subconscious of your mind is important.

We could never consciously track a millionth of what the mind does fully automatically in the recesses of the subconscious. But what we can track are our outer behaviors, triggers and instincts, when we so choose.

Do you have a glimpse of understanding of how much power you are letting slip through your hands?

Just because it is incredible, doesn't mean it cannot be controlled.

People can control elephants with a little stick. If you made up your mind (notice how language refers to the mind as separate) to learn all about elephants you would soon crack the code and never fear one.

You don't fear what you understand

The more you know about minds and their programs, etc., the more you know about yours, and the less trouble it will be able to cause you or your spouse. Do you see?

Learning how to control your mind is not optional. Only when you start doing it is optional. At some point you will have to take it over. Those who do not are victims until they do.

The mind creates instinct "shortcuts"

The behind the scenes programs that the mind has are marvelous beyond description.

As soon as the subconscious software perceives an opportunity for a shortcut it creates one. Utilizing memory and automatic calculations it quietly creates and implants 'auto-reactive programs' known as instincts and habits. Creating instincts is done by a simple software program (described later) which serves us well.

Work on improving your mind, and your marriage will improve. That should be obvious

The behind the scenes programs that the mind has are marvelous beyond description

You are the one who drops the ball

Unfortunately, what your mind does not do automatically is that it does not alert you whenever it creates a new habit.

It doesn't ask you (soul) to review for efficiency or alignment with your goals and expectations or appropriateness, any instinct or habit it just implanted. It is automatic, just like a website algorithm. So, it is rarely right on.

The reactions created are always overreactions, which may very well be established to save your life, but, in so doing also creates a lot of problems, like a reaction that makes you jump off the cliff to avoid a harmless snake.

You see, there is no quality control manager who tests or tweaks the final instinct. Because you are that missing manager, who now needs to wake up and take charge.

Your messy and unhappy marriage is your wake-up call. The most important relationship in your life, the most important vows you will ever make, none are treated in a way that demonstrates they are important enough to get your personal attention.

You have to halt the slide and you cannot blame anybody else, and you cannot really blame you; because you did not know. But now you do.

Now it is up to you to gain control over your mind and make it work for you, and your family.

Because of this hidden automatic function and lack of oversight, it could cynically be said that the mind is "you" because it makes all the "final" decisions on your behalf, without any input from you the soul

Ironically

Because of this hidden automatic function and lack of oversight, it could cynically be said that the mind is "you" because it makes all the "final" decisions on your behalf, without any input from you the soul.

Here is the problem

The establishment of random unchecked habits is the biggest problem of your life no matter what venue, but especially in your marriage! But, you do not have to be a victim any more.

You need to be more than a victim passenger, dragged through life without knowing what is happening; like some baboon, throwing up your hands, handing over control of your life to habits, the latest "good idea" or instincts.

It isn't going to change either, until you change it. As long as your instincts are in charge it lowers you to the level of an instinct driven animal. You need to take control. It must be your infallible relentless intention to govern your mind every moment of your life…. you know all too well what happens when you don't. You are living it!

Habits and instincts

There is no need to focus your intention on your marital problems, searching for this solution for this and that remedy. When your intention is to control your mind and be a giver, instead of a taker, your marriage will grow and prosper.

Pay attention to your thoughts and feelings. You will be shocked at how your reactions do not match up to what you would have your kids do in similar situations (a handy barometer). If you judged you, by your inner reactions, candidly, you might not like you very much.

You have a few tendencies that have to go. We are not asking you to change all of them at once, as it is impossible; but be realistic, without guilt and shame, and get busy changing.

Watch your reactions

There is too much fear-created defensiveness integrated in your reactions. Be honest and fearless in your self-appraisals. Nobody wants to see the list of flaws, but the ones you miss will not simply go away on their own.

Some reactions just need some toning down, and most of them need to be assigned to stay at the door when you go into your Sacred Space. You can pick them back up for when you have to deal with the rest of the world, but keep them out of your relationship.

Your self-protecting habits impose upon you and your spouse. Use your free will to contain, control and replace your automatic reactions. That is what your free will is for.

The problem is clear

So there you have it. You unfairly blame(d) your spouse for many of your troubles when it is the unfettered habit-controlled mind in your own head causing you all the grief. It does things you would never approve of if you saw someone else doing it. But to make things worse you have been a blind justifier of your instincts.

The underlying compelling forces which cause an imbalance of control are the physiological drives and instincts; the invisible forces innate in every cell; the ones that force survival and procreation.

The best protection from being a self-made victim, and/or resultant bully, is to follow the formula.

Whenever you feel tweaked, when you need to take charge of your mind because you feel anger or other emotions that makes you want to do something you will probably regret

1-Stop- Stop your mouth and mind from making matters worse with uncontrolled negative words, speech or actions. Just stop everything. Be like the director of a movie, your movie. Call cut, stop; no more action.

Pay attention to your thoughts and feelings. You will be shocked at how your reactions do not match up to what you would have your kids do in similar situations

The best protection from being a self-made victim, and/or resultant bully, is to follow the formula

2-Evaluate- See if you really need to get defensive or be reactive. Is there an actual emergency? 99.9% of the time you just react because of instinct even when a quick outward response is going to be the most detrimental. Once you stop the action; imagine and plan (evaluate) what will get the best short and long term results, while honoring boundaries and planning for a pleasant unfoldment.

3-Act wisely- Use wisdom-guided will, not instinct, to do what will help your relationship; even if it is just saying "I'm sorry" or saying "my mind is freaking out, I'm sure you are right, just give me a second to find a way to say I love you". But best is creating your next steps towards happiness.

You miss all the true fun of life by being fearful and protective...of your body! Way too much time is wasted on spats. Instincts to protect the body which reside in your mind, your central command center, are both powerful and relentless. They will never leave you alone, ever! You have to stay vigilant.

How habits are created

Habits are created by bundled default habit software which came with your mind. The habit software's agenda is to make calculations and subsequent responses speedier and less laborious. The way it makes a shortcut is simplicity, itself.

It simply does the same thing it did before, whether what it did worked for you, or not. Is this like the cookies in your computer?

The mind subconsciously remembers what it did last time so then when similar circumstances appear, which it will take as a call to action, it has an immediate solution. That way it doesn't have to "bother" you. The only check to balance, which it also does automatically, is it makes sure the new habit is not in conflict with any habit already in place.

Sometimes the check is a moral check based on an instinct you, or your parents, intentionally implanted, which was based on a decision about what is morally acceptable.

Other checks are installed as well. In some families or cultures there may be a code of some sort which is embedded. You can always tell which instincts were consciously implanted. They are the ones which are less personal and seem to challenge what you "want to do".

This is why you should do "what you should do" not what you want to do.

Habits are the ultimate time savers

Many of your activities aren't thought of as habits but they are involved in everything from breathing to speech styles.

If not for habits you would have to relearn how to walk every time you got up. Think how useful and ubiquitous the habit software is. You could quite literally, not live without it. But they are not always helpful.

All of us have some habits we would like to get rid of.

Act wisely-
Use wisdom-guided will, not instinct, to do what will help your relationship; even if it is just saying "I'm sorry"

Habits control functions you will never be aware of

Habits are not just about external behaviors. Your body adjusts secretions of chemicals to digest what you eat, adjusts body temperature to adapt to changing climates (measured in small increments), calls on different muscle groups to adjust to different workloads and regulates breath with needs for oxygenation, plus etc., all done habitually, and subconsciously.

Newborn babies are examples of what you would be like without installed habits.

Instincts and habits are the automatic pilots of our lives

Perhaps you see the automatic pilot is your life's captain.

Does that concern, or frighten you? It should when it comes to making the best choices for your psychological and spiritual life! If the drive to survive instigates all your instinctive reactions by demanding life preserving actions, you will never have an opportunity to express love. Your body will be in charge of you, like the tail wagging the dog.

Your body is a biological machine which cannot feel love so it has no use for love or its byproducts. But you do!

You have to be able to control the habits and instincts which have taken over for your social and marital relationship skills.

Breaking bad habits and instincts

Repetition of an action creates a habit; that is all it takes.

Most habits are lightly set after just one action but they become entrenched after several. In some cases when there is a buried tendency, a habit may be automatically entrenched, such as with some individuals who take just one drink, and become alcoholics; as if they worked on becoming drunks for years.

A habit which has been repeated often and in varied situations tied to a number of different stimulations (triggers) will become deeply entrenched. They even construct microscopic grooves in your brain which deepen with each repeat.

If you wish to break a habit you have to fill the groove back in. You cannot break a habit just by refusing it expression. That will only suppress it.

Habits come back if you do not get rid of it correctly.

Best and most efficient habit killer

The best way to end bad habits is to replace them with their opposite counterpart

If, for instance, you have the bad habit of being critical in thought or speech; the fastest way to eliminate it is to look for opportunities to praise.

Instincts and habits are the automatic pilots of our lives

Repetition of an action creates a habit; that is all it takes

By *consciously* looking for opportunities to praise you will begin to make praise into a habit. In fact, set a self-made alarm that has you doing it every hour. Then when your old habit of being critical is triggered you will be faced with a conflict in your mind; a sense of discomfort caused by the old habit of criticalness wanting to insert itself.

Make the discomfort into a new trigger. Make it trigger you to stop, evaluate, and act with wisdom. Recall your intention to praise, and come up with replacements for your old habit actions.

As soon as you catch the first spark of criticism in your mind force a positive reaction into its place.

Make sure it is simple, like a thought of compassion. Or search for a positive trait or accomplishment you can praise out loud. The new reaction, which you force yourself to adopt, begins to fill the groove of the bad habit you want to replace.

This approach works on all habits no matter how long they have existed in your mind. This method is fool proof. It never fails and cannot fail. It is as reliable as filling a hole with dirt to remove a hole.

The old way of battling habits with self-chastisement will wear you out, and will never give you reliable results.

If all you do is vow to fight the old habits by refusing what the trigger commands you will be in a protracted war, never annihilating the rebel habit.

But when the trigger, which used to stimulate the bad habit, is trained to waken a new positive habit, you will win, pretty quickly.

Make the trigger *your* tool

Triggers are the signals that, well, trigger reactions.

When you develop a positive habit reaction to replace an annoying or destructive reaction to a trigger, which used to stimulate a bad habit; you create a win/win.

As soon as you 'hear' a criticism in your mind, *stop it*; and *ask yourself* what triggered it; but don't dwell on that.

Force your mind to praise or forgive (did you see the stop, evaluate then act?); and embellish the ideas of praise and/or forgiveness. After a few repetitions your new habit will have replaced the old. The old habits will struggle to surface but they weaken with each of your replacements.

Another example- Let's say you are looking at traffic jamming up in front of you. Normally you might be prone to getting moody, perhaps sinking into a rat hole of continuing negative thoughts and feelings; whatever they may be; restlessness, critical internal banter, sadness or fearful ideas; whatever.

As soon as you catch the first spark of criticism in your mind, force a positive reaction into its place

Your mind was triggered by boredom, perhaps, or having to wait (impatience), or just driving all day (restlessness). Do your best to track the trigger.

When you think you pegged the trigger, instead of going down a rat hole as you are habituated, start a new habit. Whatever you choose make it a habit you will want to keep. Maybe look up a bit to notice the beautiful sky (just an example). Reset the trigger of seeing your current situation to make you look up.

Or you can make your mind think about how beautiful the sky is. Make the trigger get you to think about beautiful skies. It doesn't matter what you change your focus to as long as you use the trigger to be positive.

Be as creative as you wish and make your reaction as positive as you can imagine. Make it doable and easy. Keep it as simple as humanly possible. Ignore the mind's efforts to keep you negative.

But, don't stop there. If you do not push through, your old habits will prevail. Keep the train of your thoughts on the beauty right in front of you; reflect about birds and sweet nature and start a positive train of thought; don't let the mind slip back into the ruts of unhappiness producing habit thoughts.

If you do not push through, your old habits will prevail

Do not give up

Your mind will seem to fight you and mock you because habits have a staying power, but you will prevail if you keep on. The old habit will succumb, absolutely! It just takes time and effort.

The effort to replace the bad habit of negative, by supplanting positive thoughts and feelings, will begin to erode the old habit and establish a new habit of positive thinking.

In fact don't be satisfied with your initial improvements. Become aware of all your reactions, and improve the good ones, too. Why not?

Think of thoughts as squares you stand on

The "latest" techniques such as "thought stopping" will not work.

You have to refill the grooves. Here is one variation of how you fill the grooves. When old habit thoughts are attacking you, and you will see how attack is the right word, and you have chosen an opposite trend of thought...

Imagine a thought as a square you stand on. Create a positive thought into a square you stand on. Make it your safe, home-base. Make your next thought another positive thought which attaches to the first, so you are now standing on two positive thoughts. Add another, and then another. Watch your thoughts. The ones which are positive can add to your floor space, the ones which are less than positive you reject. If no more positive thoughts come to you, create one.

The effort to replace the bad habit of negative, by supplanting positive thoughts and feelings, will begin to erode the old habit and establish a new habit of positive thinking

Link the thoughts by theme. If your first thought was how grateful you are to have a spouse your next thought could be a thought about a positive attribute your spouse has.

Then your next thought could be how it pleases you to have a spouse with the trait you notice. Then your next thoughts should link to the previous thoughts, until all your thoughts are linked and attached creating a sense of how good things are, which your theme is.

You will soon be on a large floor of thought tiles.

Trains of thought are no less important

Once you have a floor of positive thoughts all around you, keep it up. If you think you are safe early on it is likely that old habitual negative thoughts will start popping into your mind again and you will have to start again.

Your first efforts may not be as fruitful as you need them to be because you are not used to this exercise. But you will improve with each effort

Because you are fighting habitual trends of negative thinking you have to develop habitual trends of positive thinking.

Just like individual thoughts, trains of thought are also habitual, and need the same kind of effort. Replacing thought trends you do not want with thought trends you do want, requires the same approach.

Don't be discouraged. Use useless or destructive thoughts as reminders of how your mind is so habit bound. Make them triggers. Then get busy choosing positive thoughts again.

Try, and try again

Your first efforts may not be as fruitful as you need them to be because you are not used to this exercise.

But you will improve with each effort. A good coach, if you need one, can sit with you and give you thoughts to include to avoid lapses when old thoughts slip in.

It is your goal to place one thought after another for at least six or seven minutes. No problem though if you want to do this yourself. Do not get snagged by contrary thoughts. They will give up if you persist.

Prepare for efforts in advance. Write thoughts down which you can refer to when you need the support.

As the positive thoughts multiply your mind will start to catch the negative ones easier because negative thoughts will be like rats running across a white floor. Exterminate them, they are not yours and you do not need them.

One key to success lies in maintaining an observer's view of the mind as thoughts come and go. They are not your thoughts; they are your mind's.

But it is your job to control which thoughts can come, and which can stay. It is your job to train your mind.

You are not your thoughts. You are not your behaviors

Thinking you are your thoughts is discouraging as most thoughts are not what you would call uplifting or profound.

Most thoughts, for those who are in marital turmoil, are generally pretty depressing and guarded. But don't worry; as this will change. You are going to change it!

For those who have the habit of beating themselves up, know thoughts are supposed to be selected. You do not have to go along with any kind of thinking just because it is in your mind. When a first thought or two show up you choose whether you wish to expand upon them or dump them, (by replacing them with more appropriate thoughts). You are not responsible for the first few, which are habitual, only the next ones.

You are not your thoughts. You are not your behaviors

Choose your thoughts intentionally. As soon as you notice a mood or emotion is disturbing your peace shift your thoughts to praising your spouse. The sincere expression of love, in any form, will bring you out of a foul mood into the light.

Remain persistent. Don't think a few little attempts to control your mind will change your lifetime habits.

It is your mind, and *you* control it

The goal, which your mind will argue is too simplistic, is to NEVER entertain negative thoughts but rather ALWAYS encourage positive thoughts and positive thought trends. Reach this goal as quickly as possible by making constant effort.

When a negative thought comes into your mind, be it a jealous thought, a lustful thought, a dishonest thought, an angry thought and so on; think they do not belong to you. Don't count those. Don't think your mind is rotten to the core, or something equally depressing. Use the random thought to trigger your positive intentions.

When a negative thought comes into your mind, be it a jealous thought, a lustful thought, a dishonest thought, an angry thought and so on; think they do not belong to you

You have the power to pull thoughts out of thin air. Use that power to pull in good thoughts and use the same power to reject depressing or fear-inducing thoughts.

Any thought or feeling can be rejected out of hand. So, use the power you have to make your mind a garden of beautiful thoughts, and feelings.
Remember who is doing all this? It is you. You control your mind, steering it in the direction you wish.

Practice these useful techniques

These concepts may seem odd to you, but only at first. It is only because your mind is not familiar with these new ideas as they have nothing to do with your body's survival, which is all you probably ever thought about until now.

But change your life, make it better, and this is how. Rather than just doing what it wants, you use your mind! If you are out of sorts it means your mind is using you.

When you first begin the process of replacing your old habits you may initially grasp for ideas and be clumsy. But soon you will create castles of light. You will build beautiful thoughts and feelings all around you until there is nothing but a sense of well being and happiness which are not dependent on outer circumstances.

Then you will see. You are in charge of your destiny! You will see. It is very exciting to know how to control your life. Then you will always be happy.

Be Reserved

Expect the world around you to be cynical.

Keep your efforts to yourself. If you share what you are doing you will effectively be telling others that your family has problems. Don't do that.

We at The Marriage Foundation don't want you to tell people about us unless you do it anonymously. We want you to protect your Sacred Space, not advertise what is happening within it.

Sometimes it is even better to keep it cool in your marriage. Wait until your spouse trusts you again before bringing these ideas up for much discussion.

Your goal is to have a great marriage not show off new ideas or show how you care, by study. Show how you care by action. You will not have to worry if you work at this. The changes will come.

Clean up your environment

Your closest environment is comprised of thoughts and feelings, so clean up your mental environment

Your closest environment is comprised of thoughts and feelings, so clean up your mental environment.

In religious parlance there is a technique called practicing the presence of God, where the devoted one speaks with God and focuses on the sense that God is always with them. This calls for effort, the same kind of effort. Force your mind to do what you want it to do.

It is your mind and you should have it thinking the thoughts and feeling the feelings you consciously choose. Run with your agenda of bringing reliable and permanent happiness into your life. No more polluting ideas!

Another example of those who perfect mind control is the pro ball player or golfer who intensely visualizes their goal. They don't allow anything in their mind which will distract them.

You have the same power to control your thoughts and feelings. Don't waste this great opportunity just because it is a little difficult to start it up.

Repetition is a key

People who are no better than you train for highly technical and dangerous missions such as flying into outer space by repeating the same tasks over and over, until they can do them in their sleep. Soon old triggers are switched over.

By repeating new habits under many and various conditions they can eliminate the potential for an unwanted survival reaction, like duck and cover, to take over.

When what they need to is to be triggered to go through a mechanical checklist the last thing they need is to allow their old instincts to pop up. It is exactly the same for you. Your old reactions are the last thing you need.

Repeating something in different situations embeds a habit so you can see how it will take time to go through enough scenarios to really own the new habit.

Pay attention to your mind all the time. Develop the habit of watching it process, looking for ways to improve it. If you are paying attention there is less of a chance you will slip back into old reactions.

Turn anger and other offensive emotions into triggers for self-evaluation and habit replacement. Do not accept anger or other detrimental thoughts and feelings to remain in your mind. It is unhealthy.

You cannot fail if you persist.

Start working on one habit

You do not have to wait until the New Year to make a resolution and then fail through lack of good techniques or diligent practice.

If you make a supreme effort on only one bad habit (at a time) you will literally make huge progress in as little time as a matter of days. As various situations come up and you stick to your guns the old habit will soon be in its groove grave covered under the mansion of your new joy producing habits.

Never Quit

Don't be discouraged if you forget once, or a few, or even a thousand times.

Each time you restart your efforts you will try anew with greater strength, insight and skills. How foolish to quit just because you made a misstep or because you feel discouraged.

You don't know, maybe it will be your last misstep or next to last
Finally the back of the pernicious habit will be broken

Never say die! Never trust feelings of discouragement.

People who are no better than you train for highly technical and dangerous missions such as flying into outer space by repeating the same tasks over and over, until they can do them in their sleep

You cannot fail if you persist

You have infinite resources at your disposal, and you will win. Of course if you do quit you will know you have not conquered your habits and they will, for sure, show up again. You will have no choice but to face them now, or later.

Habits do not evaporate. They hang in there even while you are making effort, for a very long time sometimes, especially if they are deep. You need to be patient as you strive.

But they have to be buried. Eventually you will have had enough of habits which rob you of your peace. Then, you will get very serious about destroying those habits.

Trust the physics

There is a science to habits. No matter how deeply any habit is set when you put forth focused attention and effort, especially in the beginning of your campaign, the struggle will be easier.

But if you ease into getting rid of a habit, trying to live with it, perhaps in some hypothetically reduced form (like alcoholics who try to reduce their consumption), you will have a harder time, just like going into a cold swimming pool a little at a time.

Pick your worst habits first

One key is to remain focused on just one habit until the habit of replacing that one is in place.

Pick one habit, the one you think is the worst (do not ask for outside help to choose, no matter what). After a couple of days (if you are really determined) or maybe as long as a month, depending on the depth of the habit you are replacing and your concentration, you will have developed a habit of catching that bad habit.

Once your new habit of catch and replace is solidly in place, you will be on your way.

Then when you are sure you are not going to allow it to reestablish itself (don't be discouraged or fooled by slips) you can select and tackle another destructive habit, keeping half an eye on the old one.

Be as methodical and purposeful as you can

Some people make a written list of all their bad habits as a first step. There are no hard and fast rules. You can experiment with different approaches. The important thing is for you to stay aware and keep up a consistent effort. This is not "one more thing to do"; it is what you are supposed to have always been doing!

Once you have a toehold on a bad habit it still can take months, years, or decades to completely get rid of it.

So, at least write down the one(s) you are working on so you have a focus. Keep your chosen habit written on a 3x5 card which you keep with you, regularly referring to it, so you can see your progress. Or track your progress in some other way. Keep your focus in a way that works, for you.

You have infinite resources at your disposal, and you will win

If you progress slowly it could be because some bad habits are more deeply grooved than others, or are supported by other bad habits, and the network of sub-habits could look like a mass of roots under a garden taken over by weeds. But watch out.

It could also be that you may be subconsciously avoiding, or it could be you have the habit of procrastination. Be honest, so you can correct your efforts when needed.

The more you are on top of this the more efficient you will be and the faster your efforts will show the significant results you seek.

Serious intentions work the best

You have to be intentional, and you have to back up your intentions with a plan that takes your instincts and habits into account, or you will not get very far.

Nobody wants to do this for thrills so don't think you will do this when it feels right, because that day may never come. Nor should you wait until your life is at the very bottom, and your choices have eroded.

Don't be like those who hit bottom and then look for a shovel so they can be sure they really hit it. Change your life. Choose a direction, and go for it.

No effort is wasted

Every sincere effort has an effect so don't quit.

A progress chart will show you how incredible your progress is, so keep one handy for the times when discouragement tries to sneak in. This is like brushing your teeth. You don't have to do it but it prevents further decay. Track your habits, and your progress with them.

As you can see, it's not about your spouse changing to accommodate your version of right or wrong, but your efforts to control your mind that will change your world; and your marriage

The way you are with your spouse, whether showing moodiness or good cheer; or how you treat your spouse, choosing adoration and respect, or treating them with indifference, is habitual; pretty much like everything else in your life; same for all of us.

Pay attention to the way you say hi, the way you say bye, the way you pass each other or ask for things. Start paying attention and see how much you can improve your interactions; it will surprise you.

But never have expectations of your spouse. Expectations are meant for use on you, nobody else is required to meet yours, no matter how "fair".

You have to be intentional, and you have to back up your intentions with a plan that takes your instincts and habits into account, or you will not get very far

Every sincere effort has an effect so don't quit

When your mind is clamoring for you to "speak your mind" or "get it out on the table" (two of the more dumb things imaginable in a marriage), recognize that the desire for that brand of so-alled "open communication" is a bad habit (culturally induced) which needs to be curtailed and replaced

Create the habit of self-awareness

Be intentionally positive with ALL your communications, your requests, your offers to serve.

Be a great spouse by looking for opportunities when none are apparent. If there seems to be an opportunity to be sweet and serviceful, or considerate and supportive, now is your chance to do it; especially if you feel like you don't want to; for whatever instinctive reason, which is working against you.

Overriding your mind's instinct driven habitual attitudes will help you in many ways

1) You will walk past what used to be inevitable altercations

2) You will catch how inappropriate your mind's attitude was
3) You will replace resentment, with love

4) You will be able to compare your spouse's reaction with what would have happened

5) You will be much happier, as you take control over your mind, your life

6) You will create harmony

7) You will create intimacy

8) You will smooth out tensions…the list can go on for a long time, but you get the idea

Don't be tricked by fad, but bad, ideas

When your mind is clamoring for you to "speak your mind" or "get it out on the table" (two of the more dumb things imaginable, in a marriage) recognize that the desire for that brand of so called "open communication" is a bad habit (culturally induced) which needs to be curtailed and replaced.

Being a complaining critical person with expectations that your desires be met is *not* some special right of intimacy. Intimacy is a connection of love, not a bundle of crude rights.

Marriage is the best, ever, incubator for positive habit development

In the case of reforming your habits, as a married person you have an unbelievable advantage over everyone else.

Not only do you have the greatest incentive imaginable, because what is more important than to have a happier relationship; but, also, you can make a billion mistakes and still not be dead.

There is another advantage, which most people mistakenly think is a bad thing.

You can't hide from your destructive thinking and behaviors

The fact that you are two people in a 24/7 space means you are living with someone who reflects your traits better than a mirror.

When you take advantage of this wonderful situation by watching your spouse's reactions to your words and behaviors you can change very quickly, as your flaws are either pointed out, or you will be hit pretty quickly with the effects you are causing.

Marriage is better than a hundred years of therapy when seen this way. Lose the habits of blame and criticism.

Some think they have a brutal marriage and they are being martyrs when they stay faithful, but we say you have a great opportunity to see your own pettiness on a daily basis, so you can change.

As long as you're sincere intention is to be selfless, your spouse will understand your mistakes; but your efforts must be sincere, or you will not be trusted.

If you screw up a job interview it may be over and you won't have a second chance; but in your marriage you have limitless opportunities to get it right as long as your intentions are selfless and sincerely communicated.

Instincts, remember, are created to protect. So if you are constantly sincere in your intentions, your partner's walls can come down, and stay down, because you will be careful to not trigger them (it takes time).

If your partner is not improving their integrity, you will be able to override your defensive instinct with love by creating new reactions like understanding or compassion.

Either way it is always up to you to creatively control your mind, to pull out benefits, where there used to be resentment.

People want to know if their spouse will change when they do. The answer is a definite probably not. Because until they change out of their own resolve, all that will happen is they will be more relaxed.

If there is a bees' nest in your backyard and you stop kicking stones at it the bees will settle down and be less aggressive; same with a crazy spouse. If you bring honey out to bees every day and speak calmly and lovingly the bees will never sting you. You get the point!

When you pay attention to where their triggers are and avoid the triggers they will calm down. But that is all you should hope for from them.

Environment and venues influence our minds

It is because "worldly" defensive habits came into your sacred space that you slip into mean thoughts which, cause movement away from the life you want.

The fact that you are two people in a 24/7 space means you are living with someone who reflects your traits better than a mirror

If your partner is not improving their integrity, you can override your defensive instinct with love, by creating new reactions like understanding or compassion

Defensive habits temporarily ruin your relationship. But with what you now know; that meanness all comes from fear, and you know you only feel fear because of the drives and instincts; you can start to see the way to have happiness.

When you establish selfless habits of thinking about your spouse in positive ways as earlier suggested (continual respect and adoration), and completely cease all mud ball launches; it will be more natural to maintain your efforts because the secure happiness within your sacred space will be sweet compared to the rest of the world.

In other words, the greater your effort the faster your marriage improves.

Constantly remind yourself of your marriage venue

You have to make sure your relationship is positively unique and uniquely positive, so your good habits do much of the work of "remembering" for you

You have to make sure your relationship is positively unique and uniquely positive, so your good habits do much of the work of "remembering" for you.

Make it a habit to think of your relationship as being in your sacred space; you will see how quickly you are able to instill habits which replace all the contrary ones which made life miserable.

Your spouse is not like anyone else in the whole world. He, or she, is bound to you in ways that give both of you huge incentives to treat each other wonderfully.

You need to start treating your spouse wonderfully and never cease…Be in charge of creating the habits that make your relationship heavenly.

Never, ever, ever argue with your spouse. It is one of the stupidest things to accept as normal.

Really, ask yourself if any argument with your spouse has ever ended well; it hasn't!

Even if your spouse is spitting in your face with rage, close your eyes, bless them with your compassion, and wait for the storm to blow over. Never argue with your spouse.

Walls

Your mind is splendidly designed to monitor, maintain and protect all bodily organs and functions, especially from outer threats; ranging from invisible microbes, to dastardly human characters, who wish to steal from you, or worse.

Walls are a great asset, as your mind's protective front line of defense.

However, you, the soul, are not important to your body (not trying to be ironic, just observable fact).

So your instinct controlled mind does not want your input, or interference. Because of this habit enforced perspective, which creates an "I got it, stay out of my way" attitude towards you, soul; your walls are antiques, fighting enemies who no longer exist (if they ever did).

Why should the mind think it needs you? It nurtures counter forces such as microbes and bacteria, to protect the body from viruses and bacteria. It maintains skin, hair and nails, despite a harsh environment, to protect from all sorts of germs. It does all sorts of things you would never imagine, to protect its body, so why should it need you?

If anything your poor judgments create all sorts of trouble for the mind as you poison, and expose your body to every imaginable threat, so maybe there is some benefit to not taking back control.

You have power you did not know about

You were probably never exposed to the notion that instincts are changeable so it never occurs that you can identify and choose your walls, (instincts and emotions); but you can. You can stop your mind from making every single decision for you. But you have to be firm.

Our situation is like Dave's, in "2001 A Space Odyssey", when the computer, (named H.A.L.) took over the space ship and killed the crew, who, in the computer's central processor (mind), were jeopardizing the mission. Dave, who escaped the fate of the others, had to disconnect its control over the spaceship or he would be killed, too.

You have to control your H.A.L.

Walls are institutionalized first lines of defense-habits

The computer on the spaceship, like the part of the mind focused only on survival, only considers its mission and its survival.

Like instincts it does not put love for another ahead of its physical survival. That ability, to consider love, is possible only for a soul (and the source of all souls?).

Walls are not thought through for benefits prior to or after being erected. They do not think or evaluate. They remain in anticipation of a trigger, alerting it to anything which might somehow destroy the body.

Without walls we would believe everything everyone says, being susceptible to all kinds of scams. We might rescue rattle snakes from drowning, not considering the probable outcome. We would leap off of thirty-foot walls to get a ball we dropped, not remembering the fall will kill. We would trust politicians as they promised us nirvana, because no wall, based on previous experiences, would stop us. Walls stop us from blind actions.

Born with hardly any fears, walls take a lifetime to create. Unfortunately too many are overreactions to subconsciously perceived fears.

You have power you did not know about

Born with hardly any fears, walls take a lifetime to create. Too many are overreactions to subconsciously perceived fears

Critical yes, and critical to keep out of your Sacred Space

You need your walls.

The world will strip you clean if it has the chance. But don't bring your walls into your Sacred Space because they block it all, literally deterring you from thinking and feeling love.

How could a feeling of love come through a wall of, essentially, distrust?

Besides, you do not need to be protected from your spouse's behaviors.

You cannot feel love through walls

You cannot feel or sense something when your mind is clouded with fear

Walls distract you from seeing things objectively.

You cannot feel or sense something when your mind is clouded with fear. Consider, you have an almost infinite number of walls in place all the time, which makes you miss the true agenda of anyone you are dealing with, but especially your spouse.

Then doubt and suspicion, natural defense tools of the mind, start bouncing back and forth.

Love can transcend walls, though. When we drop our walls at weddings and births we feel love. But mostly we feel love flow from us, not to us.

This is another example of how love is felt by the giver and barely by the recipient. Practice loving those who are mad at you. While they are being mean or stern only partially listen, and push yourself to love them anyway, even as they attack.

Yes this is tricky at first, but it is a very real way to live. When you do it you will see how your love is ignoring their behaviors, and this is what is meant by transcending their walls.

Don't expect any results from them. Just notice how your own demeanor changes to peace and calmness.

As you move closer to your spouse, by intentionally lowering your walls and intentionally reducing your threats, you will begin to feel love in both directions.

Focus on love

There is no way to eliminate all your walls even if you wanted to, and we don't think you should want to. You need them everywhere, except in your Sacred Space.

When you see a wall you can choose to ignore it. But you have to pay attention. The best advice is, figure out its purpose. If it has no immediately discernible purpose, if you have to pretend there is a purpose, or justify its existence, it is a safe bet the wall is an antique which has outlived its usefulness, and needs to be removed.

But walls are no problem in the world. Anyway, you need them. It is when you bring them into your Sacred Space that all hell breaks loose. Do not let them ruin your marriage.

In your marriage, your attention should be on building bridges. Over time bridges will be a greater part in your lives as you trigger each other with thoughts of love by thinking of each other or seeing or hearing each other. You will see how triggers can be your good friends. Build bridges, not walls

EMOTIONS

Emotions are not understood. In every case, the person emoting, and the person observing or experiencing emotional expressions from their spouse quickly lose track of where things really are in terms of context and importance. Isn't this true?

Emotions derail love and connection. Love and connection are not emotions.

Current ideas about emotions are ludicrous

You do not have to be a victim of emotions. Because uncontrolled emotions cause so many problems we need to take the fangs out of the bite.

In order to clear up the confusion completely you also need to learn about intuition and how misapplying incorrect definition to the word "feeling" causes a lot of confusion.

Learn

1) What emotions are

2) What intuition is

3) What their purposes are

4) Why the word feelings has confused everyone

5) How to identify and protect your lives from emotions, without locking yourself in the bathroom

Emotions

Emotions are the prolonger of instinctive reactions...

An instinctive reaction is instant, and instantly over. If a snake falls on you when you are walking you need instinct which compels you to grab it off of you. The instinct hits you like a shot and then it is gone. It did its job.

But what if somebody is mounting an attack on you?

In your marriage, your attention should always be on building bridges

Current ideas about emotions are ludicrous

In a situation where you are attacked, hitting the dirt or screaming a counter threat, those instinctive reactions will not be enough to "save your life". You need to be kept on high alert.

The ongoing alert, as compared with your first reaction, is what the 'emotion' software produces. Emotion keeps your awareness alive and engaged, but, unlike instinctive reactions, at a non-lethal level.

The reactions caused by instinct are too powerful for the body to sustain; the release of adrenalin and sped up heart, etc. Your body cannot take it for long. Soon, if it were kept up your exhausted body would crash and maybe die. So in cases where the subconscious mind determines you need to stay on your toes (which is too often) it passes the baton over to the other alert software called emotion.

Emotion is separate but related and connected software. It is the second step which is triggered by subconscious reaction

Emotion is separate but related and connected software. It is the second step which is triggered by subconscious reaction. It jumps right in, with a long lived, but sustainable, alert.

It could be thought of as an agitator, because it keeps you stirred up.

Do you see how magnificent the protection for your body's life is? How beautifully nature has crafted your mind for "animal" survival? Can you also see how you, as a human soul, have been left out of the process? Well, the truth is you keep yourself out of the process, by ignorance and laziness.

You can isolate your emotions, to reduce its power over you

Have you ever seen a horror or action movie, but without a soundtrack?! When you mentally separate the soundtrack from the action you will be surprised how differently the scene impacts you.

Emotions do the exact same thing to the scenes, the experiences, of your life, that soundtracks do for movies. They create sustained attention, and intensity.

Emotions are the soundtrack, the elicitor. Emotions graphically establish values of importance to what would otherwise be dry scenes in a movie. There is good reason for this mind trick. It is for your body's protection.

Emotions are not meant to own you, but they do. They are not meant to control your life, but, like habits and instincts they are produced without soul supervision or objectivity, so you get unconditionally whipped by your emotions. You think they are you; "I" am sad, "I" am angry, etc.

Emotions draw their impetus and information from your subconscious calculator of threats, people, benefits etc. So, based on its hidden calculated evaluations your instinctive emotions push your mind.

Your mind didn't have any pure thinking in forming its conclusions because you unthinkingly accept emotion as part of the equation. Like with instincts, you, soul, are out of the loop. Until you control your mind you, soul, are stuck on the roller coaster!

Some emotions are happy. They are not all misery producers, but they all control you

In cases when the subconscious deems you are safe emotions bring you a sense of "I feel good with this person" so you can securely rest. In other cases, where the mind perceives you to be threatened, instinctive emotions bring restlessness so you're on edge and alert to possible danger.

In still other cases, where the mind feels attraction to someone and detects an opportunity to procreate it creates emotions which make you want to connect.

Like instincts and habits, emotions do not need or want your input. From their point of view you, soul, can only get in its way.

Although we speak about the mind as a personality which chooses its ways we only do that to demonstrate a point. The mind doesn't come up with ways to deceive you. It is not its own person. It just seems that way sometimes.

Emotions are controllable and can be separated from you, just like thoughts

It is through misunderstanding your soul's relationship with your mind, and its functions that you have become a slave to them.

You are not your emotions

You can separate yourself from emotions and should, when you find yourself too identified with them. When you think "I am upset", "I am mad", "I am…whatever" instead of seeing those feelings as you remind yourself it is your mind. It is the action soundtrack engaging your attention.

This simple approach isn't intended to minimize the suffering you may be going through. Nobody suggests you "just detach" and everything will be fine. In fact we recognize the potential for uncontrolled emotions to make people sick mentally and physically, to the point where they cannot function normally.

But, we also know you have the innate ability to draw a line and become progressively less victimized. At some point you have to choose freedom and choose to make the effort to free yourself.

At first it may be all you can do is make effort here and there, but once you establish the intention it is only a matter of time before you are free.

First, become an observer

To really see emotions for what they are start to look at life as a movie.

Observe other people. It is ok to do so, it is educational. You aren't judging them by watching for the drives, instincts, emotions and walls, and how they take their place. See how they are slaves.

Like instincts and habits, emotions do not need or want your input

You can separate yourself from emotions and should, when you find yourself too identified with them

Look for the instant reactions, fear-driven behaviors, hard as steel habits; so you can see it in yourself, too. Watch what happens when people gets caught by their emotions. The same thing happens to you, until you change it.

Make a declaration

The best way to avoid pain from emotional imbalance is to recall your supremacy as a soul. Realize you are not your emotions, so you can choose to not identify yourself as an emotion. When you say to yourself "I am not anger, but this anger is a wall and instinctive reaction, and has robbed my free will" then you can begin to reclaim your king or queendom.

Fear and Anger

We do not believe in anger management- We believe in anger eradication

We do not believe in anger management…We believe in anger eradication

Fear and anger are the king and queen of emotions, closely followed by lust (primarily men's).

We all know these three all too well and can only find rare times when they served our needs, and then, only by chance. Ninety-nine percent of the time when fear and anger take over, and take over is what they do, they override any clear thinking. You can rid your mind of anger over time.

Stick to what you CAN do, first

Never speak an angry thought, even when you modify or gloss it over; this why your will power is essential.

Just stop, do not speak until you are well past the possibility of anger slipping into your communication. Remind yourself that the instincts are operating on their own driving you into pain and suffering.

Evaluate, and see if fear or anger will help you through your current challenge. They won't! Those two are only good for immediate challenges to your physical life!

Don't be overwhelmed. Don't think you cannot conquer, and regulate emotions; no matter how strong

When we say you will win we do not suggest your first attempts will take you past the point of any danger. These, like all tendencies, are habitual so they need to be eradicated through persistent, correct effort.

But, you will succeed if you continue your efforts; if you start again, and again, after a million seeming failures, and if you refuse to give up your life to instincts and habits.

You have plenty of evidence that winning is doable

Elite warriors who actually face the fear of death are examples of those who conquer fear, and anger.

You can also look to relatively ordinary people who do extreme sports or have to give a speech. Of course, they "feel" fear in the predicaments they place themselves, but they do not freeze up or run away, or lie or blame etc. They make the fear into inspirations to forge ahead.

You can also turn the tables by making your fears into signals to open your heart with love. Yes, you can!

Your challenges are different, as are the challenges each person faces. Fear of failure is no excuse for giving up! It makes no difference that it seems like yours are harder than what you see others going through. Your challenges are yours for reasons we cannot say. But we know from experience that yours are winnable by you.

Let's say you hear these less than sweet words "Honey, you really screwed things up, you have to admit it". If you respond with anger you might say "go to hell"; but when you separate yourself from the imposing emotions which make you think your "life is threatened" you would probably say "maybe you are right, thanks for letting me know".

Fear is not your friend

Fear is the hidden emotion, which triggers anger. Fear, as you will recall, is tied to your drive to survive…perhaps you were subconsciously afraid that screwing things up, as in the example above, makes you less valuable, or, God knows what!

But it actually makes no difference how the fear was created; it was the trigger and fear creates an instinct which creates a huge overreaction.

Once fear is allowed to take over by your inaction you are a victim, and you will react. Unless you see fear in its rawest form, the switch between drive and instinct, you will think it can be traced to an event. Events are never the switch; they are only images the mind has given substance to.

Differentiate the feelings you feel

Physical, Emotional, Intuitive

I feel the breeze… This "feeling" defines physical **sensory feeling**

I feel upset…   This "feeling" defines **emotional feeling,** the continuation of an alert

You can also turn the tables by making your fears into signals to open your heart with love. Yes, you can!

Fear is not your friend

I feel love …   This "feeling" gets confused between intuition and emotion

When it is describing how you feel towards your spouse or kids it is intuition; but what when you say "I love ranch houses you are identifying love as a description of something your subconscious has determined to fill a survival need.

You need the code

The differences between physical, also known as sensory feelings, and the other two, are easily differentiated, because physical feelings are always perceived through one or more of your senses.

But until you mentally connect instincts, habits, drives and emotions to your physical body, the distinctions between emotional and intuitive feelings are easily confused. They actually feel almost the same until you know how and when to differentiate them.

Create a system for yourself

There are individuals who think they "fall in love too easily". They lose themselves in the emotion and open their heart without any discrimination. There are also those who hate everyone they meet. They allow their self protection software to run and ruin their life. Emotions, which are mental software, are intended to be in service to the body, so categorize emotional feelings under the umbrella of physical feelings even though they are not detected by the senses.

Intuition

Intuition is very different from emotion but is often confused with emotion because you "feel" them both. Intuition is not connected to the physical senses of sight, smell etc; in any way shape or form. Intuition does not require a physical anything. It is your sixth sense, which views everything from above the physical senses.

As a result, your intuition is above the walls, instincts, drives, emotions and all other obstructions created from your drive to survive, and is part of your soul.

The bottom line is your intuition is your soul's exclusive sole apparatus

You, soul, have awareness, and of more than just yourself. It doesn't mean you don't feel anything physically when your intuition is working.

When you feel with your intuition there is often an accompanying feeling in your heart. Like, when you feel love, your heart is filled with warmth. There are no other physical conditions causing the warmth, such as increased blood or something. The feeling is intuitive.

The feeling, although felt in your heart, does not rely on a physical nerve in order to be felt.

Intuition is very different from emotion but is often confused with emotion because you "feel" them both

A breeze needs your sense of touch to be felt. Sexual feelings need nerves to be felt. The senses of taste and touch in your mouth help you identify and enjoy food, and drink. Those feelings are sensory, nerve induced, produced by something physical.

Intuitive feeling is pure and is felt by you, soul, without the need of anything physical.

Your intuition is your soul's pure view of things

Examples of your intuition include awareness of a close person too far from your physical senses, or an awareness of what has not happened yet. Just about everyone has had similar experiences and most accept them.

When you have such an experience you would say "I feel that…". Those who are comfortable with their sixth sense don't hesitate to speak about their intuitive feelings because they are reliable to them.

There can be emotion, and the simultaneous emotion being felt is a secondary feeling your instincts are catching and then reacting to. There is nothing physically felt, but there is feeling.

Pure soul feeling, which is how you should connect with your spouse, is reliable and taintless. "Life happens" because you are distracted by physical things, instinct and emotion.

In fact, if you are emoting, you will not feel through your intuition even though it is working. This is one way to know if you are emotional or intuitive. When you are emotional, you are not intuitive; period.

Love is intuitive

The feeling of love is exclusively felt with your intuition. Love cannot be detected from any of the physical senses, yet you "feel" love. Again, you use the word feeling, but there is no emotion called love, that is the biggest misnomer in history!

Love as an emotion is not love any more than flying in space is flying

Love is its own category, and though it inspires emotion it is not an emotion. Intuition is how you feel love. It is because most languages do not have a word for the feeling of love, so people have mistakenly called it an emotion.

Women can feel love easier than men

It is a normal condition for women to have a clearer sixth sense than men. Unfortunately, their sixth sense is also more easily contaminated by their emotions. They are not taught the differences or easily separate them.

Going back to how genders are physiologically defined to serve different roles in procreation; the female body creates all sorts of hormones which induce emotional impetus for women to nurture their young.

Your intuition is your soul's pure view of things

Love as an emotion is not love any more than flying in space is flying

Yes, it feels so harsh to put it that way, but it is what it is. The emotional drive is easily and usually recreated into love. Perhaps this is the gift women have, to make up for the hardships which women go through.

Men do not have a natural connection to love until they get married. And women do not have a natural connection to unconditional love, until they are married.

This is where it gets good! But we will save it for the next chapter.
Reactive; or, emotional love

We cannot just discard all the social definitions for love, so we have to give a new context, by calling some love, reactive. Remember to always look for the hidden but ubiquitous drives.

If you meet someone who appeals to you and you feel like you have fallen in love (love at first sight); be clear, it is more than likely your instinct is creating an emotion. The mind has probably, not always, conjured your elation for the purpose of procreation, or potential security (as defined by who-knows-what criteria).

Again, the emotion, which was supposed to help you has become your enemy, making you susceptible to the agony that comes from defying social norms.

This is not what we would call a negative emotion, but it can be troublesome, and you have to prevent yourself from falling into traps which are not easy to extract yourself from, like affairs or fantasies.

Your spouse is where all your love and effort needs to go

Those who seek relief from others, often complaining about their spouse as a way of justifying their broken vows of unconditional love, create more complications and dig themselves into an ever deeper hole, usually bringing their children in with them.

True love will never get you in trouble

When you confuse emotions for soul feelings you lose the benefits of either.

Our society has, as a result of this confusion, demoted love to an emotion, which it most certainly is not. Emotion, either good or bad, is a form of agitation.

You are learning all you need to have a fresh start, and your ability will increase as long as you keep at it. It won't be better to leave, or start over with someone new because your spouse isn't the problem, and neither is compatibility.

My own story is not uncommon

In my marriage I was very defensive and never let anyone tell me what to do. As a kid I was un-teachable because I knew everything. Basically, I just didn't trust anyone. As a kid I saw a treacherous world and how shady everyone is (It is dangerous to pretend the world is supportive). My answer was to be tough, be independent, a leader; so I could be in charge, or cheat whomever I encountered before they could cheat me. In general, it wasn't until I was twenty-one when I had an epiphianic experience that I decided to change my ways.

I chose to become a better person and created a plan to change myself; but I certainly didn't know anything about a sacred space of marriage or being different from the world.

So, like you, and everyone else who has a tough marriage, I unknowingly brought my walls and filters into my marriage.

Even though I was leading a serviceful life my mind was still in charge. When my wife asked me to do something my walls went up because my instincts "knew" she wanted to take advantage of me. I had not separated them from me.

My first reaction was always an anger-empowered "no". Then *after* her, or anyone else's request was perceived as harmless, or I thought the request was for my benefit, I changed my mind and responded with an improved idea. The improvement was so I could show I was in charge. My mind told me I was cool, not that I was degrading her.

Nobody could take that kind of treatment; it is amazing my wife lasted with me as long as she did!

Live and learn only counts when you learn

My next marriage came *after* I became a serious student of marriage (no way would I go through it again). I didn't want to be a husband any new wife would love to divorce so I implanted a host of preemptive habits that would protect my future wife from my stuff.

I instituted a policy of saying "sure" instead of "no" as my default response. No matter what is asked of me my first response is positive; unless the request is for me to jump off a 200-foot tower or something, but then I ask for a moment to think about it.

My intention is never say no or another discouraging remark as my first response. I trained my mind with intention, will power and follow through. I made it a point to catch my slips and correct so quickly that I soon entrenched my new positive habit.

Was this foolproof? Of course not! Sometimes I forget, but I never forget two or more times in a row. I also always look back to see if my interactions reveal unmonitored instincts.

Every single morning and sometimes at night I replay the day to see where I got caught by destructive habits.

"Live and learn" only counts when you learn

Creating preemptive habits is better than letting your subconscious create them

Determine what preemptive or two, or three habits will help curtail the inevitable reactive words or actions plaguing your marriage. Being proactive in this way is very powerful.

1) Make sure you are hitting the mark in terms of catching yourself when it is important to do so. Recall what you react to. Be clear. You want to spot the flash point; the trigger. Then you can replace the wall with a different reaction.

2) Let your spouse know what you are doing and check in with them. See if they are aware of your choice of habitual reactions as being an apropos target. If not, find a different one so you can please them.

3) Be open to your spouse if they suggest a different target. They have an objective view and can be helpful; so long as you don't flip out and react to their insights.

4) Write it down! Your mind will do everything it can to forget this information, but it will thank you later as it is able to settle down a bit more after you conquer your reactions.

5) Remind yourself every hour or more for the first couple of days and every day for a while until your preemptive is a habit...then watch for more opportunities

6) NEVER suggest your spouse should do this. Be super nonchalant if they say they are going to do it too; but they probably won't.

Using preemptives is a great start which will save you from so much grief.

Cleaning up the messes that come when you blurt out your reactions is much harder than resetting your triggers. But there is no reason to stop there.

The more you control your mind, the happier you will be. Learn how to control your mind like a pro, and be happy all the time.

Firmly decide and vow that you are *always* in charge of your mind, regardless of its old habit reactions or any outer anything; it is all on you to control your internal and external behaviors.

With your goals of a supreme marriage established the effort made to control your mind will create the marriage you desire.

Calm minds function best

You know when your mind is out of control. So, monitor your mind so you can stop when it's headed towards danger.

The most reliable measure of the state of your mind is your calmness or happiness. The best way to know your mind is out of control is when you are not happy; it is that simple; that is your gauge!

Firmly decide and vow that you are always in charge of your mind, regardless of its old habit reactions or any outer anything; it is all on you to control your internal and external behaviors

The body has indicators too, like the measure of a normal heart is its pulse or pressure. The measure of your lungs is the depth and power of your breath and so on. The measure of your mind's ability to function is your calmness and/or happiness.

Happiness and calmness does not refer to emotional happiness, which comes from pleasing occurrences or calmness that comes from exhaustion or wine. Induced surface states of the mind are false indicators.

As soon as you recognize you are neither happy nor calm you need to jump in with reason.

Don't fumble with your mind, stay honest

Don't play games with yourself or your spouse by calling yourself calm just because you have presented a calm outer appearance.

When you are outwardly composed but seething inside you need to pay attention to your inner state as the true indicator. So, as soon as you see you are not happy and/or calm you need to hit the brakes.

You will see results always come from effort

After you have been at this a long time you will constantly and habitually watch internal moods and rarely be fooled by your mind; but it still happens, so be careful.

Remember, the mind doesn't want you to interfere with its instincts because it could care less about your marital happiness; it is only concerned with your body's safety and its natural extension, procreation.

Get good at introspection, where you are monitoring your mind; and it takes time to get good at it; so don't create impossible expectations for yourself. Be patient and forgiving.

Also, be wary of the mind not being honest with you. Sometimes your mind will tell you you're calm just because it subconsciously wants to put up a wall; but don't be fooled. As soon as you see you are upset or are out of sorts, or however you want to describe your unhappiness, it is time to hit the brakes.

NEVER fuel the mind's fears

Don't listen to those who suggest venting, or hitting pillows or explaining your reasons for anger and frustration

Those are ways the mind excuses its reactions so that you get out of its way. Conditions that push you into destructive actions of mouth and mind are explainable, but not excusable.

Avoid unhappiness, including "justifiable" unhappiness. Friends show support by telling you they can't blame you for being upset, and that is nice of them. But you have to be tougher on yourself. Venting will not bring inner peace or help you become stronger. Exercising your willpower is what helps.

Don't play games with yourself or your spouse by calling yourself calm just because you have presented a calm outer appearance

Don't listen to those who suggest venting, or hitting pillows or explaining your reasons for anger and frustration

Avoid unhappiness, including "justifiable" unhappiness

You have to mindfully pay attention from now on to the best of your ability, or your instincts and habits will jump right back into the cockpit of your mind and assume control

Quit while ahead, even when behind

No matter what damage you have done you need to stop as soon as you become aware you got caught by your reaction. Don't make excuses; just stop. Don't get off on a new path; just stop. Because the mind has momentum and the negative trend will not quit until you exert serious control.

If you see what is going on and you manage to stop your mouth it may be too late to avert damage because the mind is rolling on a mindless path of destructiveness.

The only way to halt the destruction is to stop *everything*. Then focus completely on regaining your natural state of calm and happiness; before it is safe to open your mouth again.

Don't worry about the flow or anything like that. Defy the gravity of the moment collapsing all around you. Take positive control over it, and your life.

Pay attention for all kinds of reasons

Poker players watch for the signal in other players so they know when a bluff is coming. You need to see your subtle preludes to eruptions so you can catch them before they do damage. If you don't catch an obvious physical reaction you can look out for a twinge of anger, resentment, fear or resistance.

You have to mindfully pay attention from now on to the best of your ability, or your instincts and habits will jump right back into the cockpit of your mind and assume control.

Know your reactions

Maybe you are someone who broods or storms off; whatever your personal thing is identify it, so you stop yourself as early as possible. As soon as you are aware that you are not yourself stop everything.

No more excuses for your troubled marriage will do. It is on you to make and keep your marriage a sacred space. If you go along with the "it takes two" crowd that believes in "fairness" you will never find true happiness. It takes you.

Turn yourself into the best spouse who ever lived by being loving, supportive, and increasingly selfless.

Calming exercises

Your body and mind are linked by breath. You can thwart the mind's habitual tendencies by using breathing exercises.

When you manage your breath into a slow controlled rhythmic pattern, it slows your heart.

Because a calm heart reduces oxygen consumption your heart can slow even more which calms your mind. By taking control you can fool the programs (subconscious habits) which regulate the body to regulate your mind.

There are multitudes of effective breathing exercises. Any of them will calm you down. Some will work better for you than others; based on many things. Some will work better at different times so learning a few is not a bad idea.

The best sources for breathing exercises, for mind control, are the same sources used by hospitals and clinics; athletic techniques and yoga techniques.

Yoga exercises have been around forever. Like other oriental arts such as acupuncture and herbal treatments, they are effective. It may not be as easy as swallowing a pill or taking a drink of wine but among the many advantages, you remain alert, in control, and there are no harmful side effects.

Control your breath

Begin by exhaling comfortably slowly but completely through your mouth.

Then inhale through your nose, slowly and steadily, to a specific count; maybe a count of 5 or, if you have really huge lung capacity you can count to 20. Whatever the count just be sure it is paced steadily.

Next, hold the breath for the exact same count as the inhale.

Then, slowly and steadily exhale for the exact same count.

As a side note; if you close your eyes, it will calm you more quickly.

Don't hold the breath out at all after your exhale, but start inhaling right away, calmly, with the same count. Repeat this cycle at least 6 times.

End the exercise by watching your breath come in, and then go out, without controlling it; at least 3 or 4 times. Just watch the breath without controlling it for at least a few minutes; the longer the better.

Your controlled your mind

Your pulse will be slower and you will feel your shoulders relax. Most importantly, your mind will be calmer. Of course you can do this all day if you want because there are no negative side effects.

As you do breathing and relaxing exercises try to put your attention at the point between the eyebrows just above the nose. Don't use your eyes to look at the point, just your attention (you can push on the point to feel it). Also slightly lift the gaze of your eyes above the horizon line. Lifting the gaze and focusing above the eyebrows puts energy into your pineal gland which helps relax the body and mind.

The best sources for breathing exercises, for mind control, are the same sources used by hospitals and clinics; athletic techniques and yoga techniques

Don't allow your mind to engage in any kind of altercation; ever! As soon as you stop; stay stopped

After you relax enjoy your relaxed state, and don't let your mind fall back into the pit. It takes practice to maintain control but there really isn't a better anything you can do than to maintain calmness.

One more

Inhale the breath slowly and simultaneously tense the body in stages, low tension, medium and high. Then hold the breath and high tension for a count of 6 or so. Then, all at once, completely relax the body as you simultaneously push your breath out through your mouth. Do this one at least 6 times.

Be relaxed, be in control

When your imagination is at the disposal of your instincts, as it has been all your life, it will exaggerate potential dangers in order to keep your mind alert, usually to the point of causing you nervous indigestion

Focus on relaxing the body and mind so you can control it; the world will do fine without your participation for a while. This is a way you do the "stop" step.

Don't allow your mind to engage in any kind of altercation; ever! As soon as you stop; stay stopped.

The temptation to reengage will be almost impossible to resist but you will win if you refuse to go down the rat holes caused by your instincts. As you break the habits your personality will change and you will discover you are becoming a happier person.

The truth is everyone is greatly challenged when trying to control a mind that has barely been controlled in the past. It is like trying to tame a wild animal for the first time.

The thing of it is there is no other way to ever have peace in your life or relationship without controlling your mind.

Guide your imagination

Imagination is a default software program that gives you limitless opportunities to create. Like anything else it is possible to improve its power through positive use. And like anything else it will become rusty with neglect or misuse.

When your imagination is at the disposal of your instincts, as it has been all your life, it will exaggerate potential dangers in order to keep your mind alert, usually to the point of causing you nervous indigestion.

You do not have to go along with those ideas which reduce your happiness, ever again! They are there because you allowed them and you can rid your mind of them through right effort.

Better to imagine an ever expanding connection with your spouse, one that is ideal. The only thing stopping you from a life of joy and harmony are your bad habits.

It is *your* imagination. You need to take it back and use it to create the beautiful life you are entitled to.

The past is over when you say it is

People imagine they are beaten up so badly they cannot imagine a life better than what they have. Out of habit, they quickly reject the possibility of true happiness.

It is like when you get sick, you cannot imagine what it is like to be healthy; but the reverse is true, too. When you are healthy, it is hard to imagine what it is like to be sick. You need to imagine a life with your spouse that is sweet and fulfilling. Think about this and try imagining your new life in great detail, from the moment you wake in the morning till you go to sleep at night. Then think about what you need to do, not your spouse, but what you need to do to get there.

You control which thoughts come into your mind. If the direction of your thoughts is not what you intended they will change as soon as you insist. When you wake in the morning observe your thoughts and then change them if you have to. Make them positive and beneficial to what you want.

No more being a victim!

Start your day on *your* terms

Decide what your first attitude will be when you see your spouse in the morning. Exchange old negative thoughts for those which will make you both happy. Plan your thoughts. Plan your words to your spouse. Have a plan for your interactions based on what you think will please them the most, not what will get the best reaction towards you. Consider your spouse's typical communications and plan for them by bracing yourself to be compassionate and understanding. You don't have to "help" them have a better day but plan on being pleasant and loving without being overbearing.

You know your spouse pretty well so avoid saying or doing anything that might trigger them; and if they are triggered anyway have a plan to not take it personally or get in their way.

Write your plan if it will help. Go further, plan on being extra thoughtful with your actions and considerations.

Watch your mind; reprogramming it every day or every hour with habit replacement. Make it a mission of rebuilding your love and marriage.

Batteries need recharging

It helps to get some time where you can sit by yourself and maybe with a piece of paper and pencil, or not, review your behavior for ways in which to improve the connection you have with your spouse.

Find the beauty in your spouse, and blow it up in your imaginative mind.

Out of habit, people quickly reject the possibility of true happiness

No more being a victim!

You have done this with their flaws so you can do it with their positive attributes. You have looked at their flaws (as well as your own) and made them huge things which ruin your day; now look at the good qualities your spouse has and increase them in your heart and mind until it is all you see.

It is your mind; you do with it as you will. You have free will so use it.

A happy marriage of mutual adoration and service is natural. The other kind of marriage is not normal but you have to constantly work at preventing your instincts and habits from undermining your intentions.

Worry

Worry is a combination of fear and imagination fueled by not having a plan

Worry is a combination of fear and imagination fueled by not having a plan.

The supreme remedy is figuring out what you can do or waiting until things unfold enough to figure out what you can do; and then creating a plan and doing your plan.

It is no accident we placed worry as the last topic before listing the three methods of conquering the mind. Worry hurts marriages by taking up valuable time that could be spent in more positive fashion. The methods that will help are the same for all other time wasters; learn to control the mind. Chronic worry becomes depression, but no matter what you call it, by its degree, it still needs to go.

It is your mind and it is your responsibility to stop your mind from going to worry; and it is well within a normal person's ability to conquer it.

If your spouse suffers from worry it is your job to be patient and supportive; never point out what you see. Like other emotions worry is a thing, a thing you must not entertain. Replace it just as you would any other pest.

Three tried and true methods for controlling your mind

There are three general ways to redirect your mind. All three are useful at various times depending on the circumstances and your state of mind. Use all three

1) **Direct control-** This is the one you should try first. It is simple and will work immediately; when conditions are favorable.

   When you hear a thought or feel a feeling you know is not what you want you tell the mind NO. Obviously the key to its effectiveness is tied directly to the strength of your will power, and focus. It becomes more usable as it is exercised.

2) **Workarounds-** This method is like negotiating with a moody child. You offer to trade the mind's unwanted desire (these moments show how you actually have a sense of right and wrong while the mind is instinctively driven) for a better one, or you tell it you will consider the idea later; any way you can put off the undesirable action until it is not pressuring you. Then go to #1 or #3. The idea is to work around the mind's stubborn desire so you don't do what it wants. You will have to be determined.

3) **Holy indifference-** This method was introduced about 5000 years ago by the father of Psychology; Patanjali. He taught the soul is meant to enjoy its sojourn in the world and we are not meant to take the dramas here seriously (easy for him to say, right). He taught the world, and our experiences here, is a dream and the only real substance is Spirit. We are not supposed to take anything we encounter here any more seriously than we would if we were in a dream at night. This is esoteric but more and more people are open to it. We include it because it works.

These tools work and it is your job to learn how to use them; by practice. You won't get good unless you practice. Each opportunity to control the mind is going to make you smarter and happier, if you use each opportunity with the right attitude.

Try to be grateful for everything that comes your way so you make life work for you.

If you think of life challenges as life lessons you will develop the right attitude towards life as you progress more and more on a path of happiness.

Conscience

We all have sought help from others in making up our minds, but in the end it is only we, the individual, who can make the choice; and our best advisor is our conscience.

If your intention is selfless you are on as solid moral ground as you will ever stand on. Trust your conscience as the final decision maker.

Often referred to as the speaking voice of the silent God, your conscience is your ultimate yardstick for right and wrong. If you ignore the guidance from your conscience you will hear from it less. Ignoring or dodging your conscience is not wise.

Arguing with your conscience is not to smart either because you are arguing with the one who gave you free will. In the end it is your free will that will either save or destroy you. It is always best to align your thoughts with your conscience.

Sometimes though, we think it is our conscience speaking when it is actually the mind trying to trick us; and we have all have been in that place of not knowing for sure. One of the great challenges in life is deciding the difference between right, and wrong.

Two ways to confirm it is the conscience is by analyzing if the idea is reasonable and if you feel love around your decision.

We all have sought help from others in making up our minds ,but in the end it is only we, the individual, who can make the choice; and our best advisor is our conscience

One of the great challenges in life is deciding the difference between right and wrong

Do something you choose

It is better to act incorrectly (still doing your best) with will than not to act at all. Just be sure your actions are beneficial.

The more you do with specific intention the more actual control you have over future events of your life. Don't leave things to chance. Just as you are reading this book (an act of intentional will) to improve your marriage make all your actions positive efforts towards happiness,

The lesser form of change is behavior modification; the superior is personality or character change

It is better to act incorrectly (still doing your best) with will than not to act at all

Some people believe major change is as impossible as changing your DNA. But new studies have shown you can change your DNA. Some of us assumed so long before the studies. Of course you can change yourself! The very idea that you are "stuck" is as defeatist as possible.

Behavior modification means control of your natural inclinations. In order to accommodate your situation you modify your behavior on a temporary basis. You do not want to have to do that every time you are in trouble. It is better to change your habits.

In a dispute with a motor vehicle department employee for instance, after standing in line for half an hour, the clerk you see says you were in the wrong line and no one in charge will allow you to get in front of the correct line.

Everything in you wants to explain in a loud voice what you think about their systems. Instead of blasting away however, you decide it would only make matters much worse if you speak up. So you put on a pleasant face, bite your tongue, and proceed to the correct line.

You modified your behavior because your personality or character (being un-Gandhi-like) would have had you behaving in a universally destructive way. Think about a cat trained to let the parakeet sit on its head. As long as someone is reminding the cat how it must behave everything is fine.

However, if you don't force the behavior, as time passes the natural instincts of the cat will make the bird a plaything and snack. The cat will never think it did anything wrong.

The cat's character was not changed merely by repetition or training.

Change your core

A person blessed with free will can change his or her values, principles, and perspectives, and literally become a different type of person by overcoming long-embedded habits and replacing them with new ones.

**You need to have a different view of life to not be bothered
by that which now offends you**

Individuals go through life adapting to situations in ways that keep them out of trouble until they question why they always find themselves in these painful situations. They finally realize the world is what it is; and it isn't going to change.

Then (the light must go on many times before it remains on), the individual decides something on the inside must change. They realize behavior modification is a quick-fix Band-Aid, and it only masks the pain.

They realize they have to become a different person; a person who does not get affected so easily, a person who takes more in stride.

They begin changing their character or personality; by stopping the mental reactions and telling their mind that what just happened was not a big deal. They tell themselves they are better than that; more mature and evolved; and they force their minds into a peaceful state, more conducive to happiness.

Over time the individual becomes more like the kind of person they choose to be; they commit to letting go of old habits.

Simply put you have the ability to change the person you are into one who is more loving and tolerant. The person you married, who reflects both your good and bad quality traits, helps you by mirroring your flaws and weaknesses.

Don't fool yourself into a twilight zone of life

There will always be those who are not ready to accept the idea that love transcends all. They look for tricks of the mind they can use to get along better but without giving up anything that threatens them. They are simply not yet able to make the connection between their attitudes, behaviors and their suffering.

If you are married to one like this it is not your duty to show them anything other than your love.

Maybe they cannot intellectually grasp this heady knowledge but that does not matter. They are precious, and they are yours.

A person blessed with free will can change his or her values, principles, and perspectives, and literally become a different type of person by overcoming long-embedded habits and replacing them with new ones

If it is you who cannot take what you see as a leap of faith with your heart surely you can still see the logic of giving your all to your spouse. When you go through the motions even if you are not able to feel the effects right away you eventually will, because these efforts have an effect.

If you choose to be happy, nothing and no one can make you unhappy; and if you choose to be unhappy, nothing and no one can make you happy.

With all you now have been exposed to and learned about it is time to discuss sexual intimacy.

If you choose to be happy, nothing and no one can make you unhappy; and if you choose to be unhappy, nothing and no one can make you happy

- Chapter Ten -
Intimacy and Connection

◇◇

Connection and intimacy is the grand prize of marriage.
Using the knowledge you have garnered from the previous chapters
you can see how a soul-mate is much more than a greeting card concept.
You can take your relationship to place undreamed of!

◇◇

Current popular thinking about love, connection and intimacy couldn't be further from the mark. Those who have followed the advice which suggests improved sex improves relationships have not realized their goals of happiness. You are a soul. It's impossible for you to be fulfilled by a little physical pleasure, no matter how elaborately you dress it up. Learn, instead, how to have true intimacy, and use sex as just one of the many tools at your disposal.

Chapter Ten

Intimacy and Connection

By now you realize true intimacy is the connection between you and your spouse as souls. Your potential for fulfillment is far superior to any other relationship.

Those who haven't read the previous chapters, thinking you know everything, even without looking at it; you won't understand this enough to really help your marriage.

You who have read from the beginning will know exactly what we mean.

First, husband

Women's biology, which is far more complex than a man's "hit and run" instincts, initially drives them to entice men with sex appeal. The drives created instincts understand very well what gets men to procreate and then care for offspring.

These illustrations are general and illuminating but not a 100% formula

Once the man is "locked in" simple sex is not all that appetizing to women because the drives shift her attention. Her body and mind slowly shift to creating a home where her man is comfortable so she can get pregnant. She is still sexual but not as much, as her focus is on creating stability. Maintaining her husband's happiness is only a piece of her puzzle; not her mission in life. You, her husband can't figure out what happened; not without knowing about drives, instincts and gender differences.

Then after a woman becomes pregnant she focuses on building a nest for her young and learning as much as she can about child rearing so she can be a great mother. Despite the fact that her body has been invaded by a biologically foreign organism her drives cause her to protect and nurture "it". Her human aspect automatically converts the objectively speaking slavish attachment, into love (which is more natural for us humans than enslavement).

The above, naturally, and not understandably to women, makes most men, who thought they were sexually set for life, get a bit cranky.

Men's minds are adapted to their body and their body is adapted to its drives. Men don't have a context from which to understand that women are not "horny" like they are. You men only imagine what is going on. But until you incorporate the drives, instincts and gender roles, you are looking for solutions based on your experiences which miss these overriding components.

Women love their husbands and if they are able to see past their driven attitudes and allow their love for their husbands to accommodate them they seek compromise.

Women's biology, which is far more complex than a man's "hit and run" instincts, initially drives them to entice men with sex appeal.

Until you incorporate the drives, instincts and gender roles, you are looking for solutions based on your experiences which miss the overriding components

Some find solutions in mundane ways, if they are lucky! They set up date (sex) nights, or pawn the kids off on parents so they can have time (sex) together.

The so-called solutions which are very popularly advanced as fix-its only work, when they work, by compromising your wife's nature. The real solution is to have a model which works for both partners.

To have something work for both means rising above the mundane drives and instincts which exist for the purpose of reproduction.

Solution is transcendence through unconditional love

The solution is what we have talking about throughout the whole book. A man who expresses sincere appreciation and understanding based on his efforts to love his wife unconditionally will allow her to not only lower her walls but draw her heart to him, and thus, her body.

Women do not get lusty from outside stimulation the way men do (this is general, not absolute). Because men have to be ready to have sex at every opportunity his mind is trained to react favorably to any and every opportunity to copulate. Women are also familiar with lust, but only as an occasional drive, so are mentally different. They become sexual from the inside out. They are not driven by outer stimulation the way men are.

Women are "turned on" by love and connection

When you were dating your wife only appeared to be lusty because it seemed like they were turned on by sexuality; and they were. But that was because her drive was making her that way.

If you approach your wife with what you think is sexy now she will not be turned on like back in the day. She will usually reject your overtures because her desire to want to get ****** is a rare feeling for her. The fact is she might think you don't turn her on anymore; just like you. But it isn't that. It's that you are not connecting with her on her level.

What she really wants, despite what you may read in girlie magazines, is to open her heart to you, her man. So it is a rare woman who will do that when you come on sexually, unless she either has an agenda like trying to make a baby, or is willing to overlook the minimization of her heart.

Women don't know the above either, due to miss-education in our society, so you cannot blame her for not speaking out.

Her heart is the gateway to infinity

It is ironic that husbands and their wives are sitting at the door to infinite joy but keep trying to make the pebbles of lust into something special.

Sex, in correct perspective

How could sex possibly be the end all in marriage or anywhere else, as is promoted by youth oriented magazines or trendy books? How could sex toys and romantic getaways be true marital aids when they only temporarily satisfy bodies, and only accommodate survival driven psychology?

In practice false substitutes can't convince anyone of their truthfulness no matter how enticing or romanticized the words are. But, hold on.

Their inadequacies although they are lacking as a panacea, doesn't mean sex isn't an important part of most happy marriages. It just means sex needs to be under your intelligent control.

Using sex for more sophisticated purpose doesn't mean you can't enjoy the bodily excitement too.

It's where your intention and focus is, always, that makes the difference.

Sex pushed by instinct, needs be redirected for soul connection

The biological purpose of sex, procreation; is not going to let you ignore it.

Procreative energy will always find manifestation no matter how various the rituals of man or beast dresses it up, or keeps it simple. Procreative forces always strive to find a way to fruition.

The same can be said of rivers of water flowing from the mountains. The water is going to the sea, *but you can dam it and divert it.* You can make the force in the river work for you.

You can divert the flow of life energy in your body trying to create babies

That is what monks do. They use special methods to divert their sexual energy into mediation and study. It is also what some artists and athletes do.

That is what knowledgeable married couples do, as well. They use the powerful energy to lift each other to higher planes of connection.

Human sexuality is based in free-will, but only when we control our instincts

Humankind is unique when compared to all other species.

Each human individual is capable of redirecting their instincts or stifling them.

Every individual has the opportunity to explore more opportunities and solutions. We do not have to accept what is imposed on our body by its instincts.

We are not animals. We are souls.

Using sex for more sophisticated purpose doesn't mean you can't enjoy the bodily excitement too

Humankind is unique when compared to all other species

You can choose how to use sex, rather than be driven by it

Your soul awareness and guidance are not going to be included in the sex act unless you choose. You can use your drives, rather than be used by them.

Your bodily instincts don't care if you have fun or not. They don't care if you connect as souls, or not. But if you don't control it your body's drives will control your sexual experience, depriving you of incredible potential opportunities.

The sex act, even though it always builds a bridge between your souls, won't open the gates between your hearts. You have to do that intentionally and willfully.

The best news is your wife does not to be coaxed into opening her heart

The best news is your wife does not to be coaxed into opening her heart

But she has to trust you, that you are not manipulating her in order to use her as a masturbation device!

You have unfortunately, trained your wife into seeing you as a childish sexual predator (this is admittedly extreme, but only by degree). You have more than likely been very selfish in your sexual attempts and she has probably told you so. But you could not see it, or thought it is natural because you didn't consider that her body's drives manifest so differently from yours. You probably became a victim, thinking she isn't turned on by you anymore.

There is a very good solution where you will have your cake and…

Your intention is everything! Defy your drives and instincts! Put love ahead of sex!

You cannot condemn your drives or instincts and win anything. You cannot call yourself a "sinner" because you have been owned by your body's biological priorities; that wouldn't get you anything.

But what you can do is recognize the drives and how they make you shallow. You can objectively look at how you have fooled yourself into being narrow in selfish desire to consider only your body's "needs", placing them above your soul, your higher and more sensible need for love.

Here are the steps to take

1) **Don't undermine your relationship with over-familiar behavior.** Loving behavior will lower her defenses. Her instincts currently tell her you are only interested in taking her body to satisfy your physical needs, not to give her love. That message is what whores like because they are paid. It's an unbearably insulting message for your wife.

2) **Train your mind to appreciate your wife as a person.** Never see her as a sex object. Redirect your attention to her superior qualities as a soft and loving nurturer. Be on the lookout for her non-sexual and non-physical feminine qualities, and compliment her. Notice how she reacts to things, and how sweet her feminine perceptions are. Tell her what you see. She wants to be noticed as a woman.

3) **Don't call her cold or unaffectionate.** Your behavior and attitudes turned her off to you. Instead of blaming her for not having connection, lose your fear of feeling love for her. Your love will swim in her heart when you stop fearing her and start exploring your combined heart.

4) **It's better to masturbate than use your wife.** You won't have to keep up this practice and it isn't for everyone. But never approach your wife to satisfy your lust. And don't think you can pretend! Women are instinctive about protecting their body. When you are an aggressor you force her walls to come out.

The above stops you from appearing as an "enemy"

5) **Acknowledge her feminine qualities.** You need to establish that you see her for who she is rather than what she is. Her true feminine attributes are those known to children; caring, interested, supportive, compassionate, forgiving, intuitive, home-making, pretty, cute, decorating, remembering special occasions and so on. Compare her qualities to your male qualities with the emphasis on how wonderful it is for you that she is your sweeter half and how much you appreciate her.

6) **Be there for her.** Be her man! Listen to her, support her, defend her, do man stuff and jump to do what she needs you to do as soon as you hear or anticipate her needs. Never argue with her. Rather validate her ideas and efforts. Give sincere praise and compliments. Let her know how beautiful she is and how she is more beautiful than anyone else. Let her know how good she is at dressing and how sexy (she has a different definition than you) she is, and how gorgeous she is when she dresses up. Never miss an opportunity to praise or please her.

The above builds trust and bridges

7) **Get real about what sex is.** This one takes some getting used to but you have to get there. Being driven by sex is for animals. Being indifferent about sex requires you to channel your driven sexual desire towards acts of love-like admiration and appreciation. You will get more sex than you ever had when you learn this but it will be much different and way better.

8) **Approach your wife physically, without sexual desire.** You have to know what your wife likes. Some women like to be hugged and others don't. Some like to be lightly touched or kissed on the neck, or be held or have their hand held. You can experiment and you can ask her. Then you have to be able to shift at a seconds notice. One of the feminine qualities is rapid unpredictable and "impossible to know why" change. Your job is to love and listen and adjust to her moods in a supportive way, not have expectations.

9) **When sex is inevitable you cannot assume.** Just because all the indications are telling you are going to have sex doesn't mean you are. Remember that your "read" is useless. They change, they never intended, or they started thinking about your youngest child's report card. You cannot reel her back in with logic. You have to stay with her with love and support. Sometimes they stop and other times they overwhelm you with passion-**let her unfold.**

Removing obstacles is the first step towards intimacy, and building bridges is the next

10) **When it is safe to assume, don't get off the path that brought you there.** Your wife was not getting stimulated or teasing you or herself to make sex more sexual. You set the stage for her to feel safe, to open her heart, and that is the great prize! The last thing you want to do is drop down, and down it is, into an all physical state. She wants you inside her but you are coming from two different places. She wants you in her soul.

11) **"Inside her" to your wife means in her heart.** Because you're instinctively driven to only inseminate you have to bypass the physical drive with intentional effort to open your heart and pour your love into her vast heart. Don't worry about your penis remaining hard; it will.

12) **Please your wife.** When your wife's heart is open her body is open, too. Without stopping your efforts to pour your heart into hers you should slowly and methodically try to please her physically. It is not the same for every woman, and it is rarely the same for any woman from moment to moment. Over time you will discover a rhythm to your wife's body and are able to bring her to orgasm. But don't get preoccupied with orgasms. Pleasing your wife is a second to second affair. Most important is to keep your heart open and your love energy pouring into her.

13) **Don't worry about coming.** Men who simply don't care about being "satisfied" physically have the most balanced and happy sex life of all. You are pushed to come by your instincts. So you shorten the experience and leave 95% of the experience behind. Your wife will want to please you anyway. But you should learn to love her without any desire to be pleased. Some men never or rarely have an orgasm. They are the ones who have the most sex because they don't chase their wife away.

14) **Never hit and run.** The instinct to be done and run is animal. You have to ignore it and focus your loving attention on your wife.

Now, wives

As you can see, your husband has his instinct created challenges and you have yours.

Because of natures plan for keeping the population growing your role as a mother is very complex, at least from your previously uninformed point of view.

Your body prepares you for motherhood right from the start (there aren't any absolutes in creation other than change and variety, so learn these drives as creators of forces, and direction). Your special balance of hormones along with your physiological and resulting psychological specializations, directs your life all along the way.

But remember, it is your body driving for its purposes, not for your higher human potential of experiencing love. You have to use your intention and will to divert your life from nature's plan.

Unlike your husband's, whose sexual desire is simple and consistent throughout his life your compulsory desires change in stages. First stage isn't a driving force to fertilize your new eggs (like your husband's was), but a guardedness and curiosity about men.

Remember, it is your body driving for its purposes, not for your higher human potential of experiencing love. You have to use your intention and will to divert your life from nature's plan

Your mind adjusts to demands that you fulfill your female role by being the selective gender, which is how evolution moves upwards instead of randomly. Your desires were fashioned to select the "best" available. You may say "of course", as if its basic common sense to always want the best, but you don't realize that desire is implanted. It is barely there in men.

The desire of men to procreate at every opportunity makes him the selected gender, as is demonstrated by the fact that many men marry the first woman who is willing to have sex with him, or marry him.

His choices are limited to who will accept him. It may seem like the selection is equal, but those who pay attention to the subtleties are very aware that in most cases it isn't.

As the selector you sought the "best" according to your own personal chart of values. In order to win him over, however, your instincts went for his soft spot; his desire for sex. This is not to say he married you for that but his body certainly made sure it was what he noticed. If you encountered any competition for him we would make a safe bet that your competitor didn't try to win him with her math skills!

Once he was 'won' you unknowingly but instinctively moved to another stage where you prepared your new marriage home for a future human. Your sexuality was then used by your instincts to create stability by encouraging attachments to other benefits you provided him, including marriage, which provides him many things he "needs".

DON'T TAKE THIS PERSONALLY!!! We aren't suggesting you did anything wrong. You never really thought about any of this, as you were compelled by drives. But can see the undeniable truth yourself.

Until you take control over your life your drive created instincts are in charge. We only describe what happened, and why.

The stage before children is a great time to build human friendship and heart connection but too many don't do that because of worldly fears/walls. Those who never have children but seem to "fall out of love" never took the opportunity to build their relationship. Those with children went to the next stage too quickly.

During the next stage, when you got pregnant, your sexuality would have gone out of the window if not for your need to keep him around; unless you developed your bond of friendship.

Most men are completely dejected at this stage because the "promise" of continual sex evaporated, taking with it their trust. This is in fact when men decide to file for divorce or cheat on their wives. They reason that their wife left *them* because in their mind that is what happened when the sex shut off.

Many good men crush their feelings at this stage reasoning that they are building a family and that is how it is supposed to be. But the sad truth is the relationship between you and your husband leveled off in a twilight zone of dissatisfaction. Neither of you focused on building your relationship. At best, both of your focuses shifted to the child; drives win, you guys lose.

The desire of men to procreate at every opportunity makes him the selected gender

The last stage is when the child is born. Because your sexuality is driven to reproduce, unless your human mind is open to more children, you are done. Sex becomes a rarity.

The drives have done their job but you two have lost everything. Your marriage, children, security and connection are all gone. You can see how separation and divorce are inevitable when human beings remain victims of their drives and instincts. All the so-called reasons for break ups are disguises for the truth; that you and your husband are not getting the only benefit of marriage that will keep you together; happiness creating connection.

You are in a position to transcend all the drama that comes with instinctive prerequisites. As the woman you have the power to turn your marriage into the Sacred Space we discussed earlier. It doesn't fall on you. It is your opportunity. You are the heart of your family, and you can empower both yourself and your husband when you stick to a plan of love.

Build trust and bridges

Here are the steps to take to change your lives

1) **Appreciating your husband as the man you love to love and admire will enable your husband to open his heart to you.** Men, despite their physical and character strengths, are often far more fragile than they appear. If you challenge or criticize him or make him feel inadequate he will fear opening up to you. Although his vulnerabilities are mostly hidden because of his gender driven instincts he wants you to "protect" him rather than belittle him.

2) **Acknowledge his masculine qualities.** Openly admiring his masculine qualities as; protector, provider, caring, interested, supportive, strong, logical, reasonable, fearless, dependable, unemotional, and so on as positive and desirable will help him feel comfortable with you and he will talk about himself more. Even though you will want to open up too, hold off. Make it about him as often as you can, watching for ways to connect. Be his woman! Listen to, support and defend him. Never argue with him. Rather validate his ideas and efforts. Let him know how handsome he is and that he is more attractive than anyone else. Let him know how good he is at providing and how sexy (he has a different definition than you) he is. Tell him how handsome he is when he dresses up. Never miss an opportunity to praise or please him. Let him know he is the sexiest man alive.

The above builds trust and bridges

3) **Don't ever be offended by sexual overtures.** Your husband is not always just trying to release. He loves you and wants to connect with you as much as you want to connect with him. Bur he has no clue about the feelings you, as a woman, are born with. You can guide him into the soul-love he wants but never felt. Use sex as a way to expose him to the experience of love. Help him learn that it is not only safe for him to change his focus from external senses to your heart but is a vast improvement.

4) **Get into your heart not your emotions.** Your emotions aren't your heart. Because you are a woman you are often sabotaged by your emotions which are second stage reactors; but are also "feelings (go back to the chapter on the mind and reread about emotions if you do not recall). The "feelings" of emotions are agitation but the feeling of the heart is pure and uplifting. You need to work very hard at keeping your attention on the love in your heart and rejecting the agitation (with all its expectations and undesirable "feelings"). The agitation describes your fears. They will prevent you from opening your heart. When you first become aware of the distinction it is difficult to sort because of habit. But until you do your love life will be tumultuous and uncertain.

5) **Refuse the temptation to give in to the emotions.** This is repeated because it makes the difference between soul happiness and temporary emotional thrills or woes. Stay in your heart!

6) **Help your husband redirect his drives.** Guide his lust into love by setting the example. Slow him down without correcting him. Never correct him. Tell him how you love to feel him inside of you because you can feel his heart. Ask him to move slowly. Ask him to relax his body. That you will make him hard and keep him that way. When he is inside of you let him know you feel his heart. Set the pace. Never ever, ever, show disgust or disappointment. Men are very sensitive!

7) **Don't worry about orgasms.** As a woman you have the ability to feel things your husband will never feel. Women who concentrate on orgasms get sidetracked from feeling the greatest part of being a woman.

8) **Be patient.** Your marriage will become a whole instead of parts. As you open your heart to your husband without expectations, your love together will grow.

As you open your hearts without expectations, your love will grow

Wife and Husband

The choices you have when you are sexually joined with your spouse are

You can

1) Focus on your body's desire to make the male ejaculate; just like animals

You can

2) Focus on psychological perversions of domination or submission; like human "animals"

You can

3) Focus on self or spousal pleasure ; like bored uninformed humans, or

You can

4) Focus on soul connection; as you have felt at times

Those who use sex to connect as souls are, by far, making the wisest choice

Making sex a "religious" experience, by choosing the fourth intention, still allows you to add sensory fun to the mix as a sweetening ingredient. It isn't an either or situation. You can have your cake and eat it too; you can!

Your relationship with your spouse is superior to your love for your children

Those who are uninformed get sidetracked when the wife becomes pregnant. They don't realize the drives have forced their attention on child rearing so they allow their love to follow. The best idea is to recall that you have chosen your spouse, knowing them very well, and you will be with your spouse long after your children leave the nest.

Your love with your spouse is of the infinite variety. Nurture and feed it!

Your effort is all it takes

When you keep your focus on soul connection regardless of the focus your spouse has you will be fulfilled.

Your intention, alone, opens the flood gates of your love and that beckons to theirs. Your soul-mate may not be able to feel it (in rare instances) but your efforts will steadily increase your connection.

Unless your spouse is purposefully resisting your love the balance will shift as a matter of simple physics.

Protective walls are irrelevant when you give love unconditionally

When you are in the arms of your wife, or husband, and your intentional mind is pouring love upon them, even when unrequited; the walls which never go away drown in the liquid love spouting from your heart.

As long as your intention is set on purely loving them as you replace all other thoughts or emotional feelings, of expectation or resentment, you will feel the elation of your soul.

The aftereffects are often permanent. Until you allow the effects to be eroded they will remain as stair steps to infinite happiness; that is the nature of unconditional love.

**The idea of "letting go" is misunderstood until you achieve
higher states of connection**

Throughout, we have advocated the importance of monitoring and controlling your mind.

It is especially important to stay in command of your mind when you work to replace the habits which reduce marital sex to a mockery of your soul's potential.

Your habits, instincts, walls and emotions never go on vacation; so you have to always attentively defend your life from their misguiding influences.

Intoxication works against you

If you use drugs or alcohol to more fully enjoy sex you do because you desperately want to escape the emptiness of animalistic sex.

But when you intoxicate your mind you have to settle for the opposite results; mental and spiritual exhaustion.

Animal sex is fine for animals

Uninspired sex is empty. Just look at how animals do. They use sex to fertilize then get on with their day, looking for food. That's all sex is to an animal, including your animal body; a function of survival.

You are not an animal. The potential for connecting at the highest levels with your spouse, by using sex as a bridge between your souls, is wonderful. Take advantage of this amazing gift!

Sex as a physiological tool for procreation is nothing more than that. When you do not use sex for soul connection and only use it in some imaginative way to entertain or escape, you cheat yourself out of the great connection you seek.

Humankind so often misuse their great potential

Pretty much only humankind has created its own rituals around sex and made sexual enjoyment into a national pastime, even to the point of grading partners and events. People treat sex like it is some kind of competition.

However, you have the opportunity to use sex in your marriage to transcend the base physical act and its emptiness as described in the first three reasons listed above.

You have the opportunity to use sex as your bridge so you can be connected with each other, as you are meant; at your souls.

Once you try this you will understand and cherish your sexual/connecting time together.

Use sex to disarm your resistive instincts

Your instincts and walls etc. are designed to protect you from danger and propagate; that's it. But if you fool them into thinking you are doing things their way they won't pressure you.

Instincts aren't able to discern moments of soul intimacy from opportunities to procreate Your instincts will not hold a stop watch to make sure you fertilize and move on. It is true most men hurry because they are driven to complete their assignment, but your instincts won't catch on if you take a little longer. Your instincts won't catch on if you are truly loving your spouse while "procreating".

Animal sex is fine for animals

Humankind so often misuse their great potential

Use your free will to your soul's advantage

You have the ability to create new instincts and recreate old instincts.

When preparing to be with your spouse follow a plan of love. Remind yourself that this is an opportunity to silently (or noisily) open your heart. No matter how strong the physical drive is calling to you from your agitated genitalia redirect the feeling.

We often suggest to men who are too quick to please their instinct that they masturbate before being with their wives. Wives, whose husbands seem to be interested only in pleasing themselves need to understand their husbands are disconnected from their heart but can be shown a better way.

Your sex lives are the most private

Help your man take his time by putting more attention on his shoulders or chest. Tell him you cannot wait either, but you love the moment and want to extend it.

Men want to please wives who appreciate and praise them but they have been sold a bill of false goods and need to learn the facts of life correctly.

Your sex lives are the most private

Some couples seek help from sex experts, and we do not judge anything, including that. But we want to emphasize the importance of keeping your lives unconditionally private. If you choose to get guidance do so without revealing what you are doing or what "needs changing". Instead of looking for correcting look for new ideas you can experiment with.

You can do whatever you wish in the bedroom, but keep it there.

Connection and intimacy is your marital right

Connection and intimacy is your marital right

Everything you learned is for the purpose of avoiding disrupters of connection and intimacy and showing you how to create it. At the end of the day connection between your hearts is the best marriage has to offer. We wish it for you in abundance.

- Chapter Eleven -

United Parenting

◇◇◇

*Those little treasures any of us would lay down our lives to protect
are not as complicated as people think. Our fundamental thinking about our children,
when aligned with reality instead of superstition or romance,
makes raising children a loving opportunity to serve*

◇◇◇

This chapter is not meant to detract from the treasures provided by those psychologists who have spent lifetimes studying children in more detail than we can imagine. This is merely a humble offering of philosophy and a few general ideas which may be sometimes overlooked.

Chapter Eleven

United Parenting

The Marriage Foundation was conceived with a clear and singular intention; to protect children from the horrors of divorce, separation and bad marriages; by educating their parents. Teaching couples how to have an ultimate marital life brings them a long way toward fulfilling our goal.

And it's good because we and everyone else knows when you and your spouse are married well your children grow up more securely, in love's nest. They will, statistically, do far better than if you are fighting, distracted or divorced.

No matter what, you have to put your children's mental health ahead of your personal stuff

Love them and show them you love them in meaningful ways. Spend time with them, take an interest in them as people and be a parent who takes responsibility for how they see themselves and the world. It takes time but you took it on. You have to take it seriously.

An intact family is not enough

Staying together is important but it isn't enough. You agreed to more than that when you had children. Children need more than to be raised in an intact family. Yes, it creates stability, but it is not enough. Animals in a zoo have stability, too. If you were raised by amazing parents who had an amazing marriage but they did not spend enough time with you, you would understand this.

Children need to be raised by their parents who take their job as a very deep responsibility. Children need to be your second highest priority, just after making sure your relationship with each other is positively expanding.

Your kids need you to protect them and provide for them but they also need you to guide them

Human children are not meant to be raised by themselves, by caregivers, or by their peers. They need to learn rules for productive living from their parents, both vicariously and with controlled experiences, so they have a base from which to expand their lives.

Scientific methods are safest, especially when you invent them

The knowledge gathered about children through professional studies is a practical resource for many parents but sometimes the conclusions from studies are biased towards a certain way of thinking and may not be correct for your children or you.

No matter what, you have to put your children's mental health ahead of your personal stuff

The knowledge gathered about children through professional studies is a practical resource for many parents

It is up to you as their parents to observe what works for your kids. That way you can develop plans for raising them as individuals; lesson by lesson. If your first idea or plan needs adjusting, and it will, you can change it. You don't have to be afraid of messing things up. Your intention is the most important part of any life education and who could be more positively inspired and careful than you?

By crafting your children's lessons you are able to instantly determine if your idea for making a point was effective or lacking. You don't have to look any further than the results your kids enjoy.

Prioritize your goals for them

For all children discipline is of paramount importance. There is no such thing as success without self discipline. The discipline you give your kids teaches them how it feels and what it looks like. When they get older you insist on their disciplining themselves more and more.

Parents who teach their children the benefits of discipline in any situation will show them how to always fall back on that principle.

For naturally self-disciplined children the paramount quality to help them develop might be creativity. In those cases a child will be trained very differently so they are shown how to insert imaginative solutions into situations.

Another universal requirement for success is the ability for an individual to control their mind. When kids are young it is easier for them to learn that their mind is a separate "organ" which requires overseeing and attention. Kids who learn the powers of their mind are not so easily convinced to experiment with drugs. They learn to enjoy the freedom that mind control brings them.

Every human is different

Children have to be raised according to their particular bias. So, to never lose sight of their need for your attention to their special requirements, it's a good idea to start with questions.

1) Who is this person, our child? What are they going to "be" if they do it all right?

You are your child's life and career counselor.

You can see their strengths and weaknesses better than anyone else. You observe their joys as well as what they dread. You can see what turns them on and what they shun.

Nobody has the insights into your child that you and your spouse have. You see all the traits they have including those which will hurt them in the future and the traits which will take them all the way, if properly nurtured and exploited.

Who is more qualified than you to be their greatest support?

For all children discipline (not hitting them) is of paramount importance

Create a chart of your child's traits

The traits of any person can be divided into three categories-

Material traits are the worldly practical traits, like being good with their hands, having a mathematical mind, are good with people etc. Then, there are the

Psychological traits are their walls, filters, fears and attachments, which define them psychologically. No matter what course they take in life they need to be able to do so without prenatal, or post natal, obstructions. Last, but not least, are their

Spiritual traits Children who lean towards a material existence will do better when they are taught the benefits of meditation, or worship. It is too easy to "burn out" in the world if one seeks all their pleasure in worldly pursuits.

List their qualities and identify the areas your child needs to concentrate on. Remind them often that they can control their mind so they can make any changes they wish. When they are young the changes they need to make are the ones you identify, whether they agree, or not.

As your child is matures they need to be part of this process, more and more.

2) What reasonable goals do you wish your child to reach in near and short terms?

It's your job to develop a plan for success based on your child's basic character.

The earlier you get them to participate the better; some will be there sooner than others and some kids, if you start too late, won't.

This is a roadmap for their lives, and depending on the kind of person they are, their plan can be anywhere from hyper detailed to mostly directional. But it is your job to force it, not theirs to jump right in.

If a child is determined, or you believe they are suited to be a doctor or some other occupation which requires certain grades and special courses in school, then of course you need to place them on the right path right away.

Or maybe they are very creative. How it ends up manifesting is not so important, but you want them to have classes in music or art so they learn how to channel their positive qualities.

At least get them a crayon!

3) How do you help them define success for themselves based on their personality?

Every journey is made by following a map, taking the first step, and then taking another, and another.

Along the way people are either encouraged or discouraged, sometimes to the point of quitting.

What reasonable goals do you wish your child to reach in near and short terms?

How do you help them define success for themselves based on their personality?

Planning a path with someone who went before will help them lay out a growth plan. If they want to be a politician get them books on Lincoln. The plan has to have attainable goals and rewards for reaching them. They also need the tools to make it happen.

Your children need to be taught to never give up

They need to be taught that when they set their mind to something, although there will be challenges, when they are determined the challenges are only milestones.

Along the way it is your job to keep them from getting so caught up in their path that they forget to live. Introduce them to hobbies which have no hard goals so they can learn the joys of just playing.

Maybe you can introduce them to gardening or jewelry making, skiing, basketball, weight training, flower arranging…etc. Then, do it with them.

Teach them the importance of giving, loving and serving. Blend it into your conversations. Show them how to make donations of time and or money to worthy projects others have begun, but also help them choose missions of their own.

You are the most important teachers they will ever have

Yours is an obligation based on their complete dependence on you to be the best teacher you can ever imagine; even if you need to get some specialized training.

4) What should you do to help them reach their goals?

All of the above will help them develop properly as they mature; but remember, what you have learned about marriage, your mind, and everything else you learned here, is the basis for a fulfilling life.

The single most important thing anyone will ever learn is their mind can be controlled and it's their obligation to control it.

Don't allow them to be caught by the world's ignorance. Teach them the principles which you have learned.

Plans are essential tools for a productive life

Without a plan of some kind your behavior with them will be random and you will be more like a babysitter who delights in the children and loves to teach them new things but does not pragmatically guide them towards an actual destination.

Don't leave your children's future up to serendipity

Do you wish for them to know about happiness and how the world's version, focused on things and senses, is only temporary.

You need to teach them happiness comes from being in service and giving love, and how giving love is the way to get love.

*You are the
most important teachers
your children will
ever have*

Teach by your own example. It is how children learn

Children don't learn much by lecture or reward and punishment; or even well made plans. Nearly 100% of the time they learn from examples they are exposed to. You and your spouse are your children's primary models.

Copying you is the way they define their personal values, their attitudes and behaviors. Even when they hear you say "I know I don't do it this way, but I should have" or "this is wrong, but just this once" their minds are coming up with the same justifications as yours.

If they see you know something is wrong (even when you justify) they subconsciously reason, you shouldn't be doing it. So it must be "right" but you don't want to get caught!

Be good examples of good values

The ultimate relationship of your Sacred Space is what you want for your kids; so the exercises of selflessness which make your marriage so wonderful are skills your children should develop under your loving guidance, every day.

Of course they don't have the same kind of opportunities for expressing selfless service you have but they have their own continual stream of opportunities to be in service to others and put others ahead of their own needs.

You don't have to wait to go to a shelter and feed homeless people once a year to teach them the benefits. You can treat their friends as if they were your own children. You can surprise their other parent with little gifts or shoulder rubs or sweet words. You can include them in your adoration of their other parent. You can express, often, how the love they feel for you is theirs to give to others.

Include them in your efforts to be a noble and serviceful person. Make them their efforts, too.

Tell them how good you feel by making them feel loved. Teach them the power of giving love, by your example.

Know your children, and support their personalities

Children come into this world with distinct personalities. Sometimes parents get who their children are as soon as they lay their eyes on them, as if they have always known them and are picking up where they left off.

Other times, it takes some time to get who they are. Either way it is important to know them so you can be effective.

Teach by your own example. It is how children learn

Be good examples of good values

It isn't healthy for children to see their parents in disagreement

Always remind them, so they know it

The world is not going to teach them about controlling the mind or how they are souls who have a body, and mind. But these principles are natural, and make total sense to children, even teens. We have seen teens who are enmeshed in drugs and all kinds of trouble, who get these principles, respond, and change overnight. Some don't, but most do.

Everyone ultimately wants power, and where is power more important than over one's self.

Unity first

We want your children to have more than just an intact family; though that is better than what 50% of children have. We want your children to be raised with positive child-rearing intentions and wisdom based devices.

We know in many families, even those which are relatively harmonious, children are too often raised by two distinct parents who act as two different parents. Those parents compromise and agree (or disagree), rather than parent as a mom-dad coalition of consensus.

It isn't healthy for children to see their parents in disagreement

Children are meant to see their parents as one, not two. Why should a child be encouraged by the dynamics of their parents' relationship to play one off the other or choose sides because they have the opportunity?

A truly healthy relationship is seamless, from their children's' perspective, and that is the relationship you are now creating. Why not also create a purposeful environment for your children, using the same scientific principles as you do in your marriage.

What greater incentive could there ever be to become the best person you can. Of course nobody is perfect but everybody has the ability to work on themselves with the intention to become happier by avoiding trouble-making thoughts, and behaviors.

Your children should learn the first rule of life from you; strive for happiness, by being in service to others rather than selfishly striving to protect only the self.

Your child is not your creation but they are your responsibility

It is true; pride of parenthood is a bit of a trick played on us by drives to survive. Its intent, to create an intractable bond which compels good parents to do their best to protect is transparent; especially when you consider your child was a stranger at the time of birth.

But it is an instinct we want to keep in place and are grateful for the constant reminder to put another ahead of ourselves. Despite the heartfelt compulsion, it is an incredible responsibility to raise a child.

So the cultural and physiological drives all interconnected surround you with all you need to make your burden into a blessing. But, burden aside, we all instinctively want what is best for our children.

We want them to have a better life than we had, even if we have it all.

The instinct does not consider your marriage vows

Unfortunately, when couples are not harmonious or are not natural team players the instinct to protect their child works against parental harmony and can even cause rifts between spouses.

Can you see how the individual's drive to protect would include the other spouse as a possible threat?

This instinct exists so the chances of it going past its useful boundaries is high and is a great example of how unmonitored instincts cause trouble, even when their original purpose was fine.

In many families wives make husbands feel like they are outsiders. Otherwise devoted wives subtly and overtly do all they can to protect children; from their father! When you follow some of mom's all-knowing teacher attitudes to their roots you will see protection, caused by the drive. It happens in men just as often!

To make the family teeter even more you will see resentful dads try to take charge through force (there is never an excuse for a man to use his strength to control, or a woman to use her heart to control). Or you will see some moms complain that their husbands do not spend enough time with their children and on, and on, and on. All of the myriad problems are caused by not being in charge of your instincts.

Once again, the cure is monitoring the mind.

There are yet undiscovered physiological impacts

Parents of new children are completely taken aback by what often happens after the birth of a child.

They don't realize how the drive to survive is messing with them. We think a hormone or two will soon be discovered that biologically impacts women until their youngest child is about five years old. If you pay attention to mothers of young kids you will see it.

Can you see how the individual's drive to protect would include the other spouse as a possible threat?

Typically the focus moms have on their very young children creates a "left out" feeling for dad. The sex, it usually dries up, while the demands upon them, increases. Then moms, who discover raising a child has a far greater impact than they could have ever imagined, feel completely unappreciated, as do the dads.

You did not pick your children. Of course, it does not mean you can, or should, lessen your love for your children compared to your spouse, who you did choose; but it is a different kind of love with different expectations, and different obligations.

At times love for children is an easier love to identify with, especially when they are young and more dependent on you. But in your life you always have free will. So, you need to define your relationships, rather than be defined by them.

When you consider the drives and the instincts you will see that your love for your children may have begun as nature's way of protecting a new child.

It is fascinating when you think about it, how we call our children ours, with no sense of irony. Are they really ours? Nature thinks they are hers, and you are just their baby sitter! And religious, or spiritual people think of a child as God's, and we are still… the babysitter.

Avoid the pitfall of pitfalls

In most cases where couples do not control their instincts to become unconditional lovers, they are driven to a pattern of creating alliances. They do not see themselves doing it, and so they don't realize how impactful it is

In most cases where couples do not control their instincts to become unconditional lovers, they are driven to a pattern of creating alliances. They do not see themselves doing it, and so they don't realize how impactful it is.

Nor do they realize there is a domino effect which lasts until some future generation person, maybe, brings it to a halt.

Of course you can attribute it all to the drive to survive and procreate, making you a pawn in the big picture of species continuation. But that explanation does not cover it all.

There is more to it. We are not animals, like turtles, which lay their eggs and go off to sea. We are intrinsically linked to our children.

You know in your heart of hearts that this little person is a part of you and has been forever; and always will be. You are linked by a bond that cannot be broken. Those who have broken the bond have broken their own hearts. Those who have lost a child never recover.

As an act of love towards your spouse and for the best way for your children always promote your spouse to them. If you are not their biggest fan, in your kid's eyes, you are stealing an unrecoverable from your child.

Do all you can to encourage a strong relationship between your children and their other parent.

Make the relationships closest to you joyous

Sure, there is a lot of work to do and sometimes the last thing you want to do is spend time with your kids. So you find all kinds of excuses to get away. Or you may feel guilty and "spend time" by watching TV or a movie with them. Get real!

Sure, if you spend a lot of time with your kids it's ok to spend some of it in front of the screen, be it computer or TV. But don't fool yourself. You need to realize your kids need you. They need you no matter how inconvenient and they need you to be their friend. But not like a peer.

You need to be their parent first, but in this world, where there is so little real connection between people; you need to make it a point, to really connect with your kids. You need to listen to them, and give them real feedback. You need to hold them in high esteem and love them for both who they are, and who they will become.

In the end, as in the beginning

Your love is the same love as ours, drawn from the ocean of love which is the fabric of all. The more you give love, the more you will feel it, until you are love itself.

Make the relationships closest to you joyous

You need to be their parent first. In this world, where there is so little real connection between people; you need to make it a point to really connect with your kids